The Spirit of Regeneration

For Barbara
in excited anticipation
of our time in Peru
this January.

Affectionately

Frédérique

12-04-01

The Spirit of Regeneration:
Andean culture confronting Western notions of development

edited by
FRÉDÉRIQUE APFFEL-MARGLIN
WITH PRATEC

Zed Books Ltd
LONDON & NEW YORK

The Spirit of Regeneration: Andean culture confronting Western notions of development was first published by Zed Books Ltd, 7 Cynthia Street, London N1 9JF, UK and Room 400, 175 Fifth Avenue, New York, NY 10010, USA in 1998.

Distributed in the USA exclusively by St Martin's Press, Inc., 175 Fifth Avenue, New York, NY 10010, USA.

Cover designed by Andrew Corbett
Set in Monotype Garamond by Ewan Smith
Printed and bound in the United Kingdom
by Biddles Ltd, Guildford and King's Lynn

Chapters 3, 4, 6 and the first part of Chapter 7 translated by Frédérique Apffel-Marglin; Chapter 5 and the second part of Chapter 7 translated by Jorge Ishizawa Oba; Chapter 2 translated by Katie van Sant Glass.

A catalogue record for this book is available from the British Library

US CIP has been applied for from the Library of Congress

ISBN 1 85649 547 7 cased
ISBN 1 85649 548 5 limp

Contents

Tables and figures

Tables

Figures

Editor's note

The first draft of the introduction was written in January 1996. Jorge Ishizawa, now a member of PRATEC, translated it into Spanish and three members of PRATEC at the time – Eduardo Grillo, Grimaldo Rengifo and Julio Valladolid – read, commented on and endorsed it during my visit to PRATEC in March 1996. On 23 April 1996, Eduardo Grillo died suddenly of a heart attack at the age of 58. With him, I have lost the one person who more than any other is responsible for the profound change of direction my life has taken since I met with PRATEC. His loss for me and for PRATEC has created a searing wound. But as he himself often repeated, death in the Andes is the passage from one form of life to another form. We are still trying to adjust to this new form and heal the pain.

Acknowledgements

This book is the fruit of the collaboration and mutual learning that began between PRATEC and myself in 1994. PRATEC has published several books but none in English, and I have long hoped that some of PRATEC's work could be made available to English speakers. The members of PRATEC and I discussed what would go into such a book. This is the first such attempt.

I am grateful to Robert Molteno, editor at Zed Books, for insisting on a long theoretical Introduction and then sending me helpful comments and suggestions. This has given me the opportunity to reflect on this experiment and on the work of PRATEC in general.

None of this would have been possible without the generous financial support of the John and Catherine MacArthur Foundation and particularly that of Dan Martin, who attended the 1993 Bellagio conference at which the project 'Centers for Mutual Learning' was discussed. Dan Martin and the Foundation have shown remarkable confidence in the project and allowed us to forge a path through an area where there are precious few signposts. I hope they will find this book worthy of their support.

I would like to express my deep gratitude to and admiration for Dr Jorge Ishizawa Oba, who became a member of PRATEC after Eduardo Grillo's death. His translation of the book was a labour of love. We shared the bulk of the translation work; I could not have undertaken such an enormous task alone.

My gratitude to Eduardo Grillo, Grimaldo Rengifo and Julio Valladolid is profound. They have opened up a whole new way of being for me – a whole new world – with care, love, patience and laughter. They invited me to come and lecture regularly on their course, Andean Agriculture and Culture, on the topic of Gender and Development. I also wish to thank all the participants in the PRATEC course since 1994, who gave generously of themselves and their wisdom. That course as well as other meetings has made me understand the meaning of mutual learning. We began a journey together that has profoundly changed my life.

I also wish to thank my friend and colleague Kathryn Pyne Addelson whose work and conversations have been central to the development of the ideas put forth in the Introduction. Her support and encouragement have been vital to me in my academic environment at Smith College where, together, we have started a Center for Mutual Learning.

Friends and colleagues have given me invaluable encouragement and support; many of them read the Introduction and some read the whole manuscript, offering invaluable suggestions and comments. They are Leila Ahmed, John Connally, Martha Crouch, Yvonne Dion-Buffalo, Elinor Gadon, Tirso Gonzales, Søren Hvalkoff, Jorge Ishizawa, Sheila Jasanoff, Greta Jimenez, Marcela Machaca, Trilokinath Madan, John Mohawk, Ashis Nandy, Pramod Parajuli, Antonio Peña, Ravi Rajan, Marcus Raskin, Antonio Rengifo, Wolfgang Sachs, Loyda Sanchez, Marja-Liisa Swantz, Shiv Visvanathan. I am deeply grateful to all of them. Whatever short-comings are to be found in the Introduction are, however, entirely my responsibility.

Frédérique Apffel-Marglin
Amherst

About the editors and contributors

Frédérique Apffel-Marglin is Professor of Anthropology at Smith College, Northampton, USA and coordinator of the Centers for Mutual Learning in the context of which she collaborates with PRATEC and other activists and scholars in India and the United States. Previously, she was at Harvard for several years as a Research Associate in Women's Studies and later a Visiting Scholar at the Center for the Study of World Religions. Much of her fieldwork has been done in India. Her many writings include: *Purity and Auspiciousness in Indian Society* (edited with John Carman) (Brill, 1985); *Wives of the God-King: The Rituals of Devadasis of Puri* (Oxford University Press, New Delhi, 1985); *Dominating Knowledge: Development, Culture, and Resistance* (edited with S. A. Marglin) (Oxford University Press, Clarendon, 1990); *Who Will Save the Forests? Knowledge, Power and Environmental Destruction* (edited with Tariq Banuri) (Zed Books, 1993); *Decolonizing Knowledge: From Development to Dialogue* (edited with S. A. Marglin) (Oxford University Press, Clarendon, 1996).

PRATEC, the Andean Project for Peasant Technologies, is a network of several hundred village representatives, field agents and researchers who are working to revitalize Andean agriculture in terms of both indigenous techniques of cultivation and the Andean vision of the world. Its founders include the late Eduardo Grillo Fernandez and Grimaldo Rengifo Vasquez. In the course of their work, a large amount of research and other materials has been published in Spanish, notably *Desarollo o descolonizacion en los Andes* (1993) and *Crianza Andina de la Chacra* (1994).

Eduardo Grillo Fernandez (1938–96) qualified as an agronomist at the Universidad Nacional Agraria La Molina. After staying on for a time to study plant genetics, he then joined the public service where he had a distinguished career in the Ministry of Agriculture, holding a variety of posts in rural statistics, planning and agricultural research. In 1987 he took early retirement in order to join PRATEC, 'convinced that ... the autonomy of our people can only be possible by affirming their own culture which is one of nurturing and symbiosis'. At PRATEC he proved a constant inspiration to the younger generation of agronomists until the time of his untimely and deeply felt death in 1996.

Jorge Ishizawa Oba became an engineer at the Universidad Nacional de Ingenieria and subsequently did his doctorate at the University of Illinois. He subsequently worked for twenty years in the Peruvian public service, principally in the field of rural development planning. After taking the PRATEC course on Andean peasant agriculture, he became convinced that the path to autonomy in science and technology lay in cultural affirmation. Since 1993 he has worked closely with PRATEC and currently teaches at the Universidad Ricardo Palma in Lima.

Greta Jimenez Sardon has been educated in various disciplines. She holds a Master's degree in Social Work from the Universidad Nacional Autonoma de Honduras as well as a degree in human rights from the Concejo de Adultos para America Latina (Santiago de Chile). She is also a graduate of PRATEC's Course on Andean Peasant Agriculture. Gender relations is another of her prime interests. She has held posts in the Universidad Nacional del Altiplano (Puno, Peru), various state institutions as well as with NGOs concerned with rural development training, research and evaluation. She works now as a consultant in Gender, Agroecology and Sustainable Development.

Grimaldo Rengifo Vasquez holds a BEd from the Universidad Nacional del Centro, Peru, and went on to study anthropology at the Pontificia Universidad Catolica del Peru. He is currently the coordinator of PRATEC, which he founded in 1987. Prior to that, he held various posts in government and international organizations, including UNEP and FAO. He also worked for some time as a trainer at the Centro Nacional de Investigacion y Capacitacion para la Reforma Agraria (CENCIRA) at the Peruvian Ministry of Agriculture. And he followed this up by serving as the Executive Coordinator of an international project funded by the Dutch government at CENCIRA. He is the author of numerous books and essays in Spanish.

Julio Valladolid Rivera is an agronomist who has studied Andean native crops throughout his professional life. He retired from his post as Professor of Plant Genetics at the University of San Cristobal de Huamanga in Ayacucho, Peru, in 1989 and since then has been a member of PRATEC. He is the author of numerous articles on Andean agriculture and cultivation systems. In the early 1980s he participated as the local leader of an international research team applying a systems approach to the study of Andean crops. Since 1990 he has been the Director of the PRATEC Course on Andean Peasant Agriculture and has written numerous essays on Andean crops from the peasants' point of view.

Eduardo Grillo had always refused all invitations from the US due to a deep suspicion of such an imperialist stronghold. What made him decide to come was the topic of our meeting and our work involving critiques of modern Western knowledge and of development. That was, broadly speaking, the area of interest we shared.

My collaboration with PRATEC was made possible by the project funded by a MacArthur grant to create Centers for Mutual Learning.[3] That project was discussed at Bellagio and the deliberations resulted in an invitation by Grillo to several of us to visit Peru to discover whether a mutual friendship and interest would arise. The visit took place and the friendship emerged. Before turning to what happened and what I learned, I shall first explain more about PRATEC.

PRATEC was founded in 1987 by Grimaldo Rengifo. He immediately invited Eduardo Grillo and they later (in 1989) invited Julio Valladolid to join them. These three men had each spent a lifetime working for development. Rengifo was the director of a large Peruvian–Dutch development project, Grillo was the director general of the National Bureau of Agricultural Statistics and Research, and Valladolid was teaching plant genetics in the agrarian faculty of the University of Huamanga in Ayacucho. Through its extension programme, as well as through its research, that faculty was deeply involved in bringing the Green Revolution to the Peruvian countryside.[4]

These three men are part of the first generation of Peruvians from a non-élite, peasant background to have access to university training. In the late 1950s to early 1960s the universities, especially the agrarian faculties, opened their doors to wider population groups in response to the government's perceived need for more trained technicians and engineers to man the development effort. Until then the universities had been élite preserves.

Rengifo comes from Lamas in the northeastern Andes, province of San Martin; Valladolid comes from Huancayo, province of Ayacucho; and Grillo comes from the northwest coast, the Mochica region and was born in the indigenous community of Salas. All three are of native peasant background and devoted themselves to development in the belief that this was the way to help their people. In the course of their professional activities they eventually came to the conclusion it is development itself that is the problem. This realization did not come swiftly; it emerged slowly after a lifetime of professional activity in the service of development. At first they thought that things were not working because the methodologies they used were faulty. They worked hard to devise better methodologies. They lived through many phases and fashions in development: community development; participatory development; appropriate technology; sustainable development; women and development. They tried everything available, always striving to capture the reality of Andean peasant agriculture and of peasant life in general. At long last they came to the conclusion that no methodology would ever deliver and that the problem lay in the very idea of development. It is at this juncture that they left their professional activities and their jobs and founded PRATEC, a non-governmental organization. They were able to secure funding from a French foundation which has supported them until recently.[5] In other words, they de-professionalized themselves.

Rengifo, Grillo and Valladolid had come to the realization that development had failed. The physical evidence of failure lay scattered throughout the Peruvian landscape – what some have called 'the archaeology of development' – in the ruined infrastructures, abandoned to the elements after the project officials had left, uncared for by the peasants for whom they were intended, and simply left to rot. The evidence was also to be found in their experience of repeated unsuccessful efforts to devise better methodologies and the final realization that, within the professional ethos and constraints, it was impossible to approximate peasant reality and therefore make development relevant to their lives.

It is important to note that at some point in their professional experience, they felt that a better understanding of peasant reality may be available outside of their immediate disciplines. They therefore devoted themselves to reading all they could in sociology, anthropology, history and whatever other fields wrote on peasant life. They emerged from that experience feeling that peasant reality was being captured from a position outside of that reality.

The realization was not simply that development had failed, but that development consisted of a package of practices, ideas, epistemologies and ontologies that came from the modern West and were profoundly alien to the native peasantry. Extensive travels throughout the country convinced these early PRATEC members that native agriculture and culture were not only appropriate to that environment but alive and vibrant – despite the efforts of development, education and a long-term history of attempts to extirpate the native culture – and embodied a totally different mode of being in the world, of being a person, of relating to others both human and non-human, and of notions of time and space and of nature. They became aware that it is only from the perspective of development, which makes one wear modern Western lenses, that peasant agriculture and culture looks backward, stagnant and altogether lacking.

They awoke to the reality of peasant life, to the incredible richness and diversity of cultivars that are grown in this ecologically extremely variable environment. The Andes is one of the eight world centres where agriculture first emerged, according to the great Soviet geneticist Vavilov. Agriculture has almost a 10,000-year pedigree there and the peasants continue to grow an astounding variety of plants: many varieties of grains including the nutritionally renowned quinua; many varieties of tubers, the potato being very important with some 3,500 different varieties collected mostly in the Andes (Valladolid, Chapter 2); and about 1,600 varieties of maize (ibid.). Good farmers typically harvest more than fifty varieties of potatoes from their fields. In spite of the inroads of Green Revolution hybrids and packages, the peasants continue to grow their native cultivars for their own and their friends' and relatives' subsistence. The hybrids are grown for the urban market.

The members of PRATEC began to dedicate their lives to articulating these discoveries so that their personal experiences could benefit others like themselves, that is technicians and practitioners of rural development whose origins lay in the native peasantry. This effort at articulating both agricultural/cultural peasant practices as well as the epistemologies and ontologies embedded in development practice and more generally in modern Western knowledge was not undertaken as a professional activity but was engaged in as their contribution to what they were witnessing among the peasantry.

Since the 1950s (actually much earlier, but the movement picked up momentum at that time) the peasantry have been engaged in what Peruvian anthropologist Enrique Mayer has called a 'silent movement' (personal communication, 14.12.95). They have taken over the lands of the large landed properties, the *haciendas*, by direct action without forming political parties or syndicates.[6] With the agrarian reform of 1969, which made official what had been going on for a long time – namely the economic debacle of the *hacienda* system as well as the takeover or buyout of these lands by Andean peasants – that peasant reappropriation of lands accelerated. The government tried to replace the *hacienda* system by government cooperative schemes, but it took only twenty-five years to reveal the total failure of the state scheme. Andean peasants are reappropriating these lands as well and organizing themselves in their own way, namely by forming *ayllus*. The *ayllu* is a local group of related persons, and other non-human beings of the locality, the *pacha*. There, in their reconstituted *ayllus*, Andean peasants cultivate the land in their own manner, proving the vibrancy of native practices and culture.

The members of PRATEC saw this reaffirmation of Andean agriculture and culture throughout the country and wanted to be a part of that action. For them it was totally out of the question to imagine themselves as some sort of leadership or vanguard of that historical movement; such a posture would totally betray the communitarian and egalitarian ethos of Andean peasants as well as embodying an uncharacteristic hubris. Furthermore they attributed the success of peasants in reappropriating lands to the manner in which they did it: through direct action, without creating formal parties or organizations. Not being farmers themselves, they saw that their own way of participating in that cultural resurgence and affirmation would be to pass on to others like themselves what they had learned and continued learning, and thus, it was hoped, to stem the drain of young bright Andean people towards development and modernization. This would simultaneously weaken development efforts and strengthen Andean life. They chose to do this through direct action, by creating a course in Andean agriculture and culture for professionals of rural development. PRATEC deliberately eschews participation in formal politics, seeing that road as involving it in the official world of Peru, a world committed to development and modernization.

The members first dedicated themselves to writing about Andean agriculture and culture, contrasting it to development and modern Western knowledge, since – in their view – existing literature failed to convey Andean reality from within that reality. Their purpose was also to help other professionals of rural development with origins in the Andean peasantry to realize the distorting, if not blinding, effects of seeing the Andean world through the lenses of the categories of professional knowledge and to attempt to show them that world from within itself – thus enabling others to enter it and become part of the collective action of making that world. PRACTEC's publications attempt to show how both the categories of knowledge and the very notion of knowledge used in the academic professions carry within them the reproduction of industrial capitalism's institutions and status quo.

The members of PRATEC speak of industrial capitalism as 'the modern West' since this is how they experience it. They learned the knowledge of the university and for a long time bought its message of universality and objectivity; but they experienced it none the less as a foreign import. It initiated them into a different world to the one they came from. They are aware of the internal heterogeneity of 'the modern West', as they are of the internal heterogeneity of 'the Andean world'. The contrast they speak of is one that they, and many like them, have experienced as university-trained people of Andean origins. But it is only through their action of de-professionalizing themselves and of acting/writing from within the Andean collectivities – an action that philosopher Kathryn Pyne Addelson (1994) would call a 'moral passage' – that they could come to know with clarity the impossibility of participating in the Andean collective actions from within the professions. This realization brought with it an understanding of the nature of the knowledge they were taught in school and at university which, simultaneously, allowed them to see the Andean world with clarity.

They speak of this double realization as the need to decolonize their minds in order clearly to see and participate in the Andean world, sharing this double realization with others like them in the context of a course they started teaching in 1990. The participants of the course are professionals of rural development working in the universities, the government and NGOs, who are of Andean peasant origin. PRATEC has succeeded, miraculously it seems to me, in having the course accredited for the first four years at the National University of Huamanga in Ayacucho and for the last two years at the National University of Cajamarca. This seems miraculous to me because none of the three men is a member of the faculty of these two universities, although Valladolid was a member of the University of Huamanga before he resigned to join PRATEC. The participants in the course are not students at these universities, in fact many of them are professors at these universities; they all hold full-time jobs. In order to accommodate their schedules, the course is organized in three units of ten days each during one year. The units take place at a conference center outside Lima and consist of intensive seminars, the number of participants ranging between fifteen and eighteen per course. The participants have to return to their communities of origin between the units and there engage in a sort of 'fieldwork' on some aspect of the world they encounter. They present the results of these investigations in the course and finally write them up in the form of a thesis. Chapter 5 by Greta Jimenez is based on such a thesis by a PRATEC course participant. Although the course has many of the trappings of a university course – readings, lectures, exams, a concession necessary to being accredited and being able to offer a diploma of 'second specialization in Andean agriculture' – it differs fundamentally from normal university courses by not leading the participants into any profession. The participants will not further their careers by taking this course. The participants come to the course out of some experiential crisis with their work in development; something is not right and they come to the PRATEC course in the hope of figuring out what and why.

PRATEC's desire to be linked to the university stems from its sense that the time is ripe for an opening in the universities towards a different sort of knowledge. The agrarian faculties were training experts to function in the context of *haciendas* and state cooperatives. These have almost totally disappeared and now universities have no choice but to relate to the peasants. The usual forms of extension work are not working and PRATEC senses that a different way of understanding and teaching Andean agriculture may be in the process of taking shape. Things may change quickly.

By de-professionalizing themselves, the members of PRATEC freed themselves from the constraints of academic disciplines, focusing instead on the challenging task of writing on peasant agriculture and culture from an Andean point of view. For this they drew not only on their personal experience of growing up in that life but on their experience of conversations with peasants throughout the Peruvian Andes. Rengifo has had extensive experience in the field during his years as director of a rural development project. Grillo, in his official task of gathering agricultural statistics from the whole country, used to travel twenty days out of each month. Due to his own strong identification with peasants, he would

always stray beyond official duties and roam widely, striking up conversations with peasants. Valladolid's own awakening took place when he spent
three years in a peasant community studying peasant agriculture in the
early 1980s. He discovered the peasants had an incredible variety of
cultivars and an extensive knowledge to sustain and produce such diversity.
It was a revelation, for this was never taught in the agrarian faculties
where the curriculum was modelled on temperate zone agriculture,
European cultivars and hybrids – a training for running the *haciendas*, the
plantations and the state cooperatives.

In public lectures as in private conversations, Grillo has pointed out
how very slowly the three of them arrived at the point where they felt that
development, and the knowledge underwriting it, failed in articulating with
peasant life. It took them half a lifetime of professional activities to reach
that turning point. As Grillo points out, there were no guides, no signposts,
no path cleared by predecessors.[7] Having worked and lived in India on and
off for the last twenty-five years, I find this remarkable. In India there is
a long tradition debating Western science, modernization and Western
knowledge in general – one has only to evoke the name of M. K. Gandhi
to realize this.[8] Such a tradition is simply absent in Peru. This may well
be accounted for by the fact that the educated élite in Peru until very
recently has been Hispanic. Political decolonization in Peru, as in the US,
did not hand over the reins of government to the native population but
to the native-born Hispanic population. Furthermore, MacAulay's decision
in the first half of the nineteenth century to educate a native élite in India
so as to produce 'brown gentlemen' who could administer a colony too
vast for England's meagre demographic resources, created the conditions
for a critical debate on Western science and knowledge there.

The Peruvian situation has been quite different and can best be captured
by citing a well-known member of Peru's Hispanic élite, Vargas Llosa:

> There is a culture over there which has been preserved, which may be archaic,
> but which has permitted those compatriots of ours – primitive and elemental
> – to survive under conditions of extreme harshness. (1990: 154)

> ... the very notion of progress must be difficult to conceive by the communities
> whose members never remember having experienced any improvement in the
> conditions of their lives, but rather, prolonged stasis with periods of regression.
> (1983: 36)

> The price they [the 'Indians'] must pay for integration is high – renunciation of
> their culture, their language, their beliefs, their traditions and customs and the
> adoption of the culture of their ancient masters. (1990: 52)[9]

For Vargas Llosa and many others of his class, there are two Perus: one
official, modernized and civilized; the other Indian, backward and primitive,
albeit resilient. The need for the other Peru, sometimes referred to as

'deep Peru' (*Peru profundo*), to modernize and 'enter the twenty-first century' is not questioned by most members of 'official Peru'. The colonizing dynamic is internal in the country and it has taken many aspects.

One tendency that emerged in the 1930s is the movement called '*indigenismo*', which many anthropologists joined, thereby giving it academic legitimacy. These professionals 'argued against "preserving" native cultures. They worked hard at achieving new ways of integrating the Indians into national society and at revitalizing Andean cultural patterns to make them compatible with a modern nation state' (Mayer, 1992: 190–1). This was considered a progressive liberal movement. This movement is one reason why the members of PRATEC have rejected the use of the term 'indigenous' in their writings.

In the last fifteen years there have been indigenous movements in Peru, Bolivia and Ecuador in response to new legislation and regulations concerning the right of indigenous populations inhabiting nation states to their native territory, to their cultures and their language. The governments of these countries have done so in concert with the new regulations concerning indigenous rights emanating from the UN. I discuss PRATEC's response to these movements later in this chapter: 'An alternative to both progressivism and fundamentalism'.

The extreme left, including Shining Path, has an attitude not very different from that of Vargas Llosa and the liberals on the issue of Andean culture. Progress must be made and backward and feudal conditions must be overcome; the Andean peasantry must adopt Western socialist ways of life and knowledge in order to achieve progress towards a higher, more egalitarian and better future. In the name of progress, for both liberals and radicals, the 'Indians' in the 'other' Peru are condemned to disappear.[10]

PRATEC rejects these paths, arguing for a path that it names 'cultural affirmation'. They see themselves as simply supporting what the peasants are doing, their silent retaking of the lands and re-establishing there their own mode of cultivating the land and of organizing themselves. Since the term 'culture' has come under severe criticism lately in anthropology for its essentializing and colonizing tendencies and has generally been replaced by the term 'hybrid' (Clifford, 1988; Escobar, 1993; Canclini, 1990; Hall, 1990; Said, 1993; Trinh, 1994 and others), a discussion of terms would be in order.

Culture and hybrid

The criticism of the term 'culture' is a response to the essentialist manner in which culture has been depicted in most ethnographies, namely as coherent, whole, ahistorical, seamless and with no internal conflict or contradiction. Clifford's (1988: 221) matrix for the production and trans-formation of authority in both ethnographic museum collecting and in ethnographic culture collecting reveals such strategies as fulfilling needs in the anthropologist's society while simultaneously robbing the anthropologized of agency. Clifford's use of Lévi-Strauss's Indian in the New York public library wearing a feathered headdress and writing with a Parker pen illustrates the issue. To Lévi-Strauss this Indian is an occasion for nostalgia about vanishing cultures. Such a perception reveals Lévi-Strauss's 'incarceration' – to use Appadurai's (1988) word – of this Indian in a timeless, 'authentic' native culture. The anthropologist declares what is authentic, claiming his professional expertise, and simultaneously robs the Indian of agency. Clifford's rereading of the same vignette is to see it as part of the recent movement among Native Americans to reassert their identity on their own terms:

> Anthropological culture collectors have typically gathered what seems 'traditional' – what by definition is opposed to modernity. From a complex historical reality (which includes current ethnographic encounters) they select what gives form, structure, and continuity to a world. What is hybrid, or historical in an emergent sense has been less commonly collected and presented as a system of authenticity. (Clifford 1988: 231)

PRATEC's rejection of anthropology derives precisely from the latter's authoritative voice, declaring what is authentically Andean on the basis of visible traits, very much in the manner of Lévi-Strauss's Indian in New York's public library. As Fabian (1983) so eloquently put it, the Other has been imprisoned in the past by anthropology's use of tradition as opposed to modernity and Fabian urges anthropologists to find terms and ways of writing that affirm the coevality of anthropologist and anthropologized.

Another strand in this critique of culture is that it allows for the fixing of boundaries between Self and Other (Abu-Lughod 1993: 7). The generalization inevitably entailed by the use of the term culture works to make the Other seem more different, more self-contained, than the anthropologist. The anthropologist appears to stand apart from and outside of what he or she is describing. And that 'apartness' has always meant a privileging of the anthropologist's world. Anthropologists have responded to these critiques by experimenting with modes of representation, abandoning analytical authoritative prose for more fictionalized genres (Narayan 1989; Brown 1991; Abu-Lughod 1993; Aggarwal 1995). It is a welcome improvement on the weighty pronouncements of an earlier anthropology and certainly makes livelier reading. However, as Lila Abu-Lughod herself honestly recognizes, the informal conversations of Awlad Ali Bedouin women she re-creates are not the type of words these women (or their men) consider important and worth preserving. Her choice responds to the agenda set by perceptions of Arab women in general and Bedouins in particular in the US, and not to an agenda set by the Awlad Ali women themselves (Abu-Lughod 1993: 36).

To replace the term 'culture' with the term 'hybrid' is an effort to address some of the excesses perpetrated by the anthropologists who authoritatively have made pronouncements on what *the* culture of the particular group in question was all about. The term hybrid emphasizes the emergent, historical nature of what people do and in that sense obviates the all too often atemporal tradition in which anthropologists trapped their subjects. It has rightly been pointed out that such textual strategies reinforce the predominant geopolitical asymmetries of power.

We must, however, not forget that the shift from culture to hybrid is essentially motivated by critiques internal to anthropology and other social sciences and we must be wary of making this term another orthodoxy. PRATEC and the intellectuals involved in the Pan-Mayanist movement in Guatemala (Watanabe 1995; Fischer 1995; Warren 1995) reject the term hybrid and use the term culture. We cannot read their work as we read that of anthropologists; they write about their own ways of life and are involved in cultural politics in their respective countries. To censure their use of culture is to perpetuate a certain modern Western supervisory gaze that 'keeps alive the pastoral powers of European culture, transferring this role now onto secular social theorists' (Lattas 1993: 259).

It seems to me that the anthropologists' predicament is similar to that faced by the members of PRATEC while they were professionals engaged in development. No matter how much one tries to develop more sensitive, more appropriate methodologies or modes of representation, the anthropologist's agenda and that of the anthropologized are not usually the same or even similar. However self-reflective, however sensitive anthropologists' representations become, however much anthropologists try to give voice and agency to their subjects, the fact that anthropologists (and other social scientists) are located in the university means that their agenda and the agenda of the people they study cannot be the same.

The term hybrid is especially popular among those who study the new global movements which have brought members of previously localized cultures to all corners of the world. The term captures the new emergent combinations that result from those movements. The term is not dissimilar to an older term much used in Peru to refer to native religious practices after the invasion: syncretism. It refers to such things as the presence of Christ, the Virgin Mary and many saints among the Andean native pantheon as well as to the presence of such practices as going to mass. The difficulty with both terms is that it makes visible the disparate origins of various traits but makes invisible the manner in which those traits are used. This is a difficulty that the term hybrid when referring to genetically altered cultivars also displays.

'Hybrid variety' refers to a new variety formed from the interbreeding of two or more distinct varieties, many of which were originally nurtured by peasants. What is happening on a global scale is that the agricultural experimental stations and the biotechnology laboratories are monopolizing the credit for creating new 'improved' varieties. In order to use the geneplasm for genetic manipulation, geneplasm banks have been created by several nations and an international gene bank has been created and is housed by the Food and Agriculture Organization (FAO). It has gathered geneplasm from all over the Third World, much of it from cultivated plants. In this way the creativity of generations of peasants who, through open pollination, have improved seed varieties and created new ones, becomes invisible, all such geneplasm being referred to simply as 'traditional' or 'indigenous'.[11] The International Bank for Phytogenetic Resources (IBPGR), which financially supports the collection of geneplasm in the world, reports that during its first decade (1974–85) it collected 91 per cent of its geneplasm from material originating in southern countries, while the US donated only 0.09 per cent. Theoretically the IBPGR should keep one sample and send other samples to gene banks in other countries; in reality southern gene banks received 15 per cent of such material while industrialized countries received 42 per cent and the US 23 per cent (Valladolid 1993: 77). This is what Julio Valladolid says about the issue:

> We should not forget that the seeds from native varieties collected by scientists from International Centers in the peasants' fields and/or the peasants' markets, are the final product of a sustained effort of improvement achieved by the peasants who have conserved, adapted and improved their seeds since the beginning of agriculture some 10,000 years ago. (1993: 78)

Just as the knowledge, work and inventiveness of the peasants are rendered invisible in the hybrid seed, what is rendered invisible in the use of the term 'hybrid' when talking about emerging cultural phenomena is the manner in which traits originating in the West are incorporated. This may not be an issue relevant to cultural studies but is extremely important to the Catholic Church in the Andes. Sociologist and Jesuit missionary J. van Kessel (in a lecture delivered at the PRATEC course, 8.10.95)[12] reports the verdict is that evangelization in the Andes has failed. The natives basically continue with their own practices and views. A tendency within the church, to which he himself belongs, advocates the creation of an 'Andean Catholicism' and mounts on that basis a new evangelization campaign. It is clear from such a position that the church does not object to the hybrid nature of religious practice, since Andean Catholicism would clearly incorporate Andean elements. What it objects to in the current practices of Andean peasants is that they betray the central dogmas of the church. The church is sensitive to the manner in which traits are used and incorporated into the peasants' world-view and practices.

The members of PRATEC similarly view the manner in which traits originating either in Catholicism or in the modern West are incorporated as being a very important issue. Whether the trait is incorporated in a context totally different from that of its origin or whether it is indicative of a fundamental transformation of the host milieu is an important discrimination blurred by the term 'hybrid'. Whether what emerges is either a new cultural phenomenon or something like modernization is not captured by the term 'hybrid' either. Eduardo Grillo uses a deliberately embodied language to speak of the incorporation of foreign traits by Andean peasants, saying that they 'digest' alien elements, incorporating what they can use and excreting what they do not need or want. Including the Christian God and saints among the peasants' *huacas* (deities), raising bovine cattle instead of llamas, driving cars, listening to portable radios, going to school and learning to read and write in Spanish, and many other things, cannot necessarily be read as signs of these Andean peasants' 'modernization' or 'hybridization'. PRATEC argues that these are the result of conversations and mutual engagement and not the signs of a funda-mental transformation. This is how Rengifo puts it:

> Since we are not dealing with closed and autarchic peoples, their mode of being is that of dialogue with all the cultures. If to do that one has to learn to read and write in a language foreign to one's own, that will be done. Nothing is foreign to a people who nurture, including schools.
>
> Just like with the Christian saints, Western knowledge has not been syn-cretized with the Andean. In the pantheon of what the Andean have nurtured one finds the school, just like one finds bovine cattle, barley, the wooden plough, the Virgin Mary and Christ. The saints have been incorporated in their capacity of *huacas* [Andean deities] with whom one does *ayni* [reciprocates], one dialogues, but one does not worship them (as their introducers had hoped). (Rengifo, Chapter 6)

This conversationalist or interactive stance characterizes PRATEC's view of change in the Andes. A conversationalist stance *vis-à-vis* other cultures is inherently a pluralist stance, one that rejects a linear evolutionist vision of the future and entertains the possibility that industrial or post-industrial capitalism and the global market may not be an inevitable future for everyone. A dialogical or conversationalist stance is not an oppositional or essentialist stance either, rejecting whatever comes from a foreign source. Whatever has come is now part of the landscape and one simply converses with it, taking in what is useful and discarding what is not. The language of dialogue or conversation does not erase the separate reality in which Andeans live. In contrast, the language of hybrids does not help in making visible the different notions of time, space, nature, persons, knowledge and many other differences which PRATEC is intent on making visible. One could perhaps summarize PRATEC's position in terms of under-standing cultural boundaries as porous. This is a view also expressed by Ashis Nandy in the context of India:

> It is the nature of traditional India to maintain a certain openness of cultural boundaries, a permeability which allows new influences to flow in and be integrated as a new set of age-old traditions – one may call the process traditionalization – and for some cultural elements to flow out and be detraditionalized. These two processes of inflow and outflow determine, at a given point in time, Indian culture, rather than a rigidly defined set of practices or products surviving from the society's past. (Nandy 1987: 153)

The charge of essentialism grows out of the habit of seeing boundaries as non-porous. This is a habit formed in the context of Western imperialism and conquest in which the conquered was seen as wholly 'other' (Todorov, 1984). PRATEC speaks of *interculturalism*, that is, a conversationalist, mutual two-way flow between different collectivities. Such a flow would not result in what Rengifo calls a 'global hybrid soup', in which all difference disappears, but in the flowering of diversity – diversity nurtured and strengthened by intercultural cross-pollination.

The implications of de-professionalization

It is not difficult to see why the members of PRATEC who identify themselves as Andean would reject assimilationist and evolutionist views. It is more interesting to ponder why they finally came to see a more recent position, that of the 'andinistas', as inadequate. They had turned to the work of these social scientists in the hope of finding there a satisfactory approximation to Andean peasant reality. Although they learned from those readings, they saw that the andinista perspective ultimately is also an outsider's view of their culture, one capturing it in alien categories.

The label 'andinista' refers to the work of social scientists, mostly anthropologists, who set out to counter the ethnocentrism and Eurocentrism dominant in official Peru. This is how a Peruvian anthropologist, Enrique Mayer, a member of that tendency, characterizes it:

> Given the anti-Andean prejudices of the two Peru argument (of which Vargas Llosa's version is but one in a long sequence in the intellectual tradition of Peru's élite), to search for, to demonstrate with ethnographic facts, and to portray a 'living' culture rather than dead 'survivals' seemed to those of my generation of fieldworkers to be a worthwhile task. Symbolism in fiestas carried out in the village of Chuschi was analysed by Billie Jean Isbell ... Perhaps Andean anthropologists [here he means anthropologists of the 'andinista' tendency] erred a bit in overstating the case, in drawing the lines all too sharply, and in not being 'actor oriented' or self-reflexive enough. But the enterprise was worth it as a counterweight to the prevailing Peruvian national ideology. (1992: 195)[13]

I do not think that a more actor-oriented or self-reflexive anthropology, what has come to be known as post-modern anthropology, would have been any more helpful for the members of PRATEC in their search for an adequate rendering of Andean peasant reality from within that reality. The issue, as PRATEC members came to realize, is not one of better methods or greater self-reflexivity; it is more fundamental.

I think that the remarks of US anthropologist John Watanabe point us in the right direction. It is interesting that these remarks were written in the context of an article on the pan-Mayanist movement in Guatemala, a movement reminiscent of what PRATEC is trying to do:

> Unfortunately, this post-modern poetics fares no better than artless positivism in resolving the inherent political asymmetries in ethnography's problematic – indeed, inescapable – appropriation of its subjects' lives for purposes beyond the living of those lives ... [W]hatever its textual form, ethnography always diverges from the 'native's point of view', if only because anthropologists ponder worlds that other people live ...
>
> In the end, whether post-modern or otherwise, anthropologists write authoritatively about cultural otherness ... [and] such writing still carries the authority of presumed expertise ... Any attempt to deny this inescapable authoritativeness amounts to an ethically suspect evasion of accountability. (1995: 28)

I think that by probing what the 'purposes beyond the living of those lives' are for the anthropologists and other professionals who write about others' reality we will begin to gain an understanding of why Rengifo, Grillo and Valladolid felt impelled to de-professionalize themselves in order to do what they do.[14]

Primarily, the purposes for which anthropologists and other professional researchers do their work is to 'contribute to the knowledge of their professions', to use a trite but nevertheless serviceable formulation. Another way of putting this is to say that professional researchers live their work lives within the parameters and the paradigms framing their professions. The parameters and the paradigms can sometimes be changed but this is done more by pushing at the margins than by more radical reformulations (Kuhn 1962). The reason lies in the social organization of the professions and academic disciplines. To receive a PhD, then to secure a job, to keep the job and acquire legitimacy – to say nothing of prestige within the profession – one must attend to its theories, its concepts, its methodologies and so on. Such attending, furthermore, must take place in strict separation from the attending to one's 'private' life. Passion and values belong to the latter whereas sobriety and attention to facts belong to the former. Thus the facts must be presented with affective detachment under penalty of being labelled 'romantic', or 'biased', labels damaging to one's professional reputation. Furthermore, as everyone knows, it is the ability to weave these facts into theory that gains one professional recognition. In the following quote, one of the towering father figures of anthropology, Raymond Firth, enunciates unambiguously this state of affairs in his foreword to Leach's classic *Political Systems of Highland Burma*:

Some of us, for example, have not hesitated to tell our students in private that ethnographic facts may be irrelevant – that it does not matter so much if they get the facts wrong so long as they can argue the theories logically. But few of us would be prepared to say in print, as Dr Leach has done, that he is usually bored by the facts which his anthropological colleagues present. (1954: vii)[15]

As Triloki Madan commented to me, this betrays an immense gulf between the anthropologist and the anthropologized, for what are the former's 'facts' are the latter's life.[16] Furthermore, in most anthropological field situations, this life is not separated between a public domain of work and a private, domestic domain.[17] This division, as the great scholar on the making of the English working class, E. P. Thompson, has remarked, was the product of industrialization and the emergence of labour as a commodity. This is captured in his famous pithy formulation, that industrial capitalism brought about the separation of 'work and life' (Thompson 1967).[18] Life in non-industrialized and non-commoditized collectivities is not divided into a realm where passions have no legitimate place and one where they do; the whole is suffused with passion and meaning.

It is not only in the separation between work and passion, or passion and cognition that industrial capitalism has shaped the social organization of knowledge and with it the very nature of knowledge. With the fragmentation of the task at the point of production, the knowledge of making an object or completing a task was taken out of the workers' hands and put into the heads of the specialized experts. The making of an object was broken down into many separate activities performed by different sets of workers; the famous model of this form of production is exemplified by Adam Smith in his description of the making of a pin. The justification for such fragmentation of the task is efficiency. Stephen A. Marglin (1974) has presented evidence showing that there are, in fact, no efficiency gains from this manner of production and has persuasively argued that its true function is the control of the worker. I have built on that fundamental insight and argued that the skill of the workers was disembodied and transferred into the heads of the experts hired by the entrepreneur; the allegiance of these experts is to their profession and to the bosses (Marglin 1974, 1990, 1996; Apffel-Marglin 1991, 1996). This gave rise not only to a corresponding fragmentation of knowledge paralleling the fragmentation of the task, but to a disembodied and dispassionate knowledge held by experts removed from the activity of production.

The separation between knowledge and life as well as the division of labour in fields of knowledge pre-dates the rise of the factory and industrial mode of production. It has deep roots in the precursor of the university: the monastery. What the industrial mode of production brought about was an intensification of that tendency as well as a deployment throughout society of this form of knowledge. The latter was achieved principally through the creation in the mid-nineteenth century of compulsory elementary and secondary education (Apffel-Marglin 1996).

This modern view of knowledge emerged at the same time as the factory system was beginning, towards the end of the eighteenth century. With the advent of the factory this relatively new form of knowledge was deployed widely throughout society. The theoretician of the new modern university, the autonomy of which is protected by academic freedom, was Immanuel Kant. In his work *The Conflict of the Faculties*, first published in 1798, Kant advocates the separation of those faculties that should legitimately be under the control of the state – theology, law and medicine – and the faculty that should be autonomous and enjoy the privilege of academic freedom: that is philosophy and the sciences, what is now called the liberal arts. This is recognized as laying the foundation for the modern university which first took shape in Germany in the nineteenth century. It is this model of the university which was emulated in the US at the turn of the nineteenth and early twentieth century (Connolly 1995) and that now has spread globally.

At the very beginning of his famous work Kant invokes – rather offhandedly – the factory as the model for the university and the organization of knowledge (*fabrikenmässig*), with its 'division of labor, so that for every branch of the sciences there would be a public teacher or *professor* appointed as its trustee, and all of these together would form a kind of learned community called a *university*' (Kant 1979: 23).[19] The notion of academic freedom was inextricably related to that of value neutrality for Kant and in the subsequent development of the German university. Kant argued for the autonomy of the philosophy/sciences faculty because he saw its role as that of watchdog, critic and guardian of the truth, hence the title of the book:

> Its [the philosophy faculty] function in relation to the three higher faculties is to control them and, in this way, be useful to them, since *truth* (the essential and first condition of learning in general) is the main thing, whereas the *utility* the higher faculties [theology, law and medicine] promise the government is of secondary importance ... The philosophy faculty can, therefore, lay claim to any teaching, in order to test its truth. The government cannot forbid it to do this without acting against its own proper and essential purpose; and the higher faculties must put up with the objections and doubts it brings forward in public, though they may well find this irksome, since, were it not for such critics, they could rest undisturbed in possession of what they have once occupied ... and rule over it despotically. (1979: 45)

In order to fulfil the role of critic of the state-controlled higher faculties and thereby control them, the philosophy faculty must be impartial, nonpartisan and devoted only to the pursuit of truth – wherever it may lead.

This was the argument used to convince the state to relinquish its control over what now we call the liberal arts faculty. Kant's work also contains the germ of the idea of knowledge for knowledge's sake, embedded in the notion of the unhindered pursuit of truth separated from state and other controls. The notion of knowledge for knowledge's sake – or science for science's sake, that is the pursuit of 'pure' science with no practical telos – did not establish itself fully until the mid-nineteenth century along with the development of science (and other fields) as professional, salaried occupations (Proctor 1991: 68). By then, the autonomy that Kant had advocated was extended to other fields of knowledge, in particular the autonomy of the natural and later the social sciences from moral or religious questioning. 'Kantian dualism also served to insulate science from political critique' (Proctor 1991: 80). Kant's separation of theoretical and practical reason, and his vision of the new university modelled upon the factory, provided the intellectual legitimacy for the insulation of science from politics, morality, religion and passion.

My aim here is not to critique value neutrality, a task already accomplished not only by Proctor but by many of the deconstructionists (John Connolly [1995] has a good discussion of Derrida's critique of Kant's *The Conflict of the Faculties*) as well as feminist critiques of science.[20] My intent, rather, is to show the function performed by this form of knowledge in the rise and continued dominance of industrial capitalism and state power.

In his exhaustive study of the emergence of the notion of value neutrality in the context of the history of the modern German university, Robert Proctor (1991) traces how these seminal ideas of Kant eventually became institutionalized by the neo-Kantians in Germany during the nineteenth century. In the latter part of his book he focuses particularly on the rise of the notion of value neutrality in the social sciences in Germany at the beginning of the twentieth century. Proctor, unlike those who write histories of science, does not focus on the history of ideas; rather he embeds the emergence of the modern university and its notion of knowledge in the historical and political contexts of the times. His painstakingly detailed history reveals starkly the political nature of 'value neutrality':

> First, I want to suggest that at least in the case of Germany it was largely in reaction against movements *outside* the universities – socialism, the women's movement, and racialist nationalism – that the ideal of neutrality becomes important in German social theory. Neutrality emerges as a self-conscious ideology of science partly in reaction to political challenges to state power – Marxism, feminism, and social Darwinism – but also as an outgrowth of fears that practical, and specifically industrial, concerns were about to swamp the pursuit of science 'for its own sake'.

Second, I want to show that despite their protests, many of the greatest advocates of neutrality played an important role in the politics of their time. The German academic was neutral not in the abstract, but in opposition to certain ideas and social forces. Neutrality was calculated to have certain specific effects on life and society. Neutrality was political not only in the sense that it was devised to counter certain political movements, but also in the sense that it served to mask the broader political ideals of its advocates. (1991: 70)

Proctor remarks on the paradox of the notion of knowledge for knowledge's sake emerging precisely when the scientific discoveries of the nineteenth century gave industry an incredible boost. No one could be blind to the relationship between science and the growth and power of industry and the state by the mid-nineteenth century. This was particularly evident with the development of chemistry as a science and its application to the industrial production of chemical dyes and chemical agriculture in Germany in the second half of the nineteenth century (Proctor 1991: 94–5). The paradox was dealt with simply by magically invoking Bacon's dictum of the 'usefulness of useless knowledge' (ibid.: 96). But I would argue that there is a profound link between the professionalization of knowledge, value neutrality and the autonomy (or academic freedom) of the university, the rise of the specialized professional expert and the commoditization of knowledge upon which the expansion of industry and state power rested.

With the new factory mode of production, not only is work separated from the communities and houses of the workers – Thompson's separation between work and life – but the knowledge of the production process is taken out of the bodies and heads of the workers and placed in the heads of experts who themselves do not make the product or accomplish the task (Apffel-Marglin and Marglin 1996). The separation of the boss from the knowledge expert along with the ideology of efficiency and the prestige of rationality all played an essential role in the acceptance of the new technologies and modes of organizing work on the part of workers. Not only had their knowledge and know-how been expropriated, but in the process they had been made mere adjuncts to the machine, forced to work on repetitive, boring tasks at a rhythm set by the boss rather than themselves. However, all this was rationalized and legitimized by invoking the requirements of efficiency and rationality. So expert knowledge was freed not only from the criticism and constraints arising from morality and religion but also from the constraints that embedding work in the life of communities brings with it. The ideology of knowledge for knowledge's sake divorces it from the constraints and meanings arising from community life and its purpose of regenerating itself, that is of continuing to live. The well-being and continuity of particular communities ceases to be tied to the production of goods or of knowledge. Goods and knowledge become ends in themselves. The well-being of communities where factories or universities are located is irrelevant to those institutions. Neither the relocation of factories which destroys local communities nor the presence of prosperous universities – such as Yale and Columbia – in the midst of extreme urban poverty are any longer viewed as scandalous by most people.

The combined force of the separation between work and life and between knowledge and life had a profound effect on that domain where the continuity of life is attended to, namely the domestic sphere. The private, domestic sphere where the regeneration of individuals, kin and wider interpersonal ties is relegated, by becoming separated from work and the making of knowledge, was gutted and made dependent on the public domain. Another way of saying this is that procreation understood in its broad sense of 'a social activity that includes the care and love and raising of the new generation', which is the work of communities that generate the future by carrying on the work of the past (Addelson 1994: 36), becomes subordinated to economics and the imperative always to produce more. The material wherewithal of life ceases to be a procreative issue and becomes an economic issue. This is how procreation and regeneration have become biological reproduction, medicalized and in-dividualized (Apffel-Marglin 1996; Davis-Floyd 1992; Martin 1987).

The professionalization of knowledge made knowledge a commodity as well as an individual pursuit. What is bought on the market – the academic market as well as the industrial, military and government markets – is an individual's ability to produce knowledge, and in order for this to be bought and sold on the market it must be held indivisibly by an individual, just like the labour of a person must be owned individually for it to become a commodity (Apffel-Marglin 1996). Each knowledge pro-ducer is pitted against other knowledge producers. Anybody who has looked for a job in academia knows this. Individualism is the very condition of the commodification of this knowledge, which is why it is so strictly taught at all levels of education from elementary school to graduate school where rules and regulations policing the individualized production of knowledge are euphemistically referred to as 'honour codes' and plagiarism has become an indefensible sin.

The philosopher Kathryn Pyne Addelson points out a deeper form of individualization in professional knowledge. In the context of discussing a different way of acquiring knowledge, using the example of the direct action engaged in by the anarcho-syndicalists in the US at the beginning of the twentieth century, she writes:

> The anarcho-syndicalists advocated revolutionary social change through direct action. Direct action was a paradigm of knowing and doing, and direct action was a *collective action*. Knowledge was needed to make the change, and knowledge was made in direct action. Coming to have knowledge required the emotion and bonding necessary to a 'gestalt switch', because new relations had to be

made, and a new kind of self. The knowledge wasn't 'objective' in the sense of being open to any individual (as in the individualist perspective). (1994: 26)

In the collective action way of making knowledge, emotional bonding with particular others is what generates new insights and knowledge. Knowledge here is not separated from emotion. Furthermore, these others need not be only humans but any aspect of the environment that becomes part of the collective action. In Addelson's theory of knowledge, where the unit is the act, meaning and reference are released from a narrow connection with thought and language (ibid.: 146). This is a feature that I shall come back to later since it is one close to the world that PRATEC writes of.

The theoretical egalitarianism of 'objective' knowledge – its vaunted epistemological egalitarianism – is precisely what makes this form of knowledge a universal one and frees it from particularity and localism. But this feature hides the particular way this knowledge is embedded in the institutions of modern Western industrial capitalism. Addelson's alternative view of knowledge – one based on *collective action*, which in turn means that knowledge emerges out of particular encounters and relationships in particular localities – goes a long way towards making a shift from an evolutionary paradigm of knowledge to a diversity paradigm.

The autonomy of the university along with the ideal of value neutrality reassures everyone – the workers in particular – that this knowledge is the best available and designed neither to enslave them nor to empower the bosses. It is presented as knowledge that serves neither Mammon nor God; it serves only unsituated, transcendent and value neutral rationality. This is how knowledge for knowledge's sake is legitimized and knowledge is disembedded from the regenerative (procreative) collective actions of local communities.

As Addelson has shown (1994), this individualist, passionless, factual expert professional knowledge reproduces the existing social, political and economic orders. She discusses in particular the double participation of researchers in the laboratory or the field on the one hand and in the activities of their professions on the other. This is particularly relevant to the case of the professional anthropologist who is a 'participant/observer' in the field and a participant in the profession. Like Watanabe (1995, cited above) she underlines the difference between participation in the field and in the profession. Unlike Watanabe, she devotes a good part of her book to probing what the purposes of professionals are in appropriating their subjects' lives.

As I pointed out above, the explicit purposes are clear enough: the advancement of knowledge. Such purposes, however, take for granted the nature and legitimacy of that knowledge and of its social organization. In the process it veils the manner in which professional expert knowledge is embedded in institutions which are instruments of governance:

The unquestioned right to know in terms of one's disciplinary concepts and methods is at the foundation of the cognitive authority of scientists and other professionals. It places them in the *local* sites of laboratory and field, not as participants but as 'judging observers' who are themselves to be unjudged. The outcomes of their work extend beyond the boundaries of their disciplines, professions, and institutions. This is because the institutions in which professionals make and transmit knowledge are instruments of governance. In the broadest sense, the double participation of scientists and other researchers is a participation in the local activity as hidden agents of governance. Except in special circumstances, whether any particular professional wills it or not, the participation is in support of the existing social, political, and economic orders – loyalty to these things is embedded in the institutional folk concepts of profession and university. (Addelson 1994: 161)

Rengifo's, Grillo's and Valladolid's de-professionalization meant not only that they abandoned the right to know the Andean world in terms of their disciplinary concepts and methods, and thus abandoned cognitive authority, it meant a total change in their lives. Their writing emerges from their own passionate bonding with Andean peasants, first experienced in their families and communities of origin, and subsequently in a wider set of friendships with particular peasants and particular places. Their de-professionalization meant that there was no longer a double participation for them; the world of which they write is their own world, to which they are passionately bonded through a multitude of particular relations. In other words, writing about that world and living the lives of that world have become for them a unified field of action. This is precisely why they left their jobs; they realized that, irrespective of their wishes, in their professional roles, they were agents of governance – specifically of the state's purpose of developing the country. They also realized that switching profession and becoming, for example, anthropologists would not change that fact significantly. Another way of saying this, and a way which I think would be closer to the way they themselves would talk of it, is: they joined the collective action of the Andean peasants engaged in retaking possession of lands and re-establishing their own forms of organization and practices. They repossessed their Andean selves and ways of being by ceasing to practise the double participation that professional knowledge making had required of them. They speak of the Andean world not as judging outsiders but as insiders bonded to that world. They write books and articles like professional knowledge makers do, not with the intention of adding to the fund of knowledge of their professions, but as their chosen field of action. They do not publish through the usual professional channels; PRATEC publishes its own writings. They write of the Andean world not primarily as a world to *know* or study but as a world to live in, to participate in, to be a part of and collectively to make.

In order to clarify many of the issues discussed so far – the issue of the professional as a judging outsider, the professional's right to know using the concepts and tools of the profession and in general the role of the professional as a hidden agent of governance – I will take the example of the assessment of PRATEC's work made by a Peruvian anthropologist quoted above, namely Enrique Mayer.[21] Mayer starts out by stating how important he considers the PRATEC proposal to be:

> I was invited to consider the proposal of PRATEC to strengthen the *chacra* [the peasant's field] and see it as an extremely interesting point of departure in the context of contemporary Peru. In it, I think one can find the germ of a project of investigation – the basic ideas for a programme of technical, social and political action. (1995: 513, my translation)

He then goes on to contextualize PRATEC historically and points out how a desire to 'return to the grassroots' is eminently understandable given the failure of the government's agrarian reform of 1969, which aimed to liberate the productive forces of the country and modernize it. This failed reform has left Peru, twenty-five years after its introduction, gripped by economic, political and social crises. Furthermore, the unforeseen and unwanted result of the reform has been the *'campesinizacion'* (the 'peasanticization') of almost all of rural Peru. He then proceeds to criticize PRATEC for not being scientific:

> I have read with care, attention and sympathy almost all the publications of this group of intellectuals [he cites publications from 1987 to 1991]. My verdict is that, lamentably, until now there is very little in what has been published by them which has any scientific value. (ibid.: 514)

Mayer goes on to detail how PRATEC's work fails to test the factual truth of what their 'informants' tell them, of not using quantitative measures, and of confusing peasants' articulation of their world-view with 'our real knowledge of ecologic processes':

> The mere assertion of a postulated harmony does not demonstrate the existence of healthy or balanced ecological processes. There is a confusion in asserting without explanation or analysis informants' statements as if they were factual material results ... They do not mention possible mechanisms that might be relevant in the explanation nor are direct observations made in the field or quantitative measures given with which one might begin to create some evaluative criteria ... To demonstrate that Andean culture (or Andean cosmovision) also supports balance adds nothing to our real knowledge about ecological processes. (ibid.: 514–15)

Mayer finds fault with PRATEC's work because it fails to use the conceptual and methodological tools of his profession. Most ironic is his use of the anthropological term 'informant', which captures precisely the relationship between anthropologist and anthropologized. This is a term

explicitly rejected by PRATEC because it reproduces the double participation which they have abandoned, not as a conceptual choice but as a
life change. Mayer is clear where *real* knowledge lies; not with what peasants
say but with what the professional researcher can empirically verify using
his methodological and other conceptual tools. Here is a clear example of
professional knowledge having cognitive authority and being a judging
outsider (Addelson 1994). Mayer wants PRATEC members to be scientific
professionals of an empiricist bent and judges them negatively for failing
to measure up to those criteria. In the process, he is blind to the different
epistemology and ontology that PRATEC tries to articulate, partly through
a contrast with modern Western knowledge. The contrast is necessary
precisely in order to make clear that what they are talking about is *not* a
better methodology to get at the 'facts'. In their presentation of Andean
peasants' worlds, wisdom arises out of mutual nurturing and conversations
between all the beings of the locality. They prefer to use the term 'wisdom'
rather than 'knowledge' because knowledge is so associated with concepts
and language. Their view is much closer to that presented by Addelson in
that wisdom arises out of acts between particular beings, be they humans
or non-humans. Just as for Addelson, viewing the unit of knowledge as
the act decentres concepts and language; in PRATEC's account of the
Andean world the conversation and mutual acts of nurturance are not
only between humans but between humans and the other beings in the
world: the stones, stars, sun, moon, animals, mountains, rivers, plants and
so on.

Mayer also chastises PRATEC for not referring to the 'conditions of
poverty, scarcity of resources, exploitation, and the damaging integration
into the market' (ibid.: 516). What in fact PRATEC has tried to do is to
show that these categories – 'poverty', 'resources' and 'integration into
the market', as well as many others – carry with them a whole way of
making (and of course of perceiving) a world. PRATEC's whole effort is
aimed at speaking of a world from within that world so that the knowledge,
and ultimately the world in which that knowledge is embedded, namely
industrial capitalism, is not reproduced.

Mayer's role as an agent of governance reveals itself most clearly in
the following sentence:

> The hypotheses must lead to an experimental work and a work of potential
> development which can be given back to the *comuneros* [members of peasant
> communities] in efficient and absorbable form. (ibid.: 517)

There is absolutely no doubt that Mayer has no intention of relinquishing
cognitive authority to the Andean peasants. Their practices and views will
be taken as hypotheses by the professionals, well chewed up methodo-
logically and then generously given back in absorbable and efficient
development pills.

Mayer concludes his ambivalent assessment of PRATEC's work in the following way: 'To refuse, due to purist principles, to practise certain forms of our professions is to fall into sectarianism and extreme positions which are less than useful in these times of crisis' (ibid.: 517). Mayer's own inability or unwillingness to de-privilege his own professional tools and point of view – that is the privileged, unsituated, Archimedean stand-point of empiricist social sciences – makes him blind to what PRATEC is doing. PRATEC is entering into the non-dualist Andean world, one in which organism and environment are not separate, pitted one against the other, but one in which they make each other. Eduardo Grillo states this unambiguously:

> Science is founded on a clear separation and opposition between humans and nature, and between the knowing subject and the known object. For science, culture is an exclusively human attribute and is precisely the quality that makes humans and nature different ...
>
> Here [in the Andean world], conversation cannot be reduced to dialogue, to the word, as in the modern Western world but rather conversation engages us vitally: one converses with the whole body. To converse is to show oneself reciprocally, it is to share, it is to commune, it is to dance to the rhythm which at every moment corresponds to the annual cycle of life. Conversation assumes all the complications characteristic of the living world. Nothing escapes conversation. Here there is no privacy. Conversation is inseparable from nurtur-ance. For humans, to make *chacra*, that is to grow plants, animals, soils, waters, climates, is to converse with nature. But in the Andean-Amazonian world, all, not only humans, make and nurture the *chacra* – all nurture. The human *chacra* is not only made [or nurtured] by humans; all, in one way or another, participate in the creation/nurturance of the human *chacra*: the sun, the moon, the stars, the mountain, the birds, the rain, the wind ... even the frost and the hail. (1994b: 34, 35)

Grillo is passionate and strongly emotionally bonded to his Andean-Amazonian world.[22] He rejects the scientific method because of its dualism and objectivity and what these bring with them. He speaks of a world in which organism and environment make/nurture each other. Such a re-jection is also voiced by two Western scientists, Richard Levins and R. C. Lewontin, biologists at Harvard University:

> The demand for objectivity, the separation of observation and reporting from the researchers' wishes, which is so essential for the development of science, becomes the demand for the separation of thinking and feeling. This promotes moral detachment in scientists which, reinforced by specialization and bureau-cratization, allows them to work on all sorts of dangerous and harmful projects with indifference to the human consequences. ...
>
> Science entered the Third World as a form of intellectual domination. After the troops depart, the investments remain; after direct ownership is removed, managerial skills, patents, textbooks, and journals remain, repeating the message

that only by adopting their ways can we progress, only by going to their universities can we learn; only by emulating their universities can we teach. (1985: 225–7)

An anecdote told to me by Trilokinath Madan, an anthropologist from India, captures the 'moral detachment' that Levins and Lewontin are talking about. Madan, being a specialist in kinship, attended an international meeting on that subject. There the topic of the kinship system of the Purum, a tribal group from northeastern India, came up. The Purum's kinship system has challenged the ingenuity of generations of anthropologists. Madan at one point asked the assembled anthropologists if they knew what had happened to the Purum. His question was greeted by an awkward silence. Professional anthropology transmutes the Purums into occasions for elegant anthropological theorizing.[23]

The danger of such a posture of emotional and moral detachment in science has nowhere been better revealed than in Zygmunt Bauman's book *Modernity and the Holocaust* (1991):

> Perhaps the most spectacular was the failure of science – as a body of ideas, and as a network of institutions of enlightenment and training. The deadly potential of the most revered principles and accomplishments of modern science has been exposed. The emancipation of reason from emotions, of rationality from normative pressures, of effectiveness from ethics have been the battle-cries of science since its inception. Once implemented, however, they made science, and the formidable technological applications it spawned, into docile instruments in the hands of unscrupulous power. The dark and ignoble role which science played in the perpetuation of the Holocaust was both direct and indirect …
>
> What truly mattered to German scientific (and more generally, intellectual) élites, and to the best and most distinguished individuals among them was the preservation of their integrity as scholars and spokesmen of Reason. And that task did not include (and did exclude in case of conflict) concern with the ethical meaning of their activity. As Alan Beyerchen found out, in the spring and summer of 1933 the luminaries of German science, people like Planck, Sommerfeld, Heisenberg, or von Laue, all 'counselled patience and restraint in dealing with the government, especially regarding dismissals and emigration. The primary goal was to preserve the professional autonomy of their discipline by avoiding confrontation and waiting for orderly life and procedures to resume.' (Bauman 1991: 108, 127)

Bauman also points out that the Nazis did not change the rules of professional conduct and that German universities – which were then the best in the world – continued carefully to cultivate the ideal of science as a value-free enterprise.

The latter part of the quotation from Levins and Lewontin states rather bluntly that the model of the university today is a hegemonic enterprise of the modern West. The model of the German university spread not only to the US but worldwide, and with it the notions of knowledge for knowledge's sake and the separation between knowledge and life (or theory and practice). That separation may tell us something about the seeming paradox of an exponential growth of knowledge about both the natural and the human world coupled with an exponential growth in species extinction and other threats to both the natural and the human environment.

Representational thinking versus conversation and mutual nurturance

Rengifo makes a distinction between dialogue (which he uses synonymously with conversation) and nurturing on the one hand and representation and transformation on the other:

> If a world, like the Andean one, is constituted by persons and not by subjects and objects, its members are not interested in 'knowing' the other, because they do not see the other as a thing or an object and also because they are not interested in acting upon it and transforming it. The focus is on mutual attunement ... for inasmuch as mutual conversation flowers, nurturing flows. Dialogue here does not end in an action that falls upon someone, but in a reciprocal nurturing ...
>
> One converses with the mouth, the hands, the sense of smell, vision, hearing, gestures, flowerings, the colours of the skin, the taste of the rain, the colour of the wind, etc. Since all are persons, all speak. The potatoes, the llamas, the human community, the mountains, the rain, the hail, the *huacas* [deities] speak. Language is not a verbal representation which encapsulates the named person ... The word makes present the named one, it is not, as it is said, a representation. (Rengifo, Chapter 3)

Rengifo's words echo those of Grillo cited above: 'one converses with the whole body'. Rengifo highlights a profound difference between 'representation' which is verbal and conceptual, and conversation and nurturing which involve the whole body. It is clearly not a matter of speaking metaphorically when they say that Andean peasants converse with the stars, the moon, the plants, the rocks, etc. Understanding such conversing as metaphorical or symbolic emerges from situating oneself within representational thought. Rengifo continues with a quote by Castelnuovo and Creamer: 'strictly speaking in order to be able to speak of "thought" there must exist a discrimination between the internal and the external world, between symbol and symbolized'. In other words, for it to be representational thought there must be a dualism between organism and environment.

According to environmental philosopher David Abram, the withdrawal of human senses from the world and the subsequent silencing of the non-human world began with the widespread use of the Greek alphabet and its offspring, classical Greek philosophy. In his deeply insightful book (1996) he shows that for all oral collectivities, the world itself speaks:

In indigenous, oral cultures, nature itself is articulate; it *speaks*. The human voice in an oral culture is always to some extent participant with the voices of wolves, wind, and waves – participant, that is, with the encompassing discourse of the animate earth. There is no element of the landscape that is definitely void of expressive resonance and power: any movement may be a gesture, any sound may be a voice, a meaningful utterance ... To directly perceive any phenomenon is to enter into relation with it, to feel oneself in a living interaction with another being. (Abram 1996: 116–17)[24]

David Abram is greatly influenced by French phenomenologist Maurice Merleau-Ponty, who also inspires the work of feminist philosopher Carol Bigwood. Representational thought, according to Bigwood, has character-ized Western philosophy from its beginning:

From the very beginnings of philosophy, Being has appeared as the ground, *arche* (principle), and *aition* (cause) from which beings as such can be known and can be at the disposal of reason ...

The peculiar representational nature of metaphysical thinking becomes prom-inent with modern, post-Cartesian thought ... To represent is to set a being before oneself in such a way that one can account for and be certain of that being. By means of the ground, interpreted now as ratio, what-is comes to stand in such a way that it is certified as an object for a representing subject. The ground guarantees that the object is firmly placed and secured as a calculable object for representational thought ...

What-is in the modern age thus becomes solely what can be represented, what can be referred back to the power of self-consciousness. Representational thinking assumes *that the rational human subject is the stable, relational center of what-is.* (1993: 27, 28; emphasis added)

Representational thinking is not only anthropocentric but rationalist. Know-ing consists of linguistic and conceptual *representations* in an individual's *mind*. The kind of conversing that Rengifo, Valladolid and Grillo talk about is simply not countenanced. Rather, when 'informants' report such conversations, they are classified as 'symbolic' or 'metaphorical'. Unless what-is can be penetrated by reason, defined and measured, it does not really exist or only exists in people's minds as 'beliefs'.[25] The anthropo-centrism of representational thought is how the organism/environment dualism manifests itself in the field of knowledge. The stable human subject is the centre of what-is; the stability of that centre, that human subjectivity at the centre, means that the subject is not affected in the process of knowing. The relationship is not mutual; it is not a conversation, not an act of mutual nurturing/caring; it is simply not an act. The dualism of organism versus environment is related to the mind/body dualism since the stable centre, the ground, is a *ratio*. Rationality is the stable centre for which the body becomes an object, a part of what-is – to be known, defined and measured. The body cannot become a source of knowledge. In fact at the beginning of experimental science, the senses were seen as 'infirmities'. The senses were to be remedied and rendered trustworthy by the use of experimental devices and instruments. Nature does not speak directly; it can be interrogated in the laboratory through experiments and it 'answers' or 'speaks', but these are metaphorical expressions. To 'hear nature speak' one has to be a specially trained person – today's professional expert – and be taught how to construct mechanical devices properly to interrogate nature. As Robert Boyle – the first experimentalist and inventor of the air pump in the seventeenth century – put it, the experimenters must be 'priests of nature' (Shapin and Schaffer 1985: 319). The analogy was a precise one since as lengthy an intellectual training is required to become a legitimate, professional interrogator of nature, as is required to become a priest. By ingenious devices, certain aristocratic and wealthy European men – women were kept out of this new priesthood as they were kept out of the old – were able to interrogate nature and receive its answers. The judicial vocabulary of interrogation is deliberate since Bacon, one of the founding figures of the scientific revolution, used the language of interrogation – even of interrogation under torture as in the trials of witches – to speak of the manner in which the secrets of nature must be wrenched from her (Bacon cited in Merchant 1980: 167).

In other words, in representational thought the body and the world are at the disposal of the representing subjective mind. This *ratio* can measure, define, weigh, manipulate and use the body and the world with its conceptual, linguistic and instrumental tools. As Descartes had seen clearly, this new *ratio* gave one power and control over nature (Descartes *Discours de la Méthode* 1961 VI 61–2). Eduardo Grillo specifically links representational thought and modern notions of time and space with industrial capitalism:

> As Heidegger put it, modern Western culture, the culture of capital, is characterized by making an image of the world: the world is not as it is but rather as I represent it. But, of course, not any image but an image functional to capital, which permits it to manipulate nature, to exploit it, to reduce it to productive resources. The image of the world for modern Westerners is constructed on the basis of the instruments of space and time. These instruments assure them of a world that is apprehensible, that one can appropriate, that one can make use of, a world that can be bought and sold ...
>
> Descartes himself constructs analytical geometry in order to contribute to apprehend, to measure, nature. Leibniz (1646–1716) and Newton (1643–1727) construct infinitesimal calculus thus completing the instruments to measure the *res extensa* ... with infinitesimal calculus the world becomes a continuous quantity, susceptible to being cut up as needed, susceptible to being measured ... Paniker ... notes: '(...) With the arrival of modernity and industrialization, emerged a purely commoditized time, a time entailing the sale of labor, a quantitative time, linear, abstract'. (Grillo 1993: 38–9)

It is clear from this quotation that Grillo – and this is true of the other two members of PRATEC – does not reject the tools of the professions out of 'purist principles', as Enrique Mayer imagines, but from a realization that these tools are profoundly implicated in the world of industrial capitalism. He and the other members of PRATEC have done the work of making visible such an implication. They make it clear that the utilization of such tools reproduces the world of industrial capitalism, a world whose internal dynamic leads to the disappearance of worlds such as that of the Andean peasants. This kind of work is rendered unnecessary – if not illegitimate – by the professional posture of the right to know using professional conceptual tools and instruments. This kind of work is not done in the professional training of those who come to the PRATEC course. In their professional training, the right to know using professional conceptual tools and instruments is not examined; it is taken for granted. Such a posture obviates the possibility of rendering visible the fact that such tools are not located in an unsituated universal domain, but rather are implicated in the emergence and reproduction of a particular world. They reproduce the world that emerged in Western Europe, which eventually became industrial capitalism. The work that PRATEC has done and continues to do, furthermore, shows that the conceptual tools and the nature of representational thought not only have particular cultural-historical roots but are only one way of being in the world, not necessarily the way that should prefigure everyone's future. By using the alternative notions of conversation, of mutual nurturing and others, PRATEC attempts to show a different world. The issue of the rejection of professional tools is crucial to that endeavour for, through their use, the Andean world appears to be lacking, pre-scientific, backward, poor, and as having any number of other unfortunate characteristics. Alternatively, using a professional perspective, that world can be shown to be exotic, quaint and interesting, full of rituals, myths and symbols, and fascinating as a museum exhibit of some precious and distant cultural artefacts but not as a world to live in, collectively to make a future in.

The members of PRATEC offer the Andean mode of being in the world, with its very different notions of space and time, of personhood, of nature, and others as a viable alternative in the Andes to Western modernity and development. They constantly emphasize that this alternative vision is not offered as a universal panacea for the ills of modernity. They constantly reiterate that this is a viable alternative to development and modernity *in the Andes*. They are engaged in transmitting what they have learned to people of Andean origins or Andean residence who, through university training and professionalization, have more or less accepted the dominant view that development and modernization are not only desirable but inevitable; the ultimate evolutionary destiny of human-kind. University training also has the effect of making them perceive the Andean world through the categories of their professions.

The impact of PRATEC's course on its participants is enormous. I have been able to witness it not only in my participation in the course but in talking with many PRATEC graduates throughout the Peruvian Andes. A common comment made by participants in the course goes something like this: 'these things were there all the time but I neither could see them nor hear them; I was deaf and blind; this course has enabled me to see and hear'. The course has changed their lives, not only their perceptions. Some of them have returned to their communities of origin and there engage in farming and/or herding and in activities to strengthen Andean practices.

Before turning to conversation and mutual nurturing and other key notions PRATEC's writings introduce us to, it is necessary to address another alternative to representational thought and foundational thinking, namely the post-modernist critique. Derrida replaces the notion of a stable, unified origin with a notion of *différance* (Derrida 1982). This is how Bigwood explains this term:

> [*D*]*ifférance* is text generated and is always differing/deferring, divided from itself. In the Derridean search for origins we discover only traces making continual referral to other traces. A sign is not a homogeneous unit, bridging an origin or referent and an end or meaning, but is haunted by the trace of another sign that is absent. Thus, *différance* is not ultimately a genesis but a perpetual play of traces. (Bigwood 1993: 34)

As Bigwood points out, although Derridean post-modernism (also called post-structuralism) has mounted a radical critique of 'regimes of truth', or metaphysical foundationalism, it shares with traditional Western metaphysics its privileging of culture over nature and the body:

> A sign of post-structuralist disregard of nature is the very language some post-structuralists use. Their talk of cultural inscriptions, plays of significations, signifiers and signifieds, deferring/differing, referring, referent – in short their semiotic terminology and textual metaphors – is alienated from embodied existence. The fleshless abstractness of their terminology and the nihilistic playfulness of deconstruction display an intellectual intoxication ...
>
> When post-structuralists make epistemological and ontological claims about our being, moreover, they generally place too much weight on language as a constituting force and on cognitive meaning (for example, Jacques Derrida's emphasis on the textual) and thereby disallow any true being to the nonlinguistic. (ibid.: 46)

Post-modernists understand nature as the production of given historical discourses, rejecting foundationalist notions of nature as a pre-cultural, fixed and unchangeable given. The body as a biological entity is an object of enquiry treated like other objects by representational thought. It is defined by fixed anatomical, genetic, hormonal and other scientifically established features. In the process of criticizing the givenness of what anthropologist David Schneider has called 'the facts of life'[26] – a view that privileges scientific knowledge of nature and the body – the post-modernists have done away with nature and the body altogether, seeing them as purely cultural constructions.

I think the manner in which Bigwood steers a path that avoids both the extremes of representational thought and foundationalism on the one hand and those of post-modernism on the other can help us to approach the Andean notions of conversation and mutual nurturance. Bigwood turns to the philosophy of Maurice Merleau-Ponty (1962) to speak of the body.[27] By making a bridge between Bigwood's feminist reading of Merleau-Ponty and the manner in which PRATEC writes about the Andean world, it is hoped simultaneously to de-exoticize that world as well as not read it in terms of the categories of either representational thought or deconstructionism. For Merleau-Ponty, the body is not a passive recorder of sense impressions but rather a sentience with a unique sensitivity to its environs. The emphasis is on the *lived* body that experiences rather than merely records phenomena. The body's sensitivity to its environs is due to the body's openness. The body is in constant contact with its environs through touch, breathing, ingesting, smelling, seeing, hearing, tasting, moving through the environs and more. The following passage captures Merleau-Ponty's understanding of the body and its relation to the world:

> let us take the example of sensuous contact such as that of looking deeply at the sky. If I fully attend to the sky, gazing up into its blue, my body gradually adopts a certain bodily attitude in response to the spacious blue. My eyes and my whole body slowly yield, relax, and enter into a sensuous rhythm of existence that is already there and that is peculiar to the sky in its blue depths. In its contact, my body adopts a 'certain living pulsation' of the sky itself that is not its own but that it lives through and that also lives through it and becomes my body's being of the moment. My living situation becomes one of blue. I can feel the blue profundity and become immersed in it because of a bodily openness that lets the sky pulse through me and, in the same trembling stroke, lets my sensing breathe life into the blue sky. Existence realizes itself in the body because of this incarnate communion with its surroundings. I am not a passive spectator of the sky; I commune with it, or rather, a coition takes place where the sky and myself are only abstract moments of a single incarnate communication. (Bigwood 1993: 50)

This body in communion with its environment is the living body not separate from its environment, not external to it, but inextricably of it. The environment is not external, a distanced object of observation, rather it flows in and through the body. In the actions of seeing, smelling, eating, breathing, moving and so on, the body and the environment are changing, mutually affecting each other. Neither is a fixed, bounded entity. The world is always latent in all our actions and experiences. The world and the body are a unified field, always mutually intertwining and mutually affecting, creating, changing each other. In this coition, to use Merleau-Ponty's arresting term, it is the pre-linguistic, pre-cognitive body that is highlighted.

This is very close to Grillo's words: 'conversation cannot be reduced to dialogue, to the word ... here conversation engages us vitally: one converses with the whole body. To converse is to show each other reciprocally, it is to share, to commune, to dance to the rhythm which in every moment corresponds to the annual cycle of life' (see above). The Andean peasant does not experience her gazing at the rising of a particular constellation in a particular region on the horizon as a unidirectional act on her part. Rather it is experienced as the constellation and the gazer being united in a conversation. These conversations lead to wisdom rather than knowledge; wisdom emerges from the body–world interface; it is not an intellectual, conceptual, or symbolic 'knowledge' or set of 'beliefs' held in the mind. As the members of PRATEC constantly reiterate, in the Andean world there is no dualism between humans and the world.

Grillo continues by saying that 'conversation is inseparable from nurturing [*criar*]'. Conversation is a reciprocal act that brings about 'nurturance'. The Spanish verb *criar* is used to speak of raising children, of growing plants, of raising animals, of making a cultivated field (*chacra*). It too is a fundamentally reciprocal action. PRATEC captures this by the oft repeated phrase '*criar y dejarse criar*', to nurture and let oneself be nurtured. Nurture connotes a caring relationship that lets the nurtured one come forth freely, emerge from the dark, invisible earth or womb, and unfold according to its own rhythm. In the word nurturance, there is no sharp distinction between the internal bringing forth of nature and the external human actions of making or helping. In nurturing we bring forth through the one being nurtured; we attend to the nurtured one's rhythms of growth and are responsive to it in its integrity. The attitude of nurturing requires attentiveness and sensitivity to enable the nurtured one to grow into the fullness of life. In so doing the nurturer is not unaffected. The very act of nurturing, of caring for, nurtures oneself – allows the nurturer to participate in the unfolding and growth. Such responsiveness happens through conversation, through the openness one has towards the one being nurtured and towards the world. It is that openness that implicates one in the processes that one attends to. The nurturer does not remain unchanged by the act of nurturing because fundamentally one is not separate from what one nurtures. The principle of reciprocity (*ayni, minka*) pervades relationships in peasant communities, where people work on each other's fields and tasks. But that principle is one that pervades all relationships, not only those between humans.

It therefore follows that nurturing is not the sole prerogative of humans. A person who nurtures a field is in turn nurtured by the plants grown in that field, or the animals raised there. Alpaca herders will say 'Just as we nurture alpacas, the alpacas nurture us' (Rengifo, Chapter 3). In a first fruit ritual in the Puno region, the wives of the ritual leaders take out the first fruits or seeds at the time of the harvest and they have them embrace the fruits and seeds preserved from the ritual of the previous year. The ritual leader, becoming the voice of the old seeds and fruits, addresses the new fruits and seeds as follows: 'as we have nurtured these people, now it is your turn to also nurture them' (Valladolid, Chapter 2). Nurturing is made possible by conversation. This is how a Bolivian peasant formulates it:

> We have great faith in what nature transmits to us. These indicators are not the result of the science of humans nor either the invention of people with great experience. Rather, it is the voice of nature itself which announces to us the manner in which we must plant our crops. (Rengifo, Chapter 3)

This last statement could have been uttered by one of the new 'grass' dairy farmers in Wisconsin. In an article reporting on this new phenomenon, Hassanein and Kloppenburg (1995) tell how the primary focus of dairy farming there has been maximizing milk production per cow throughout the year. Milk production is based on year-round feeding of stored forage to livestock kept in confinement. The forage is grown in the farm's fields as monocultures that replace the natural prairie grass that grew there. A hundred years of scientific investigation and technological invention has provided a steady flow of technical innovations that have kept the farmers on the technological treadmill. To stay alive, dairy farmers have been forced to produce more milk by running ever faster on the technological treadmill. In the past decade or so a growing number of dairy farmers have stepped off that treadmill and begun rotational grazing and seasonal milking. As Hassanein and Kloppenburg show, this shift has profound implications. One of them is that farmers are no longer dependent on expert knowledge from the land grant universities but need to develop their own powers of observation. As one farmer puts it:

> You have to look ahead and determine when to graze and that requires experience and observation ... There aren't any rules or regulations. You gotta look at the pasture. You can't look at a calendar and know what to do. The whole thing is observation. (Hassanein and Kloppenburg 1995: 10)

Another farmer says: 'I simply cannot understand why nobody has challenged the university and their assumptions about dairy farms ... None of these people are performing the functions that I need.' These farmers engaged in what Addelson calls direct action and simply walked away from high tech dairying and into pasture grazing on their own. This has led them to a complete change of outlook, even of cosmology. This can be captured by what yet another farmer is quoted as saying: 'You let Mother Nature put the plants where she wants 'em ... you are farming in harmony with nature; you are not fighting nature' (ibid.: 13) and another even spoke of letting nature speak!

This example from the 'new' dairy farmers in Wisconsin is invoked both to de-exoticize the Andean manner of being in the world as well as to show that more technology, more expert knowledge, and more production does not seem an inevitable future even in the US, let alone in the Andes.

An alternative to both progressivism and fundamentalism

PRATEC is committed to what it calls 'cultural affirmation', namely to strengthen Andean culture and peasant practices, and this they do mainly through their course. Many of the graduates of that course engage directly with peasants, getting involved in sharing seeds, practices and wisdom from one community to another, gathering the wisdom of the elders in particular in an effort to counter the influence of schooling which trains its pupils to leave their world, a world portrayed as ignorant and backward.[28] Simply by the fact of questioning development knowledge and seeing Andean reality with new eyes, technicians of development strengthen Andean culture by not working towards transforming it. This should not be confused with a desire to 'preserve culture', frozen in time and static. The perception of change and dynamism as being equated with modernization is one of the more unfortunate to come out of the tradition/ modernity dichotomy. It cannot be sufficiently emphasized that at any given time, a 'culture' is made up of the inflow and outflow that the process of digestion entails; it is not a 'rigidly defined set of practices or products surviving from the society's past' (Nandy 1987).

The term 'cultural affirmation' also means to take up a particular stance towards the world. This is how Grillo puts it:

> We are a living world. We live nurturing and letting ourselves be nurtured. We live the immediacy of familiarity, of nurturance, of tenderness; we love the world as it is. Here there is no separation between man and nature. Here we do not want to transform the world: we are not a world of knowledge, we are not the world of technology. Here neither subject nor object, nor ends and means, nor abstraction belong. (1994b: 35)

The expression to 'love the world as it is' expresses a radical rejection of the modernist stance towards the world. This modernist, scientific stance is articulated by Grillo as follows:

> Science is the crystallization of an attitude of profound discontent and lack of trust toward the world as it is. The world is decidedly confronted in order to transform it into 'what must be'; that is into what is convenient to power. (ibid.: 34)

This statement is remarkably similar to a statement made by the Indian philosopher-saint Gopinath Kaviraj:

> Such an attitude of doubt, however, which in the West was first clearly stated by Descartes, involves a breach of faith towards everything that is. This breach entails the hostility of all against all and against all things. Nothing can be sure and immediately certain any more except one thing, the doubting ego.[29]

Eduardo Grillo and Gopinath Kaviraj's statements are made within a cosmology that does not separate humans from the world and that views the world as being alive. The attitude of transforming the world into 'what must be' can be illustrated by Hassanein and Kloppenburg's example of dairy farming in Wisconsin. Modernist dairying aims to get the maximum production of milk from the cow. The problem is defined and solved not by the farmer, but by experts at the land grant universities. In other words the expert does not live the life of the farmer, and does not care for the land or the cows; farming is not a way of life for the expert. Thus his or her solutions are purely rational, efficient ways of reaching the goal of maximum production. The landscape is transformed, the natural prairie eliminated and replaced by monocultures of feed grains with intensive use of pesticides and chemical fertilizers. Heavy machinery is needed to sow and reap these feed crops. The cows are confined and the feed taken to them. The manure must be removed with heavy equipment. It is not used on the fields. The cows' stationary existence makes them more susceptible to diseases and they must be given antibiotics and hormones. Nowadays, the cows are given bovine growth hormones to increase the milk yield. The landscape is totally altered and heavy machinery is a necessity. The farmer is dependent on expert advice and does not rely on his or her own observations and senses as well as experience. Many species of plants that grew naturally become defined as 'weeds' and need to be eliminated. The whole is viewed as a 'production system' rather than as a way of life. As a production system, there is no room for emotion, attachment or mutual caring. The land, the waters, the soils, the plants, the animals are only inputs in a productive system. The people are 'human resources' – another kind of input into the system.

This model is generalized to all food production in the US and in many other places all over the world. It is now well recognized that this manner of producing food is both ecologically and socially destructive (Kloppenburg et al. forthcoming). The world, both natural and human, is transformed into inputs into the productive system and the economy. Life – the complicated webs between people and between people and place that regenerate themselves over time – has no integrity. Work – understood as commoditized work that feeds into the productive system – is dominant, and 'life' is relegated to an individualized private and dependent domain. This is not only so in agriculture but in all walks of life. In that production-driven world, there is no place for care and nurturance. These are relegated to the devalued margins and the feminized sphere of the home. The regeneration of life – both human and non-human – cannot happen without nurturance. We are ontologically interdependent with all that is, and this means that mutual nurturance is the only way that life can regenerate itself.

The progressivist attitude of distrust towards the world betrays a profound anthropocentrism. The world is there to fit human needs and desires. It is not allowed to dwell in its integrity. It is currently common to speak not only of 'natural resources' – that is parts of the non-human world seen only in terms of their utility for (certain) humans – but also of 'human resources'. It is not only nature that must be transformed into 'what must be' but society as well. Everything must be transformed, changed, improved, so that ever greater productivity can be attained. In the human sphere, anthropocentrism becomes Eurocentrism, where different people are not allowed to dwell in their integrity but must be 'developed' and 'studied'. Greater productivity, ever since Mandeville's *Fable of the Bees* (first published in 1714),[30] has been seen as the key to progress and greater 'happiness'.

Within this broad view, there are differences as to how exactly the goal can be achieved and how much weight is to be given to issues of equity and distribution, but these are internal disputes. The impetus to change, transform, and jettison pre-modern and non-modern ways of life is fundamentally ongoing, whether it wears a democratic, a socialist, a communist, or a national socialist face. All of these political forms are united in the desire to transform the world into 'what must be'. The latter is of course defined differently by diverse tendencies within modernism but all share a determination to improve and transform, a vision of a better and radically different society. The impetus to transform the world into 'what must be' corresponds of course to the ideology of progress. In the field of improving society, the vision of a better society can, and has, justified the worst horrors of the twentieth century. Bauman makes this explicit:

> Getting rid of the adversary is not an end in itself. It is a means to an end: a necessity that stems from the ultimate objective, a step that one has to take if one wants ever to reach the end of the road. *The end itself is a grand vision of a better, and radically different, society.* Modern genocide is an element of social engineering, meant to bring about a social order conforming to the design of the perfect society ... [O]ne can and should remake society, force it to conform to an overall, scientifically conceived plan. One can create a society that is objectively better than the one 'merely existing' – that is, existing without conscious intervention. (1991: 91, emphasis in original)

This approach to the world, for which Bauman uses the garden metaphor – that is to make the world conform to a plan and eradicate the weeds

– is as true of democratic industrial capitalism and communism or socialism as it is true of national socialism.

With the break-up of the former Soviet Union, the enormity of Stalin's
internal genocide is now common knowledge.[31] Similarly the famine in
China in the late 1950s and early 1960s, caused by the government at the
time of the 'great leap forward', is now known to have killed between
16.5 and 29.9 million people (Dreze and Sen 1989: 210). In the US, one
example is the recently released information about the military's experiments on civil populations – including retarded children – on the
effects of radiation without the people's knowledge. Other examples could
include the services offered by American universities to Dow Chemical
Minneapolis, Honeywell, Boeing Aircraft or to ITT in the re-establishment
of fascism in Chile (Bauman 1991: 126–7).

There is another modernist tendency that adheres to the garden metaphor but does not belong to the above three types of regime. I am speaking
of the various fundamentalist movements of the twentieth century.
Although fundamentalists often define themselves as anti-modernists and
many outside the West as anti-Western, they do share with the modern
West a commitment to transforming society through social engineering.
The rhetoric is emphatically not secular, but social engineering is definitely
part of the programme. The garden metaphor dominates in the language
of the eradication of whatever is not the true, or pure, or authentic.
Whether we are talking of the Islamists in Iran, Algeria, Egypt, Pakistan
or India, or the Hindu fundamentalists, or the Christian fundamentalists,
what unites them is the determination, at whatever cost, to establish or
preserve the 'true' or 'pure' version of their faith and society. Fundamentalist movements or governments have been as quick to use violence to bring
about their vision of the good society as have the secular Western political
forms discussed above. For fundamentalists, typically, the better society is
not in the future but in the past, which explains their often anti-modernist
rhetoric. Generally, this past is enshrined in some sacred textual canon.
The zeal with which fundamentalists go about eradicating what does not
correspond to their version of the good/true/pure is quite in keeping with
the zeal with which the classless society, or the Aryan nation, or the free
market society have been pursued. In that zeal, the fundamentalists have
not hesitated to use all the technological and scientific devices that the
West has spawned, considering that the ends justify the means.

In their study of the Ramjanmabhumi Hindu fundamentalist movement,
Ashis Nandy et al. (1995) contrast its version of Hinduism with that of
M. K. Gandhi. Gandhi, like PRATEC, had a well-articulated critique of
Western science and technology. He took his inspiration from what Nandy
et al. call 'vernacular Hinduism': the non-Brahmanical, non-Sanskritized
folk practices of the majority of the rural peasantry. The Hindu fundamentalists – most of whom revile Gandhi – according to these authors

favoured Brahmanical, textual Hinduism; they characterize it as a variant
of modernism:

> One reaction [to nineteenth-century colonialism] took the form of a defensive
> attempt to redefine Hinduism as a 'proper' religion along Semitic lines and to
> make this redefined Hinduism the pillar of a second, nativized theory of
> modernization of mind and society in India ... [T]he ideology of nationalism
> was nativized in a form that could sanction the attempts to convert the Hindus
> into a conventional, European-style nation. (Nandy et al. 1995: 57)

Hindu fundamentalism, like Islamic fundamentalism (see Leila Ahmed
1992 for the case of Egypt), is nationalist and rejects any 'traditional
technology or skill that diminishes or subverts the power of the state of
its centralizing thrust'. Hindu fundamentalism has shown no interest in
traditional Indian concepts of state craft or artisan skills (ibid.: 62). Fundamentalism is a modern phenomenon that uses religion instrumentally for
nationalist purposes.

A central characteristic of fundamentalism is the demonizing of the
Other. This is often achieved by making appeals to righteous anger and
the status of the victim.[32] PRATEC has taken an uncompromising stance
in rejecting victimhood, in spite of 500 years of often brutal colonization.
This is how Eduardo Grillo phrases it:

> Just like when frost or hail falls in the fields of our peasant communities it is
> because some of us have disrupted the harmony of the world with our incorrect
> conduct, similarly the apparition of the Spanish invaders is due to the perturb-
> ance in the harmony of our own world. To free ourselves from colonization we
> have to recuperate our internal harmony. Then it will be impossible to colonize
> us, just like in a healthy and strong person, in whom life flows fully, illness
> cannot penetrate. It is not a question of acting directly against the invader
> because while we remain perturbed another can always come and invade us.
> (Grillo 1994a: 24; see also Chapter 4)

Such an attitude leads to a non-oppositional as well as a non-vindicatory
stance. Misfortune, conflict, any kind of obstacle is not attributed to an
outside force but is seen as emerging from actions within. This precludes
the demonizing of the Other, the one who is different – a stance regularly
employed by fundamentalist movements. PRATEC refuses for itself, and
for the Andean world of which it speaks, the position of victim. Furthermore, an oppositional stance belongs to a dynamic where the opponent
and the one opposed are locked together. The oppositional stance for
colonized peoples has been labelled by Dion-Buffalo and Mohawk (1994)
one of 'bad-subjecthood' which they reject in favour of 'non-subjecthood',
a stance very close to PRATEC's.

This non-oppositional stance leads PRATEC to reject all manner of
formal political organizing and violence. In Grillo's words:

it is not a matter of forming another political party because such formalism would fetter the decentralized creative capacity required by the task of decolonization.

Nor is it a matter of using violent means to deactivate the apparatus of colonization. We consider that what is adequate is to affirm ourselves each time more in our own Andean culture, dispensing with having recourse to the colonial authorities, breaking with the colonial authorities, leaving them thus without function and obsolete ... [W]e believe that violence justifies the presence and the action of the police, the army, the magistrates and the rest of officialdom. (Grillo, Chapter 4)

This position is one that makes for a radical contrast with most fundamentalist movements, which are characterized by a thirst for power (Madan 1997; Nandy et al. 1995; Ahmed 1992). PRATEC's non-oppositional stance is similar to the position articulated by a group in the US who are trying to create alternatives to the global food system. These alternatives are seen in regional food production and consumption, what Kloppenburg has called 'foodsheds' by analogy with 'watersheds':

What these diverse people and groups share is that their activities and commitments involve various degrees of *disengagement* from the existing food system and especially from the narrow commodity and market relations on which it is based. We follow Wendell Berry and David Orr in our conviction that a fundamental principle of the foodshed is the need for 'secession'. The principle of secession is based on a strategic preference for withdrawing from and/or creating alternatives to the dominant system rather than challenging it directly ... A primary strategy of the secession principle is 'slowly hollowing out' the structures of the global food system by reorganizing our own social and productive capacities. (Kloppenburg et al. forthcoming)

This position of secession, of hollowing out, can also explain PRATEC's rejection of the politics engaged in by various 'indigenous' groups of Peru, Bolivia and Ecuador to have their territory recognized by the state, and gain other concessions from the state such as bilingual education and the like. These politics recognize the legitimacy of the state, create artificially bounded, non-porous units, and set the stage for potentially disastrous inter-ethnic competition and rivalries since they are all competing for handouts from the state. More fundamentally, such politics are based on a self/Other exclusive dichotomy which – according to PRATEC as well as to Ashis Nandy et al. – betrays the essentially fluid and porous boundaries characteristic of the vernacular native world-view. PRATEC does not exclude people of Japanese, Chinese, African, European or any other origin from participating in the making of the Andean-Amazonian world: after Eduardo Grillo's death Jorge Ishizawa, who is of Japanese descent, became a core member of PRATEC; he is married to a woman of European descent and Grimaldo Rengifo is married to a woman of

African descent. The self/Other dualism is modelled upon the dualism and exclusivism characteristic of Western modernity. It has characterized not only much of anthropology but colonialism and imperialism, ethnic conflict, genocide, forced assimilation[33] and the like.[34]

PRATEC's writings are of course a 'reading' of the Andean world, and PRATEC are the first to say so. They are acutely aware that what they are doing, namely putting down in discursive prose the living reality of a diverse and oral world, is in no way the equivalent of living that world. They reiterate that their writings reflect their own understanding of the Andean world and reject the status of canonical truth for their statements. However, since they are no longer involved in a double participation, in writing of the Andean-Amazonian world they participate in making it. They belong to that world and speak from within it and – as with all such speaking and acting – it is part of making that world. Their reading of and speaking of the Andean-Amazonian world is also their participation in making that world. They speak of their course as their *chacra*. There, through conversations, they nurture each other. They have chosen their *chacra* to fit their lives; they are former professionals of development who have retaken possession of their Andean selves and rejected the double participation that professionalization entails. They have rejected the knowledge system of their former professions and emphatically do not see themselves as teaching the peasants, to whom they have nothing to teach rather they see themselves as learning from the peasants.

The Andean world is not one frozen into 'structures', 'kinship systems', 'economic organizations' or whatever social scientific categories are currently in vogue. It is a dynamic world, a world of events, constantly making itself, creating itself through innumerable acts of conversation and nurturing. There are here no knower and known, no subject and object; rather there are actors in relationships of mutuality. By acting one affects not only the world but oneself as well. Therefore it is a fundamentally dynamic world – always moving, always changing, always in flux. There is no simple act of knowing, for such knowledge-acquiring activity presupposes that there is something to be known, irrespective of who knows it. There is not a knowable, more or less fixed, 'tradition' lying there as an object available to the criticisms of an observing and judging subjectivity separated from what it judges. There are continuities and some perennial facets to the Andean world, but these continuities are incessantly remade, in flux, regenerated. But regeneration is not transformation. The dynamic of regeneration emerges from the attitude of loving the world as it is, as a parent loves a child, not wanting to transform him or her into someone else. Regeneration, unlike transformation, emerges from an unbroken faith and connection with what-is. The doubting ego, this pillar of modernity, does not exist.

Conclusion: knowledge and life reunited

In coming to know PRATEC and in collaborating with them since 1994, I have abandoned the stance of 'studying the Other', the classical anthropological stance. I abandoned fieldwork.[35] This collaboration has been a long conversation and a mutual nurturance. Deep friendships and passionate attachments have been forged. What we have done together emerged from these conversations and friendships; it did not result from project proposals and planning sessions and, of course, not from doing fieldwork.[36] The genesis of our collaboration or, more aptly expressed, our conversation and mutual learning/nurturance goes back to the conference Stephen A. Marglin and I organized in Bellagio in August 1993.[37] The conference had two parts: the first part consisted of presenting papers and commenting on them; the second part was dedicated to a planning session on what the Centers for Mutual Learning Project would be. The contingents from India (four persons), from Tanzania (two persons), from Thailand (one person), Scandinavia (one person) and from PRATEC (one person, Grillo), were all invited to submit proposals for setting up these centres in their regions. People went off to caucus and prepare written proposals. Grillo reacted differently from everyone else. He told us that at PRATEC they work on the basis of consensus; since his friends were not present he could not speak for them. He added that in the Andes, people first came to know each other, conversed to see if a friendship emerged, before embarking on a path together. So he invited several of us to visit them in Peru, get to know them and the place, and let things emerge from the conversations. Right from the beginning Grillo refused to separate knowledge from life.

I and Witoon Permpongsacharoen from Thailand visited PRATEC in Peru for the first time in March 1994. We travelled to many places in the country and met with graduates of the PRATEC course. The trip was full of conversations with the people and the land. From those conversations emerged an invitation from Witoon to Jorge Ishizawa to visit Thailand and participate in a workshop Witoon's organization (Project for Ecological Recovery [PER]) was organizing, and an invitation from Rengifo, Valladolid and Grillo for me to go and lecture in the third unit of their course in the following October. What we have done together – the mutual translations of our work,[38] the visits of PRATEC members to the US for conferences, lectures and meetings with Native Americans, my visits to Peru (and those of others we invited from the US), my (and others') participation in PRATEC's annual assembly, in regional workshops and in the course – all emerged spontaneously from our conversations and our friendship. We made a path by walking it.

The impact on me has been deep. I no longer see the critique of the concepts and tools of my profession and the form of knowledge to which it pertains or self-reflexivity or the attempt to give voice to subjects as being the answer to the anthropological dilemma. The answer to that dilemma requires of one nothing less than the questioning of the very notion of knowledge and of the social organization of its production. The dilemma of the anthropologist became visible with the political decolonization of the former colonies. The anthropologized have talked back and made it clear that the one-way gaze of anthropology is not particularly to their liking. As a result of such critical assessments, the profession of anthropology has engaged in a remarkable process of self-questioning. Of all the social sciences, anthropology is the discipline that has questioned itself most thoroughly and most searchingly. This questioning and searching has produced many valuable results. It seems to me, however, that as long as the discipline itself – along with the social organization of the production of knowledge in the value-neutral, autonomous university – continues to be taken for granted, the dilemma will not really be addressed.

The dilemma of anthropology became visible and articulated because of geopolitical events. However, it is not fundamentally different from the situation in the other social sciences and even in the natural sciences. The similarity consists in this: in all the sciences – social and natural – the gaze is one-way. The knower's *ratio* is the stable centre from which everything and everyone is observed and known. The world to be known is separated from the world to be lived; knower and known are divided as are self and Other, cognition and emotion. Knowledge is pursued for knowledge's sake so that regenerative (or procreative) concerns have no place. The non-human world is not an interlocutor, not a sentience with whom one converses, not a being (or beings) whose integrity must be respected, not a sentience to nurture and be nurtured by. Knowledge is not an activity, not a living, not a mutual interaction.

As far as anthropology is concerned we simply cannot assume a right to know, however self-reflexive and self-critical the tools used to achieve that knowledge may be. To act responsibly, our engagements with people living lives different from our own must result first of all from a *mutual* desire for interaction. We must stop arriving uninvited in people's back yards. If interaction does take place, it must involve all of ourselves, and must be lived in mutuality so that shared nurturance, interactive learning, and mutual regeneration emerge from it. We must approach such engagements with the willingness to have our lives and our selves profoundly affected and be prepared for a life-long commitment if that is what is required by the circumstances; our commitment must shift from profession and career building to mutual nurturance – and this requires the abandonment of the pursuit of knowledge for knowledge's sake. In anthropology, the size of its scholarly archive bears no relationship to the well-being of the people studied (the situation is very similar in the natural sciences).[39] In fact the fate of the people studied has not overly concerned the profession as a whole. Those organizations that emerged in the late 1960s and early 1970s, such as IGWIA, Cultural Survival and Survival International, are all NGOs functioning outside of academia. As David Maybury-Lewis – founder of Cultural Survival – put it, his appeals to the profession to intervene in the dire fate that had befallen the Xavante, whom he had studied almost twenty years before, floated like lead balloons.[40] This prompted his decision to create Cultural Survival. Such an incident is nothing short of scandalous. However, according to the tenets of the social organization of knowledge and the separation of knowledge from life – that is, the credo of knowledge for knowledge's sake – not only does such human indifference not appear shameful; it is seen as the proper thing to do.

Knowledge for knowledge's sake or the pursuit of 'pure' knowledge/science requires the autonomous university. It gives the knower, the enquirer, total freedom in the enquiry, constrained only by the enquirer's intelligence and vision. This unfettering of the pursuit of knowledge has given rise to an unprecedented explosion of knowledge. At the same time (beginning in earnest in the mid-nineteenth century) there has been an explosion in the industrial, commercial and military uses of that knowledge – giving industrial societies enormous power. The pure scientist is not responsible for the applications his or her knowledge is put to. Harvard biologist Ruth Hubbard has put it this way:

> Scientific writing implicitly denies the relevance of time, place, social context, authorship, and personal responsibility … The assumption is that if the science is 'good', in a professional sense, it will also be good for society. But no one or no group is responsible for looking at whether it is. Public accountability is not built into the system. (Hubbard 1990: 13, 24)

Whether one refers to the atomic bomb, the accelerated and rather alarming rate of extinctions of animal and plant species, acid rain, the ozone hole, and many other natural and social environmental degradations, no one is responsible for those; they are just unfortunate by-products of the application of knowledge. So the unfettering of knowledge is a double-edged sword. The wonders of modern technology that we are all so addicted to are also implicated in natural and social environmental degradation.

The separation between theory and practice or pure science and its application is necessary to a world where not only pure knowledge is pursued in the autonomous university but its applications are carried out by experts trained at the university hired by industry, commerce or the military. Both applied scientists and pure scientists have an unquestioned right to know in terms of their disciplinary concepts and methods. They are responsible only to their professions and their bosses, not to those who are affected – adversely or otherwise – by their knowledge. The starkest example of this situation is that of scientists under the Nazi regime referred to by Bauman, who worried mainly about being able to continue their professional work without interference (see above). The process is one-way; there is no mutuality, no conversation, no engagement. The pursuit of pure or applied knowledge is divided from the passions of embodied, full-blooded life. In this sort of enquiry, no new relations are made and, as a result, no new kind of self emerges, brought about by the interaction. The body and the emotions – not to speak of the spirit – are closed off; there is no sensitivity to the environs, no flow through the enquirer's body, no openness. The knower/known dichotomy becomes a self/Other dichotomy. Objectivity, the bracketing of values and emotions, objectifies the known – Othering it. Such a stance is functional to a world where regeneration is marginalized, and production and accumulation have become the ends of existence.

In my collaboration with PRATEC I have not had the freedom to decide unilaterally what I would focus on, what questions to ask, what our path would be, or how to go about walking it. I have been constrained by the priorities, wishes and life circumstances of the members of PRATEC as well as by my own. What guided us at the beginning was the general idea of mutual learning, of a two-way flow between equivalents that would strengthen both parties. But there were no models, no beaten paths. We made the path by walking it. There has been a conversation, a mutual learning, a mutual nurturance that has left both parties affected. We have opened to each other and in the process I have experienced a kind of gestalt shift. I feel responsible for what has emerged and cannot abandon it for greener academic pastures. In fact, as a result of this collaboration I have negotiated a part-time appointment at my institution so as to have the time to live up to the responsibilities I have acquired. Part of these are to create the conditions where I live that will foster and strengthen this new understanding of learning and living, a task I intend to carry out in conversation with PRATEC. My collaboration with PRATEC cannot be separated from committed friendships, from deep emotion as well as from deep insights. It has affected the way I live my life and I have undergone profound changes.

Notes

1. Organized by the Intercultural Institute of Montreal, director Kalpana Das.

2. Three books have been published from that collaborative group which started in 1985 under the auspices of the United Nations University World Institute for Development Economics Research (UNU/WIDER) in Helsinki. They are: Frédérique Apffel-Marglin and Stephen A. Marglin (eds) *Dominating Knowledge: Development, Culture, and Resistance* Oxford University Press, Clarendon, 1990; Tariq Banuri and Frédérique Apffel-Marglin (eds) *Who Will Save the Forests?* Zed Books, London, 1993; and Frédérique Apffel-Marglin and Stephen A. Marglin (eds) *Decolonizing Knowledge: From Development to Dialogue* Oxford University Press, Clarendon, 1996.

3. We are deeply grateful as well as admiring of the way Dan Martin of the

Foundation supported the exploration of an untested and novel idea, that of mutual learning.

4. Grimaldo was initially also working with François Greslou, a Frenchman married to a Peruvian, who had to leave the country in the late 1980s due to the danger posed to him and his family by Shining Path. Another early collaborator at PRATEC was Enrique Moya who also left the group.

5. They are now partly funded by the European Community, Terre des Hommes, Bolivian Office and Oxfam America, Lima office.

6. Two leftist Marxist parties, the Confederacion Campesina del Peru (CCP) and the Confederacion Nacional Agraria (CNA), arrogated to themselves the leadership of a peasant movement with the intention of establishing communal land holding. The silent movement Mayer and PRATEC speak about refers to the direct action of Andean peasants inspired by their native culture and modes of relating to land (the re-creation of the *allyu*). According to Danish anthropologist Søren Hvalkoff (personal communication), the CCP and the CNA never succeeded in their aims. I am grateful to Søren for this information.

7. Søren Hvalkoff, who has worked with the indigenous movements in Peru and Ecuador for the last twenty-five years, tells me that no tradition of debating science and modern Western epistemology exists in South America as a whole.

8. In a course I co-taught with Shiv Visvanathan at Smith College in the spring of 1992 on precisely that topic, I learned a great deal about the nature of the debate and its lengthy pedigree in India. I cannot do justice here to that complex information and refer the interested reader to forthcoming publications by Shiv Visvanathan of the Centre for Developing Societies in Delhi.

9. Cited in Enrique Mayer 1992: 193–4.

10. Marcela Machaca, who is from Quispillacta in the province of Ayacucho, and Julio Valladolid, who lives in Ayacucho city, told me that in their region Sendero has systematically killed the Andean native 'priests'.

11. For a detailed analysis of the Green Revolution and its precursor, the development of Hybrid corn in the US, see the excellent work of Jack Kloppenburg Jr, 1988.

12. J. van Kessel teaches at the Free University in Amsterdam in the department of sociology. He has done research as well as missionizing in the Andes for at least twenty-five years. He is a visiting lecturer in PRATEC's course and the author of many works on Andean culture.

13. Enrique Mayer's remarks are made in the context of debating the position of a US anthropologist, Orin Starn (1991), who has criticized andinismo as romanticizing, not focusing on the Indians' poverty, hunger and desire for a 'better life', and thus failing to predict the rise of Shining Path. I will not discuss this view since it is a variant of the radical views I do discuss.

14. This is not the path that Watanabe pursues. He falls back on a rather conventional advocacy of anthropologists' comparative advantage with regard to the pan-Mayanists or any other native intellectuals, and argues for anthropologists supplying the comparative perspective.

15. I thank Trilokinath Madan for reminding me of this passage.

16. Triloki Madan, a student of Derek Freeman, when faced with a choice of field, simply could not reconcile himself to studying strangers and opted to study his own people, the Kashmiri Pandits.

17. On the absence of this separation, see especially Roy Wagner's discussion in *The Invention of Culture* (1981), Chapter 5.

18. See Louise Tilly (1978) for a critique of the use of the public/domestic

dichotomy by certain feminist anthropologists to account for non-commoditized and non-industrialized societies.

19. I am grateful to John Connolly for sending me his essay on Kant's *The Conflict of the Faculties* which alerted me to this quote. It is also thanks to Connolly that I have the more exact translation of the German *fabrikenmässig*, which Mary Gregor translates as 'mass production'. See Connolly 1995.

20. Marcus Raskin produced many years ago a searing critique of the production of knowledge in the universities and characterized that system as a colonialist one. See Raskin 1973.

21. Enrique Mayer now teaches in the anthropology department of Yale University. I am grateful to Tirso Gonzales for sending me this article by Mayer.

22. Not only Grillo but other PRATEC members often use the phrase 'Andean-Amazonian'. Such inclusiveness has been criticized by some. It can be defended by pointing out that at the rather general level at which they speak, the principles apply to both regions, which are otherwise quite differentiated. The Andean world is itself a diverse one made up of various ethnicities. In this diversity, PRATEC members focus on some generally shared cosmological traits.

23. Organizations such as IGWIA, Cultural Survival, and Survival International were created in the late 1960s and early 1970s out of a critique of anthropology's amoral stance. All three organizations are NGOs outside academia.

24. Abram's theory of language corresponds closely to that held by PRATEC.

25. On this issue see also my discussion of 'beliefs' in 'Rationality, the body and the world: from production to regeneration' in Apffel-Marglin and Marglin (eds) *Decolonizing Knowledge: From Development to Dialogue* 1996.

26. Schneider (1980) has criticized the view of kinship as biology in anthropology and shown it to be a cultural artefact. However, even he, in the last instance, has recourse to a universal truth about the biology of the body, what he calls the 'facts of life'. See Sarah Franklin 'The Virgin Birth Controversy in Anthropology' MA thesis, Dept of Anthropology, NYU, 1988.

27. The anthropologist Pierre Bourdieu has also approached the body in a non-reductionist manner. In *The Logic of Practice* he argues that cultural orientations and preferences are inscribed in the body. That the body through something like kinaesthetic formulae – akin to the verbal formulas that oral bards employ – what he calls *habitus*, encodes sociocultural norms. Bourdieu, as the title of his book reveals, tries to give a theoretical, rational, intellectual account of the body. His endeavour is closer to those of the post-modernists than to that of Merleau-Ponty.

28. This has been reported by many participants in the course, either from their own childhood memories or from their practice as teachers.

29. In Medard Boss *A Psychiatrist Discovers India*, translated from the German by Henry A. Frey, Rupa and Co. Calcutta, Allahabad, Bombay; 1966: 108. The author does not identify the name of the philosopher saint whom he interviews. Giri Deshingkar (personal communication) assures me that his identity is well known in India to be the late Gopinath Kaviraj.

30. On Mandeville's *Fable of the Bees*, see Louis Dumont *From Mandeville to Marx* 1977.

31. Reported in the *Sunday Statesman*, Calcutta, 17 June 1990. Sharansky is quoted as saying that: 'not only dissidents but also official sources now admit that 60 millions died under the Soviet regime'.

32. An example is the pamphlet distributed by the VHP in Ayodhyah in 1990 entitled 'Angry Hindu! Yes, Why Not?' (in Ashis Nandy et al. 1995: 55). The

murderous rampage against Muslims and the eventual destruction of the Babri Masjid is one of the results of such a sense of victimization and anger.

33. Such as the US policy towards the native population until the 1950s where young children were forcibly taken to boarding schools and taught to forget as well as despise their own culture.

34. This tolerance and openness to mutual nurturing does not mean that, in particular circumstances where transnational companies such as Texaco in Amazonian Ecuador and Peru are exploiting and often destroying the territory where some groups live, a strategy of demarcating territory on the part of native groups and gaining sovereignty over it may not be necessary for survival. But these are actions required by dire conditions and circumstances.

35. I was involved in fieldwork in Orissa (India) from 1975 to 1992.

36. I and PRATEC are deeply grateful to the MacArthur Foundation for having faith in us and allowing us to forge a path while walking it. This freedom and this support made all the difference. Without it this new vision could not have come to fruition.

37. The conference, funded by the Rockefeller Foundation, was entitled: 'Alternatives to the Greening of Economics'. The book *People's Ecology, People's Economy* Stephen Gudeman and Stephen A. Marglin (eds) (forthcoming) has resulted from it.

38. Jorge Ishizawa translated seven essays of mine and PRATEC published them as a book: *El Bosque Sagrado: Una Mirada a Genero y Desarrollo* 1995 (The Sacred Grove: a perspective on gender and development). I have written an initial essay on PRATEC that was first published in John Mohawk's and Yvonne Dion-Buffalo's magazine *Daybreak* (Winter 1994); it was also published in *Interculture* (Summer 1995) and in *Futures* (Fall 1995). *Daybreak* published some of the proceedings from our conference at Smith College in May 1995. *Daybreak* is preparing an issue in memory of Eduardo Grillo as well as preparing a book of translated lectures given by members of PRATEC during their visits to the US in May 1995, December 1995 and May–June 1996.

39. This is what prompted Native American author Vine Deloria to quip that Mesopotamia disappeared as a civilization because it must have been overrun by anthropologists (Deloria 1969).

40. Maybury-Lewis, lecture delivered at Smith College, spring 1987.

References

Abram, David. 1996; *The Spell of the Sensuous: Perception and Language in a More-Than-Human World*, New York; Pantheon Books.

Abu-Lughod, Lila. 1993; *Writing Women's Worlds: Bedouin Stories*, Berkeley, Los Angeles, Oxford; University of California Press.

Addelson, Kathryn Pyne. 1994; *Moral Passages: Toward a Collectivist Moral Theory*, New York; Routledge.

Aggarwal, Ravina. 1995; 'Haunted histories: experimental ethnography and feminism in the marketplace of Leh', ms.

Ahmed, Leila. 1992; *Women and Gender in Islam*, New Haven and London; Yale University Press.

Apffel-Marglin, Frédérique. 1991; 'Development and repression: a feminist critique', *Lokayan Bulletin*, 9: 1.

Apffel-Marglin, Frédérique. 1994, 1995; 'Development or decolonization in the Andes?' *Daybreak* Magazine, Winter 1994; also in *Interculture*, Spring 1995; also in *Futures*, Fall 1995.

Apffel-Marglin, Frédérique. 1995; *El Bosque Sagrado: Una Mirada a Genero y Desarrollo*, (*The Sacred Grove: A Perspective on Gender and Development*), Lima; PRATEC and CAM (Center for Mutual Learning).

Apffel-Marglin, Frédérique. 1996; 'Rationality, the body and the world: from production to regeneration' in *Decolonizing Knowledge: From Development to Dialogue*, F. Apffel-Marglin and S. A. Marglin (eds), Oxford; Oxford University Press, Clarendon.

Apffel-Marglin, Frédérique and Stephen A. Marglin (eds). 1990; *Dominating Knowledge: Development, Culture and Resistance*, Oxford; Oxford University Press, Clarendon.

Apffel-Marglin, Frédérique and Stephen A. Marglin (eds). 1996; *Decolonizing Knowledge: From Development to Dialogue*, Oxford; Oxford University Press, Clarendon.

Appadurai, Arjun. 1988; 'Putting hierarchy in its place', *Cultural Anthropology*, 3: 36–49.

Banuri, Tariq and Frédérique Apffel-Marglin. 1993; *Who Will Save the Forests? Knowledge, Power and Environmental Destruction*, London; Zed Books.

Bauman, Zygmunt. 1991; *Modernity and the Holocaust*, Ithaca, NY; Cornell University Press.

Bigwood, Carol. 1993; *Earth Muse: Feminism, Nature, and Art*, Philadelphia; Temple University Press.

Boss, Medard. 1966; *A Psychiatrist Discovers India*, tr. from German by Henry A. Frey. Calcutta, Allahabad, Bombay; Rupa and Co.

Bourdieu, Pierre. 1990; *The Logic of Practice*, tr. Richard Nice. Stanford CA; Stanford University Press.

Brown, Karen MacCarthy. 1991; *Mama Lola: A Vodou Priestess in New York*, Berkeley, Los Angeles, London; University of California Press.

Canclini, Garcia Nestor. 1990; *Cultural Hibridal: Estrategias para Entrar y Salir de la Modernidad*, Mexico; D. F. Grijalbo.

Clifford, James. 1988; *The Predicament of Culture: Twentieth Century Ethnography, Literature and Art*, Cambridge MA; Harvard University Press.

Clifford, James and George E. Marcus (eds). 1986; *Writing Culture: The Poetics and Politics of Ethnography*. Berkeley, Los Angeles, London; University of California Press.

Connolly, John. 1995; 'The Academy's Freedom – The Academy's Burden', lecture delivered on the occasion of Ruth Simmons's Inauguration, Smith College, September.

Davis-Floyd, Robbie E. 1992; *Birth as an American Rite of Passage*, Berkeley, Los Angeles, London; University of California Press.

Deloria, Vine Jr. 1969; *Custer Died for Your Sins: An Indian Manifesto*, Norman and London; University of Oklahoma Press.

Derrida, Jacques. 1982; 'Sending: on representation', *Social Research*, 49, no. 2: 294–326.

Descartes, René. 1961; *Discours de la Méthode*, Paris; J. Vrin.

Dion-Buffalo, Yvonne and John Mohawk. 1994; 'Thoughts from an autochtonous center', *Cultural Survival Quarterly*, Winter 1994: 33–5.

Drèze, Jean and Amartya Sen. 1989; *Hunger and Public Action*, Oxford; Oxford University Press, Clarendon.

Dumont, Louis. 1977; *From Mandeville to Marx: The Genesis and Triumph of Economic Ideology*, Chicago; Chicago University Press.

Escobar, Arturo. 1993; 'Hybrid cultures and post-development: "The alternative" as a research question and social practice', to appear in *People's Ecology, People's Economy*, Steve Gudeman and Stephen A. Marglin (eds).

Fabian, Johannes. 1983; *Time and the Other: How Anthropology Makes Its Object*, New York; Columbia Press.

Fischer, Edward F. 1995; 'Essentially Maya: Ethnic Theory and Practice in Guatemala' ms. delivered at the AAA meetings, Washington DC, 13 November.

Franklin, Sarah. 1988; 'The Virgin Birth Controversy in Anthropology: biology and Culture Revisited', MA Thesis for the Department of Anthropology, New York University.

Grillo, Eduardo Fernandez. 1993; 'La cosmovision Andina de Siempre y la Cosmologia Occidental Moderna', *Desarrollo o Descolonizacion en los Andes?* Lima; PRATEC: 9–61.

Grillo, Eduardo Fernandez. 1994a; 'El Paisaje en las Culturas Andina y Occidental Moderna', *Crianza Andina de la Chacra*, Lima; PRATEC: 9–45.

Grillo, Eduardo Fernandez. 1994b; 'Sabiduria Andino-Amazonica y Conocimiento Cientifico', *Revista Peruana de Epidemologia*, 7 (2): 34–5.

Gudeman, Steve and Stephen A. Marglin (eds). *People's Ecology, People's Economy* (forthcoming).

Hall, Stuart. 1990; 'Cultural identity and diaspora', *Identity: Community, Culture, Difference*, J. Rutherford (ed.); London; Lawrence and Wishart: 392–403.

Hassanein, Neva and Jack Kloppenburg, Jr, 1995; 'Where the Grass Grows Again: Knowledge Exchange in the Sustainable Agriculture Movement', ms.

Hubbard, Ruth. 1990; *The Politics of Women's Biology*, New Brunswick and London; Rutgers University Press.

Kant, Immanuel. 1979; *The Conflict of the Faculties*, tr. and intro. Mary J. Gregor; New York; Abaris Book Inc.

Kloppenburg, Jack Jr. 1988; *First the Seed*, Cambridge; Cambridge University Press.

Kloppenburg, Jack Jr, John Hendrikson and G. W. Stevenson. 'Coming to the foodshed', *Agriculture and Human Values* (forthcoming).

Kuhn, Thomas. 1962; *The Structure of Scientific Revolutions*, Chicago; University of Chicago Press.

Lattas, Andrew. 1993; 'Essentialism, memory and resistance: aboriginality and the politics of authenticity', *Oceania*, 63: 240–66.

Leach, Edmund. 1954; *Political Systems of Highland Burma*, Boston; Beacon Press.

Levins, R. and R. C. Lewontin. 1985; *The Dialectical Biologist*, Cambridge, MA; Harvard University Press.

Madan, Trilokinath. 1997; *Modern Myths, Locked Minds: Secularism and Fundamentalism and the Religious Traditions of India*, Delhi; Oxford University Press.

Marglin, Stephen A. 1974; 'What do bosses do?', *Review of Political Economy*, 6: 60–112.

Marglin, Stephen A. 1990; 'Losing touch: the cultural conditions of worker accomodation and resistance'. In *Dominating Knowledge: Development, Culture, and Resistance*, F. Apffel-Marglin and S. A. Marglin (eds); Oxford; Oxford University Press, Clarendon: 217–82.

Marglin, Stephen A. 1996; 'Farmers, seedsmen, scientists: systems of agriculture and systems of knowledge', *Decolonizing Knowledge: From Development to Dialogue*, Oxford; Oxford University Press, Clarendon.

Martin, Emily. 1987; *The Woman in the Body: A Cultural Analysis of Reproduction*, Boston; Beacon Press.

Mayer, Enrique. 1992; 'Peru in deep trouble: Mario Vargas Llosa's "Inquest in the Andes" re-examined'. In *Rereading Cultural Anthropology*, George E. Marcus (ed.); Durham and London; Duke University Press: 181–219.

Mayer, Enrique. 1995; 'Recursos naturales, medio ambiente, tecnologia y desarrollo', *Peru: El Problema Agrario en Debate* SEPIA V. Oscar Dancourt, Enrique Mayer and Carlos Monge (eds): 479–532.

Merchant, Carolyn. 1980; *The Death of Nature: Women, Ecology and the Scientific Revolution*, San Francisco; Harper and Row.

Merleau-Ponty, Maurice. 1962; *Phenomenology of Perception*, tr. Colin Smith; London; Routledge & Kegan Paul.

Nandy, Ashis. 1987; 'From outside the imperium: Gandhi's cultural critique of the West'. In *Traditions, Tyranny and Utopias*, Delhi; Oxford University Press; 127–62.

Nandy, Ashis, Shikha Trivedy, Shail Mayaram and Achyut Yagnik. 1995; *Creating a Nationality: The Ramjanmabhumi Movement and Fear of Self*, Delhi; Oxford University Press.

Narayan, Kirin. 1989; *Saints, Scoundrels and Storytellers: Folk Narrative in Hindu Religous Teaching*, Philadelphia; University of Pennsylvania Press.

Proctor, Robert N. 1991; *Value-Free Science? Purity and Power in Modern Knowledge*, Cambridge, MA; Harvard University Press.

Raskin, Marcus. 1973; *Being and Doing*, Boston; Beacon Press.

Said, Edward. 1993; *Culture and Imperialism*, New York; Knopf.

Schneider, David. 1980; *American Kinship: A Cultural Account* (2nd edn), Chicago; Chicago University Press.

Shapin, Steven and Simon Schaffer. 1985; *Leviathan and the Air-Pump: Hobbes, Boyle and the Experimental Life*, Princeton; Princeton University Press.

Starn, Orin. 1991; 'Missing the revolution: anthropologists and the war in Peru', *Cultural Anthropology*, 6(1): 63–91.

Thompson, E. P. 1967; 'Time, work, discipline, and industrial capitalism', *Past and Present*, 38: 56–97.

Tilly, Louise. 1978; 'The social sciences and the study of women: a review article', *Comparative Studies in Society and History*, 20 (1): 163–73.

Todorov, Tzvetan. 1984; *The Conquest of America*, Cambridge, MA; Harvard University Press.

Trinh, Minh-ha, 1983; *Woman, Native, Other*, Indiana; University of Indiana Press.

Trinh, Minh-ha. 1994; Lecture delivered at Smith College, 15 April.

Valladolid, Julio Rivera. 1993; 'Las plantas en la cultura Andina y en Occidente moderno', *Desarrollo o Descolonizacion en los Andes?*, Lima; PRATEC: 63–94.

Vargas Llosa, Mario. 1983; 'Inquest in the Andes', *New York Times Magazine*, 31 July.

Vargas Llosa, Mario. 1990; 'Questions of conquest: what Columbus wrought, and what he did not', *Harper's*, December 45–6.Wagner, Roy. 1981; *The Invention of Culture*, Chicago; University of Chicago Press.

Wagner, Roy. 1981; *The Invention of Culture*, Chicago; University of Chicago Press.

Warren, Kay B. 1995; 'Reading History of Resistance: Mayan Public Intellectuals in Guatemala', ms.

Watanabe, John M. 1995; 'Unimagining the Maya: anthropologists, others, and the inescapable hubris of authorship', *Bulletin of Latin American Research*, 14(1): 25–45.

CHAPTER 2

Andean Peasant Agriculture: Nurturing a Diversity of Life in the *Chacra*

Julio Valladolid Rivera

This chapter is an introduction to the growing of the heterogeneity of life in the Andean *chacra* (field marked off for cultivation). It is written for those people who – having been educated according to the norms of modern Western culture and having confronted its evident inability to provide for the well-being of the majority of the populations of countries with millenary cultural traditions like ours – are looking for space to reflect, a reflection that may also allow them to realize that there are other 'paths' to 'seeing', 'feeling', and 'living' the Andean reality. The cement-covered roads, pavements and traffic lights that the modern West proposes and imposes upon us, in order to achieve the dreamed of progress by means of its development proposals, is not the only or the most certain way to live the 'sweet life' (*la vida dulce*) of the Andean countryside.

It is not easy to come to an understanding of the nurturing of the heterogeneity of life in the *chacra* solely through readings like this one. How to convey the profound feeling of affection and respect that the peasant feels for the 'Mother Earth' (*la Pachamama*), or the joy and gratitude towards his or her mountain protectors ('*Achachilas*' or '*Apus*') the peasant experiences on the birth of an 'alpaca' who is treated like a 'new daughter', is a truly difficult challenge. One must live the life of the Andean country-side in continuous conversation with the stars, rocks, lakes, rivers, plants and animals both wild and cultivated, with the clouds, the frosts. One must relish the taste of the rains, listen to the corn growing, observe the colour of the winds – feeling oneself at all times accompanied by our deceased ancestors. The nurturing of the *chacra* is the heart of Andean culture which, if not the only activity carried out by the peasants, is the one around which all aspects of life revolve.

The characteristics of nature in the Andes are pointed out in the first part of this chapter, highlighting its diversity (heterogeneity), density and variability; in other words, its capacity to generate new forms of life from those already existing. The Peruvian Andes (Central Andes) have the greatest ecological density in the world; in a short distance of 200 linear kilometres it is possible to find close to 80 per cent of the 103 Zones of Natural Life proposed by Holdridge for the entire planet (ONERN 1976).

In the second part of the chapter, the diverse ways in which the peasants nurture the heterogeneity of life in their *chacras*, allowing themselves in their turn to be nurtured by the soils, microclimates, waters, animals, hills, rivers and stones are shown.

The third part deals with the ways in which the members of the '*Ayllu*' converse among one another in order to nurture the *chacra*.

Throughout the chapter attempts are made to explain in clear detail what Andean living is all about, most of the time in an emotive form suggestive of our own Andean way of 'seeing', 'feeling' and 'living' life. As the historian Pablo Macera (1993) states: 'perhaps some in their eagerness to rationalize everything would prefer something more rigid and square' – something more scientific – but life in the Andes, happily, is not that way.

Nature's mode of being in the Andes

Nature in the Andes is the soils, the climate, the waters, the plants, the animals, the heavenly bodies, the mountains, the rocks; it includes humans and all that is present here and now in the area that the diverse Andean ethnic groups share.

This Andean nature is characterized by its great heterogeneity or diversity, variability and ecological density determined above all by the presence of the Andes mountain range, with its perpetual snow in the midst of the planet's tropical zone. This mountain chain crosses South America from south to north. The Andes of Venezuela, Colombia and Ecuador are called the Northern Andes; those of Peru, the Central Andes, and those of Bolivia, Chile and Argentina are called the Southern Andes. The Central Andes are the highest mountains of the tropics where the lives of crops such as bitter potato (*papa amarga*), *cañiwa* and *maca*, and those of animals such as llamas and alpacas and of the people who raise them, unfold at 4,000 metres above sea level.

In a cross-section from west to east of this mountain chain, one appreciates a very rugged physiography with eight natural regions (Pulgar Vidal 1987), that stretch both altitudinally and latitudinally throughout the Andes. This uneven geography is just as irregular when a south to north cross-section is taken. In general terms it is observed that the Andes of southern Peru, where the high plateau of Puno is found, are on average higher than those known as the Central Andes, and these in turn are higher than the Andes of northern Peru. Natural evidence of this is that the major rivers that flow through the Andean valleys run from south to north. If this is the case, then for us Andeans, 'up' is south and 'down' is north and, therefore, a reading of a map of Peru more in accord with our reality would place the south at the top and the north at the bottom. An additional argument backing this up is the fact that the oceanic current known as the Humboldt or Peruvian current also runs along the coast from south to north – from 'top' to 'bottom'. For greater historic precision and detail about this matter, see Maria Rostworowski (1992). Moreover, the Andeans of yesterday and of today orient themselves and 'converse' with the Andean constellations of the southern sky to grow their *chacras*: they converse with the brilliant constellation of the *Chacata* and the dark constellation of the *llama* with its eyes formed by the stars Alfa and Beta of Centaurus, which in Quechua are called '*llamapa ñawin*' (eyes of the llama). In other words, the Andean world looks to the south, because its terms of reference are in the south. The official way in which the map of Peru is oriented and read is further proof of cultural domination.

The characteristics of heterogeneity, variability and density of Andean nature are also shared by the climates and soils, which in turn contribute to enrich the heterogeneity, variability and density of the plants, animals and human beings that inhabit the Andes.

The climate is one of the elements of this particular nature that most influences life in the Andes; not only is it diverse and dense, but each of the climates is quite variable as well, both throughout the years and from month to month in each year. Periods of drought, frost and hail, and of excessive rains are frequent, making the Andean climate even more variable.

The Andeans of the past and the present know the mode of being of the climate and are not surprised by the occurrence of one year catalogued as 'dry' or another as 'very rainy'. They have the knowledge that allows them to 'converse' and 'reciprocate' with any class of climate in such a way that they obtain harvests to survive, even in the years of greatest climatic difficulty.

The peasants recognize two periods clearly delimited in the climate of a year: one cold and dry period in which the nightly minimum temperature can reach zero degrees centigrade and precipitation is minimal; and the other hot and rainy in which the minimum temperatures and pluvial precipitations rise, making possible the growth and development of plants and animals both wild and cultivated. In this period, life in the Andes 'blooms' at its fullest. The duration of each period, that is to say, the months of the calendar year included in each one, varies from place to place and also varies in the same place as a result of the climatic character-istics of each year. In the Quechua language the cold and dry period is called *Usyai uku*, and in the Aymara language, *Auti pacha* or *auti urasa*; the hot and rainy season is *Puquy uku* in Quechua and *Jallu pacha* or *Jallu urasa* in Aymara.

The Andeans give the name *Usyai wata* to the kind of year in which the *Puquy uku*, or period in which the crops grow, is characterized by precipitations that occur irregularly and are scarce and when the period includes frequent droughts, hail and frost. In this kind of year the precipitations are scarce in general and it is considered a year of scarcity or *Muchuy wata* – that is, a year of great difficulties for cultivating the *chacra*. The harvest in these conditions will be scant, but sufficient to nourish the peasant and his Andean family or *Ayllu* frugally, as is customary even in years of good harvest. It is useful to point out that the peasants get a harvest both in a *Usyai wata* (dry year) and in a *Para wata* (rainy year), but a much greater yield is harvested in a year with rains distributed regularly throughout the growing season (*Allin wata*). In such years they reach levels of production which allow them to conserve food for several years.

It is not a matter of resigning oneself to alternations between 'good' years (rainy years) and 'bad' years (dry years); the Andeans of past and present accept the year as it is, they converse with it through a large repertoire of knowledge in such a way that they always obtain a harvest. If this were not so, Andean peasants would have disappeared from the Andes many years ago and, with them, the Andean culture. Nevertheless we can see that neither in the pre-Hispanic era nor afterwards has this occurred. For the Andean peasant there is no 'good year' or 'bad year'; in both he receives a harvest for himself and his *Ayllu*.

Another element which, jointly with the climate, shares the characteristics of heterogeneity, variability and density is the agricultural soil. Official statistics say that, nationwide, agricultural soil is the scarcest resource. Less than 6 per cent of the territorial surface area can be used for agricultural purposes. If we add to this the rugged landscape of the Andes which allows the planting of crops only on small parcels with shallow soils situated at different altitudes in the mountain chain, and on hillsides with steep slopes and thus exposed to flash floods, we see that this entire diagnostic, referring to the soil, contains sufficient argument to hold that Peru is a country 'without agricultural vocation'. Furthermore, if one considers that nearly 80 per cent of the country's agriculture is rainfed – in other words, exposed to the variability of the Andean climate – the above affirmation seems to be conclusive ... but what is forgotten is that here the Andean peasant has always tended the soil, water and microclimate, together with plants and animals, and has nurtured them in order to increase the heterogeneity, variability and density of nature and of all life in order to foster a natural harmony that provides well-being for all.

The peasant understood that the soil was limited and, therefore, nurtured it by constructing *andenes* (terraces), and slowly forming terraces, *qochas* and basins, *waru warus*; and as he nurtured them and still nurtures them, he knows full well their diversity and variability. Expressions such as *Sallqa allpa* (soil from the highlands), *Qichwa allpa* (soil from the lowlands), *Yana allpa* (black soils), *Puka allpa* (red soils), *Yurac allpa* (light coloured soil), *Uqi allpa* (greyish soils), *Aqu allpa* (sandy soils), *Llinku allpa* (clayey soils), *Purun allpa* (virgin soils), *Purmag allpa* (soils which have begun a long period of fallow), *Chacra allpa* (soils under cultivation), *Ruruq allpa* (soils that release a pleasant odour and are therefore fertile), or *Qamya allpa* (soils that have the odour of rock and consequently are not very fertile), are evidence of a meticulous knowledge of their soils.

Table 2.1 summarizes the most relevant characteristics of climate and soil in the Andes with relation to its great variety.

Table 2.1 Characteristics of Andean climate and soil

---

1 Great variability in climate

a. Year to year

Year with a deficit of rain = *Usyai wata*
Year with an excess of rain = *Para wata*

b. Within each year (month to month)

Month with a deficit of rain = *Usyai killa*
Month with an excess of rain = *Para killa*

2 Great variability in soil

a. In the soils of the highlands = *sallqa allpa*

Yana allpa paqway ñutu = Black soil with fine particles, not appropriate for cultivation.
Ruruq yana allpa = Black soil with larger particles, appropriate for cultivation.

b. In the soils of the lowlands = *qichua allpa*

Puca allpa paqway ñutu = Dark red soil with fine particles, difficult to cultivate.
Ruruq puca allpa = Light red soil with granular structure, convenient for cultivation.

In the months of little rain or *Usyai killa*, corresponding to the hot and rainy period of the year or *puquy uku*, when the crops grow, there arise periods of drought with strong insolations during the daytime and frost at night. Alternatively, severe hailstorms occur after a period of strong insolations, and after the hailstorms severe frosts fall at night, damaging the crops even more. The peasants know about this sequence of climatic events and say that the hail is the elder brother of the frost, because when hail falls in the afternoon, the probability of frost that night increases.

In these periods of drought the incidence and severity of attack of certain insects or pests increases. Incidence is understood to be the number of plants attacked in a given area of cultivation and the severity of the attack is the percentage of foliar area destroyed by an attack. For example in potato cultivation, and above all, in the initial phases of growth, the occurrence of a drought increases considerably the degree of incidence and severity of the insect Epitrix called *illaqu* by the peasants of Quispillaccta-Ayacucho.

In contrast, in the months of *puquy uku* with periods of excessive pluvial precipitations, the degree of incidence and severity of diseases produced by micro-organisms increases, especially those caused by phyto-pathogenic fungi. For example, in potato cultivation, the peasants know that in this period of high humidity, the disease they call *Rancha* of the potato – caused by the fungus of the Oomycetes class, *Phytophthora infestans* – will appear.

Aside from causing direct damage to crops in these periods of humidity, in deficit or in excess, climatic conditions also damage the crops indirectly through the influence that climate has over the biological cycle of insects and phytopathogenic micro-organisms.

In addition, the rugged relief of the soils and the variability of the climate make the soils, of even the same region and of the same fields, diverse and heterogeneous. This diversity is also nurtured by the peasant who increases it deliberately, in such a way that in spaces relatively close to one another, in the same region, he may have diverse classes of soil. In other words, he may have many *chacras* each with a different type of soil.

The Andean peasant nurtures the diversity, propitiates the variability and increases the density not only of the soil, but also of the microclimate of the *chacra* and of the landscape in general. Andean culture is a culture that nurtures heterogeneity based on the *chacra*.

Nurturing heterogeneity in the *chacra*

The *chacra* is the piece of land where the peasant lovingly and respectfully nurtures plants, soil, water, microclimates and animals. In a broad sense *chacra* is all that is nurtured, thus the peasants say that the llama is their *chacra* that walks and from which wool is harvested. We ourselves are the *chacra* of the *huacas*, that is the deities who care for, teach and accompany us.

One part of this act of nurturing, the part that only has to do with the nurturing of plants and animals, modern Western science calls agri-culture and says that it began in the Andean valleys around 8,000 years ago, beginning with the domestication of plants (Bonavia 1991; Silva-Santisteban 1990; Kaulicke 1985). But, as we have said, the Andean people have always nurtured not only plants and animals, but also the soil, the waters, the microclimates – the land in general – and surely all of this took place long before 8,000 years ago.

The evidence shows the Central Andes of South America to be one of the world's four centres of primary origin of agriculture, where, independently and without influence from other places, agriculture began. It is said that the same thing happened in Central America (Guatemala and Mexico), Indochina (Thailand, Burma and Laos), and in the Middle East and Africa (Turkey, Iran, Afghanistan and the mountains of Ethiopia and Somalia). From these four places it expanded to other places, now known as centres of secondary origin. This whole process took place when, 12,000 years ago, the climate began to change, becoming more favourable to the emergence of a greater diversity in all plants, among those the wild ancestors of the plants cultivated today.

The higher temperatures and increased precipitation in those remote times, especially in the tropical zone, made possible the intensification of the cultivation of plants and the breeding of animals by the ethnic groups that inhabited these areas. Three of the four primary centres of origin are situated in the midst of the tropical zone and the fourth is close to it. Agriculture originated in the tropics and from there extended to the planet's temperate zones.

In the Central Andes, agriculture was born with the nurturing of the *chacra*. To nurture a *chacra* is not merely to domesticate plants and animals; it is to nurture lovingly and respectfully, in other words, to nurture ritually, together with the plants and animals, the soils, waters, microclimates and, in general, the whole land.

To understand what this act of nurturing means for the peasant, it is necessary to make an effort to empathize; in other words, to put oneself in his or her situation, considering the characteristics of the environment where he or she lives. This is not easy for those of us who have been raised to be individuals in a society such as the modern West; on this matter the historian Pablo Macera says: 'and so are we made and it is difficult to change ... It is clear that we are made, not by our mothers or fathers, but by something much larger and unnamed which has its own interests ... call it system, culture, society or whatever you like' (Urbano and Macera 1992).

Recognizing our limitations, we must make this effort beginning with the way the Andean 'sees', 'feels' and 'lives' his or her reality, in other words, from the Andean conception. In order to assist the reader, what has already been explained very well in another document (Grillo 1993) will again be explained, highlighting the concepts of *Pacha, Ayllu* and *Chacra*.

The *Pacha* is the house of the *Ayllu* and the *Ayllu* is all that lives in the *Pacha*: the stars, the rocks, the plants, rivers, animals, human beings dead and alive, all is *Pacha*.

The *Pacha* and all that is part of it is alive, has all the characteristics of a living being; even the dead are 'alive' and are present. A peasant expresses this eloquently: 'whatever little thing ... land, rock, plant, little animals ... they say that all speak, cry, dance ... even the dead don't go far they say, they stay around ... (for this reason) we also call to the spirit' (Machaca 1992).

The *Pachamama* is also *Pacha* but refers more specifically to the land that offers us its fruits, the land that nurtures us as a mother does her children and in return she is loved and respected like a mother. The testimony of Jesús Urbano, a peasant from Huanta (Ayacucho, Peru), responding to the question, 'Who are the children of the *Pachamama*?' makes very clear what the peasant considers and feels for the *Pachamama* when he answers: 'Everything, all are her children. I myself am the son of my parents, may they rest in peace, but I am also a son of the *Pachamama* ... of the potato, the *olluco* [...], the corn. ... But the harvest of the *Pachamama* is also born of the *Pachamama* and is her daughter and not only because we work, but because nothing is done without her' (Urbano and Macera 1992).

Before beginning any agricultural labour, such as preparing the land for fallow (*barbecho*), the sowing, the hilling-up (*aporque*), the harvest, permission is asked of the *Pachamama*. Modesto Machaca of Union Potrero (Quispillaccta-Huamanga) says: 'to open a *chacra* I must ask permission of the *Pachamama* so that she will allow me to work this soil ... [A]side from offering *coca* and liquor (*traguito*) I tell her that ... I will cultivate this soil with love, without mistreatment and the fruits that she gives me we will all eat ... at least we will taste them' (Machaca, Marcela 1991). The peasants of Conima-Puno also make an offering (*pago*) for making fallow which is called *Qhollitaki mayt'asiña* in the Aymara language. They present a small quantity of coca to the *Pachamama* in an act called *Chillt'asiña* or *K'intt'asiña*, saying: '*Pachamama*, holy earth, please pardon us, excuse me ... saying this we kiss her on our knees' (Chambi 1991). In these testimonies made by Quechua and Aymara peasants from places as distant from each other as Ayacucho and Puno, a profound respect and love for the *Pachamama* is revealed, a respect and love that is also felt for the guardian mountains which are considered protectors of the *Ayllu*. They are those which accompany, teach, counsel: in Quechua they are called *Taita Urqu, Taita Huamani, Apu*; and, in Aymara, *Achachila, Uywiri, Llaullani, Mallku-Marani*. A Quechua peasant says: 'We should not forget about the *Urqus* and the *Pachamama* ... we must always remember ... They are the patrons of our *kancha* (corral where animals are raised) and of the *chacra*' (Machaca, Magdalena 1993).

Since we are all children of the *Pachamama*, we are all relatives. In the Andean mode of thinking, *Ayllu* refers not only to relationships between human beings but to the relationship between all the members of the *Pacha* – the stars, the sun, the moon, the hills, lakes, rivers, mountains, meadows, the plants and the animals of the *sallqa* (wild) and of the *chacra*, along with the rocks and the human beings or *runas*, are all relatives and are at once children, parents and siblings. This deep sense of familiarity is evident in the report by Chambi, Quiso and Tito (1992) of *Uywa K'ichi* (branding) of alpacas and llamas in Puno, when they say that as part of this ritual the best pair of animals are chosen to be married 'godparents are designated, keeping in mind that this is a real matrimony, it is no play, ... two children of the family are married here'.

This same feeling of love, respect and kinship is felt when the *chacra* is nurtured; the *chacra* is not merely the place where the soil, the water, the microclimate, the plants are nurtured, but is also the ritual space where one converses and reciprocates with the *huacas*: Pachamama, *Huamanis*, *Achachilas*, with our ancestors, with the sun, the moon, the *suchu* (the Pleiades), the *Amaru* (the constellation known as Scorpius) and the *Chacata* or *Chacana* (Andean constellation of the Wiracocha), and also with the other members of nature – wild plants and animals, clouds, winds, rainbows. In other words, because everything is alive and everything 'speaks', in the *chacra* the peasant has the capacity to converse with everything. As Jesús Urbano says, referring to what happens in the *Pacha*: 'everything is settled ... it is only a matter of just seeing' and this 'just seeing', in the eyes of an Andean, is to understand the subtle message of the stars twinkling, of the flowering of wild plants or the flight of birds, the colour of the winds, the taste of the rain. At all times they 'tell' us what is happening to the soil and furthermore what will happen to the climate.

We call these stars, meteors, plants and animals 'climate prediction indicators' or 'soil condition indicators'; for the Quechua peasants they are simply 'signs'; and for the Aymaras '*lomasas*'.

Moreover, the *chacra* is a place where one works in an atmosphere of *fiesta*. When the potato is hilled in *ayni* or *minga* (mutual help between families) it is done with music, dancing and plenty of good food. The work in the *chacra* is done joyfully.

For the Andean all of this represents the *chacra*; it is not merely a parcel or several parcels of agricultural soil, it is much more than that. The peasant expression '*Chacra Sunqulla*' (the *chacra* is my heart) can be understood as the all-inclusive expression of love for the *chacra* where one nurtures crops, called *kawsay* in Quechua, which also means life, to live. In other words, on the *chacra* all of life is lovingly nurtured but this nurturing is not done only by people. Just as the *runas* or human beings participate in this nurturing, the *huacas* (deities) and nature also nurture. For this reason the products of the *chacra* are from and for all the communities of the Andean *ayllu*.

The *chacra* is not made at any old 'time': to do the labour of making fallow, weeding, hilling-up as well as sowing and harvesting one waits for the moon to mature; the *chacra* is worked in synchrony with the living rhythm of the *Pacha*.

Figure 2.1 shows the moon phases recognized by the Quechua Andean

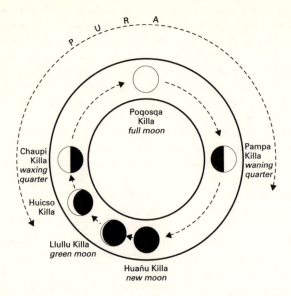

Figure 2.1 Phases of the moon in Quispillaccta (*source*: Marcela Machaca)

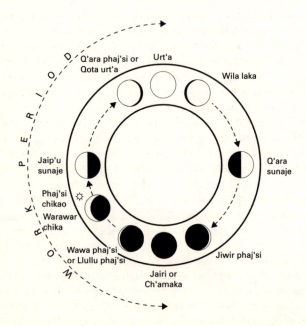

Figure 2.2 Phases of the moon in Conima (*source*: Nestor Chambi)

peasant of Quispillaccta-Ayacucho. The mature or '*Pura*' moon begins with and includes *huicso killa* (moon before the quarter crescent) and ends with the *pampa killa* (waning quarter). Starting in *huañu killa* and until after *llullu killa* no work is done on the *chacra*. Work is not done on the *chacra* simply when people are disposed to do it, but rather following the rhythm of the life of the *Pacha* – conversing in this case with the moon, at other times with the sun, the stars, the plants, the animals. Thus one converses with everyone at all times and at all places.

Another example of the Andeans' extensive and detailed knowledge of the moon for the growing of the *chacra* is given in Figure 2.2. The Aymara peasants from Conima, Puno are familiar with no fewer than nine moons.

1. *Jairi* or *ch'amaka*   = new moon
2. *Wawa phaj'si* or *llullu phaj'si*   = moon one or two days after the new moon
3. *Phaj'si chikao* or *warawar chika*   = moon before the waxing quarter accompanied by a bright star
4. *Jaip'u sunaje*   = waxing quarter moon
5. *Q'ara phaj'si* or *qota urt'a*   = moon one day before the full moon
6. *Urt'a*   = full moon
7. *Wila laka*   = moon one day after the full moon
8. *Q'ara sunaje*   = waning quarter moon
9. *Jiwir phaj'si*   = moon one day before the new moon

The period when one works nurturing *chacra* lies between *jairi* or new moon and *urt'a* or full moon, but during this period no work is done in *wawa phaj'si* and *phaj'si chikao*. The period of rest is situated between the full moon (*urt'a*) and *jiwir phaj'si*. This is not to say that during this period nothing occurs: housework and weaving are done, farm tools and the *chacra* fences are repaired, and so on. In *jairi* or new moon, agricultural and pastoral work start again. For example, in *jairi* livestock are paired, most importantly the llamas and alpacas. The mating done during this moon 'will take' and most of the offspring will be female. The sowing of crops such as the potato is started after *wawa phaj'si* and continues until *wila laka*, one day before the full moon and, especially, in *jaip'u sunaje*, the waxing quarter.

One also converses with the moon in order to fish in Lake Titicaca; the peasants fish around the time of the new moon, especially on the day of the new moon and on cloudy nights. At these times the fishing is best.

In the Andes all of life revolves around the nurturing of the *chacra*; Andean culture is agrocentric. All the activities of the *chacra* such as sowing, weeding, hilling-up, harvesting and even the storage, transformation and consumption of harvested products are ritual activities. Ritual is understood as the Andean's attitude of utmost and heartfelt love and respect, shown with greatest intensity at specific times and places. The West calls this attitude religiosity. For the peasant who lives this ritual there is no such religiosity; it is not lived in the way it is understood by Christian religiosity, in which there is an attitude of adoration of a supreme being or God. The peasant does not adore his or her *huacas*: he or she converses and reciprocates with them on terms of equivalence; he or she recognizes that the *huacas* are incomplete just as he or she is, that they make mistakes, and the peasant views the Christian God, the Virgin and the saints – all of whom have been incorporated without much problem – as *huacas* with whom they also converse and reciprocate on equal terms. Examples of this relationship and testimonies to it can be found at all times and in many places in the Andes. In some villages when there is a prolonged period of drought, the villagers bring out their patron saint in a procession so that he will make it rain. If he does not succeed give him the lash.

It is difficult to understand what the peasants feel for their *huacas*. Jiménez Borja (1992) says, 'The idea of a supreme being, creator spirit, omnipotent, omniscient, eternal, etc. does not seem to fit into what the Andean world has expressed from the beginning to doctrinaire Christian chroniclers and idolatry extirpators ... but neither is it obligatory that it should fit in.' He also says that in the Andean world 'there is no divine figure that incarnates the absolute'. Lastly, he expresses the following reflection: 'to my judgment what the aborigenes (the Andeans) think of him is more important than what we ourselves are capable of imagining. For them *Pachacamac* was *huaca* and nothing else.'

Taking into consideration the fact that the mode of being of Andean nature is diverse, variable and dense, and that it is the right thing to do to converse and reciprocate with it for the greater enrichment of hetero-geneity by means of nurturing in the *chacra*, the members of an *ayllu* carry out this nurturing each in their own way but, in general, always conversing and reciprocating with everything.

The following reports summarize the way in which the peasants of Qasanqay and Quispillaccta in Ayacucho do it, mentioning also examples from Chetilla-Cajamarca and Conima-Puno. This does not in any way mean that all of the communities in the Andes cultivate the *chacra* in the same way. It is understood that each *Ayllu* has its own ways of cultivating the *chacra* according to its own reality.

Qasanqay is a peasant community located in the valley of Vinchos, Ayacucho (see Figure 2.3) extending altitudinally from 3,100 metres up to 4,000 metres above sea level. The Quechua, Suni and Puna regions are included in its territory. Each peasant family cultivates 7 to 12 *chacras*, the size of each being one *yugada* (a day's ploughing with a yoke of oxen), about 1,800 square metres located at different altitudes in the Quechua and Suni regions. On average there are two or three *chacras* planted with maize and associates, in the Quechua region, four *chacras* of potatos and associates and three of barley and associates in the high Quechua and Suni regions. Both the maize *chacras* and the potato *chacra* are sown along

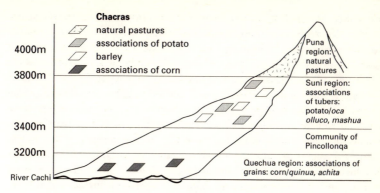

Figure 2.3 Qasanqay–Ayacucho peasant community

with other species, with grains such as quinoa (*Chenopodium quinoa*) and achita (*Amaranthus caudatus*) in the case of maize. Tubers such as *oca* (*Oxalis tuberosa*), *olluco* (*Ullucus tuberosus*) and *mashua* (*Tropaeolum tuberosum*) are grown with potatoes.

The nurturing of the *chacras* is undertaken according to a continuous conversation and reciprocity with the members of the local *Pacha's Ayllu*, by means of the 'signs' that can be stars, wild plants and animals, meteors and other physical phenomena and, finally, dreams. There are 'signs' to converse with the climate and others for conversation with the soil. As an example of a climatic 'sign' related to the stars we can cite the case of the moon (see above) which 'tells' us when to make and when not to make *chacra*. The sun, according to how and where it 'walks' as it rises on the Eastern horizon, tells us about the conditions of cold and dry of *Usyai uku* and when they will increase (June solstice) or when the intensity of the rains will increase (December solstice) for the best raising of the crops.

The brightness of the stars that make up the Pleiades or 'seven little goats' also 'tells' us about the conditions of the climate. In the Quechua of Ayacucho this constellation is known as *Suchu* or *Jarampa*. In the Quechua of Qosqo it is *Colca*, in Aymara, *Cheje* and in the Quechua of Cajamarca, *Qoto*; it is a constellation known to all Andeans. In Huamanga (Ayacucho) it is observed on and around 24 June (the feast of Saint John), the June solstice. At this time the *Suchu* rises on the northeast horizon at around four in the morning. If the little crowd of stars that make it up is bright, so that it is possible to distinguish one from another, this 'sign' 'tells' us that the climate of *Puquy uku* with which the plants will converse and reciprocate will be rainy. If the *Suchu* looks like a little whiteish stain, diffuse and one star being indistinguishable from another, the peasant expects a climate with insufficient rain; in other words, a *Usyai wata*. But the peasant does not only observe this one constellation, but rather he or she also converses with others, like the dark llama constellation with its bright eyes (*llamapa ñawin*), with the *Qasa Puyu* which are two bright small 'clouds' that appear in the southern sky beneath the stars *Achermar* and *Canopus* and which modern astronomy calls Magellan's 'greater cloud' and 'lesser cloud'. These are also observed on and around 24 June. If they appear 'standing up', vertical and bright white, the year will have few frosts; if it looks dim and 'reclining', horizontal, the year will bring severe frosts – in other words, a *Qasa wata* (year with frosts).

The more abundant or sparser flowering of certain wild plants in the month of August are also 'signs' of the climate. In Qasanqay a 'sign' for the Quechua region is the columnar cactus, *Sankay* (*Trichocereus sp*); for the Suni region it is the thorny bush, *Taqsana* (*Colletia spinossisima*) and for the Puna region the *Waraqu-kichka* cactus (*Opuntia floccosa*). A more abundant presence of buds and flowers indicates a *Para wata* (rainy year) and a sparser flowering a *Usyai wata* (year with few pluvial precipitations). These plants are not the only 'signs'; many more exist in each region. These are also observed meticulously not only at the time of bloom, but both before and after then; among other characteristics, the plant's strength, the height it attains and its fructification process are also observed.

In the peasant community of Chetilla in Cajamarca – where an excess of rain and not its deficit, like in Qasanqay, damages the crops – there are 'sign' plants that 'tell' whether the year will or will not be rainy. Among others, the peasants converse with a red-flowered begonia called *Tamia tucto*. Each place has its 'sign' plants for each region and for each instance of excess or deficit rain.

Wild animals are also 'signs' of the climate; thus the skin colours of toads and snakes are observed. If the colour is darker than usual one expects a rainy year; if it is lighter, a year with scarce rain is forecast. The presence and flight direction of certain wild birds are observed, as well as the place they choose to lay their eggs, and the number of eggs, the presence or absence of certain fish. The sound of the fox's howl is listened to very carefully, as well as the chirping song of the cricket, the croak of the toad and the presence, size and number of certain insects such as ants.

The appearance, colour and intensity of certain meteors and meteorological phenomena such as the wind, clouds, rainbow, hail, frost and the taste of the rain are observed.

Dreams are also taken into account as 'signs' of the climate. In the community of Conina-Puno, when the peasant dreams that he or she is lighting a candle or stirring a fire or embers, it is a 'sign' of a dry year (*Lupi mara*), with severe periods of drought (Chambi 1991).

These few examples of 'signs' of the climate give us an idea of the Andean peasants' richness of knowledge for 'predicting the climate' which their crops will converse with. They do not consider a single 'sign', but many, which are 'read' continuously at different times and in different places. These 'readings' are socialized in the fairs, the *fiestas* for patron saints and above all the Andean pilgrimages, such as the one to Apu Ausangati (Our Lord of Qoillur riti) in the Ocongate region in Qosqo, in the month of June.

The Andeans also have 'signs' that indicate the condition of the cultivated soil. Thus in Chetilla when the presence of a wild plant known as *Chupika kewa* increases in the *chacra* it is the moment when the soil is asking for rest. When the number of certain gramineous wild plants increases in fallow land, it is the soil that is asking to be sown once again. In addition, there are wild plants that 'tell' us that the soil they grow in is appropriate for this or that crop. In the community of Quispillaccta-Ayacucho, the gramineous *Saylla* is the 'sign' of maize, while the shrub *Tankar* is the 'sign' of potato (Machaca, Marcela 1991). According to his or her dialogue with the 'signs' of the climate and soil, the peasant can say which soils are suitable for sowing, what tillage methods are best to use, what species to cultivate and even when it is best to plant.

An ample repertory of knowledge is available to the peasant to prepare and sow the soil in accordance with the 'climatic prediction'. For a *Usyai wata* (year with little rain) a larger area is planted in the highlands and less in the lowlands. In other words, in a *Usyai wata* the crops move up. For a *Para wata* (rainy year) a greater area is planted in the lowlands and the planting area in the higher regions is reduced; so, in a *Para wata*, the crops move down.

Not only do the crops move up or down, but in addition to this a particular type of soil preparation and ploughing is used. For a 'dry year' one plants in the depressions and the furrows are made diagonal to the slope of the terrain, in such a way that the little rain that falls may be retained and better used – not lost in runoff. On the other hand, for a 'rainy year' one plants on the hillsides and the furrows follow the slope of the terrain according to a system called *huaccho* with short, alternate furrows, the objective being that the soil may not suffer erosion from the runoff caused by excessive rains, and also that the water does not form puddles creating humid microclimates that could favour an increase in the incidence and severity of fungal diseases such as the '*rancha*'.

In each *chacra* a diverse group of plant species, varieties and ecotypes is grown in order to enrich the genetic heterogeneity and 'broaden' the crops' genetic base – the objective being the ability to converse with the diversity and variability of the soil, and, most importantly, with that of the Andean climate.

The peasants know very well that one converses and reciprocates with the diversity and variability of the climate by means of a diversity and variety of plants. At all times and in all circumstances the peasant consciously tries to increase the diversity of his or her cultivated plants and

Table 2.2 Number of collections of crops in each Germplasm Bank of Peru (1985)

	Puno	Qosqo	Huancayo	Ayacucho	Cajamarca	Sub-total
Grains						
Quinua	1,500*	198	48	425	425	2,596
Kañiwa	330	–	14	47	–	391
Kiwicha	–	570	32	109	17	728
Tarwi	228*	1,200*	1,500*	325	126	3,379
Tubers						
Bitter potato	68	130	42	257	–	497
Oca	120	610	168	122	30	1,050
Olluco	40	18	118	61	18	255
Mashua or isaño	65	14	47	107	–	233
Total						9,129

* Includes data from other Andean countries. *Source*: Tapia and Mateo 1990.

for that end he or she gets and 'tests' new varieties and/or ecotypes. The peasant is a consummated 'wooer' and 'tester' of plants, and does it without obligating the new seed 'to get accustomed by force'. It is accepted for a seed which does not 'accustom' itself to move away – the peasant says simply: 'this seed does not get used to me' and he or she continues 'testing' others to see 'if they follow him or her' (Asociación Bartolomé Aripaylla 1992).

In its report about the nurturing of seeds in the community of Quispillaccta, Ayacucho, the Aripaylla Association shows the varied and meticulous knowledge that the peasants possess for the nurturing and enrichment in the *chacra*, and the diversity and variability of the species cultivated by them (Machaca, Marcela 1993).

The Andean climate's extreme variability, along with the physiographical characteristics of its soil's relief set in the planet's equatorial zone, makes the Andes display a varied and dense ecology that favours mutations, natural hybridizations and the maintenance of a genetic diversity in the plants and animals that inhabit it. However, these characteristics of the Andean natural environment do not in themselves constitute sufficient explanation for the great richness in cultivated species and forms that the peasant raises.

With love and dedication, Andean culture nurtures diversity in its crops, and it is thanks to the unique way of life of Andeans throughout history and today, that the Andes are considered to be one of the richest regions in terms of the numbers of both cultivated species and forms within each species. In other words, it is one of the regions of highest plant diversity or biodiversity. Proof of this assertion is presented in Table 2.2.

Table 2.3 Species and samples of the potato collected in Chile, Bolivia and Peru from 1966 to 1972 (Ochoa 1972)

Solanum species	2n	Samples			
		Chile	Bolivia	Peru	Total
S. ajanhuiri	24	–	10	5	15
S. goniocalix	24	–	–	30	30
S. phureja	24	–	2	13	15
S. stenotomum	24	–	59	215	274
S. chauca	36	–	–	37	37
S. x juzepczukij	36	–	48	55	103
S. tuberosum sub. esp. tuberosum	48	30	–	–	30
S. tuberosum sub. esp. andigena	48	–	220	1,407	1,627
S. curtilobum	60	–	11	35	46
Total		30	350	1,797	2,177

Maize and potatoes are not included in Table 2.2, which lists indigenous Andean grains and tubers. In the case of maize, in the 1950s the Co-operative Maize Research Program from the National Agrarian University, La Molina, collected 1,600 entries which were grouped into forty-eight strains, making Peru the country with the world's greatest genetic variability and diversity in maize (Manrique n/d). The number of strains of maize found in the Andean region is almost equal to the number of strains in the rest of the world combined in spite of the fact that the genetic diversity in the Andean strains is smaller than that found in strains of maize of Central America – possibly the original centre of this important cereal. Wherever maize's original centre may actually be, it remains certain that the Andean peasant nurtured and conserved the greatest diversity of maize strains in the world.

The case of the potato, an important tuber of Andean origin, is similar to that of maize. In 1972 Carlos Ochoa showed that of the 2,177 species and samples collected in Chile, Bolivia and Peru, 82 per cent belong to Peru (see Table 2.3).

Furthermore it is reported that, of the 6,000 entries of native cultivated potato collected throughout Latin America and maintained in the early 1980s by the Germplasm Bank of the International Potato Center (ICP), 80 per cent are from Peru (Vásquez 1988). In 1991 Huamán reported that originally the ICP's cultivated potato germplasm 'consisted of more than 13,000 native culture samples collected throughout Latin America. The identification of duplicates in the cultures allowed for a reduction down to 3,500 different cultigens.' Moreover, the same author reports that the ICP maintains more than 5,000 *Ipomoea* entries which includes 3,200 sweet

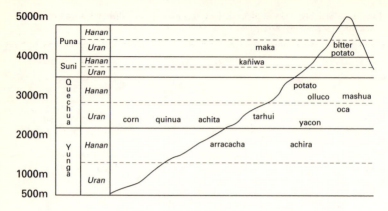

Figure 2.4 Distribution of Andean crops in the central regions of southern Peru

potato (*Ipomoea batatas*) entries, a root cultivated in the Andes since the pre-Hispanic period.

The richness of genes in the germplasm banks is due to the peasants. What is not generally said or is commented on in a 'hushed voice' is that all of these plant collections created by the scientists come from the *chacra* of the peasants who, without claiming any 'right of intellectual property' over them, have given them as gifts and will continue giving them to any collectors who visit them, so that they may keep on spoiling them in their germplasm banks.

It seems that the worst genetic erosion occurs not in the peasants' *chacras*, but rather in germplasm banks and especially in biotechnological laboratories for 'in vitro' conservation.

The peasants do not only maintain their plant varieties in their *chacras*, but they also continuously enrich them. It is not surprising then that Don Manuel Tafur, a peasant from Sorochuco, Cajamarca, shows us more than one hundred classes of potato which he grows in one *chacra* or that the peasants Don Luis Tomaylla of the Barrio (quarter) of Pirhuamarca and Don Juan Mendoza of the Barrio of Cuchuquesera, both from the community of Quispillaccta, Ayacucho, grow thirteen and fifteen species, each one with 129 and 111 ecotypes respectively (Machaca, Marcela 1993).

The above examples eloquently confirm that the Andean culture is one that nurtures plant diversity.

Figure 2.4 and Table 2.4 show the Andean plants cultivated by peasants since the pre-Hispanic period and the altitudinal distribution of the most well known ones. Not included in these data are the Andean species of medicinal plants, dyeing plants, natural grasses and shrubs found in the mountains, which would at least double the number of plants raised by

Table 2.4 Principal Andean plant species, original and/or cultivated from the pre-Hispanic period to the present

Species	Latin name	Natural region of greatest cultivation
1. Tubers		
Mashua	*Tropaeolum tuberosum*	Upper Quechua and Suni
Oca, apilla	*Oaxalis tuberosa*	Upper Quechua (Aymara) and Suni
Olluco, papalisa	*Ullucus tuberosus*	Upper Quechua and Suni
Potatoes	*Solanum tuberosum spp. Andigena*	Yunga, Quechua and Suni
	Solanum ajanhuiri	
	Solanum goniocalyx	
	Solanum phureja	
	Solanum stenotomum	
	Solanum × chaucha	
Bitter potato	*Solanum juzepczukij*	Suni and Puna
	Solanum curtilobum	Suni and Puna
2. Roots		
Achira	*Canna edulis*	Yunga, Upper Quechua
Ajipa	*Pachyrrhizus tuberosus*	Yunga, Quechua
Arracacha, racacha	*Arracacia xanthorriza*	Yunga, Lower Quechua
Camote	*Ipomoea baratas*	Chala, Yunga, Lower Quechua
Chagos, mauka	*Mirabilis expansa*	Yunga, Quechua
Maca	*Lepidium meyenii*	Puna
Yacon, llakuma	*Smallanthus sonchifolius*	Yunga, Lower Quechua
3. Grains		
Achita (Huancayo, Ayachucho), coyo (Cajamarca), achis (Ancash), qamaya (Arequipa), kiwicha (Qosqo)	*Amaranthus caudatus*	Yunga, Lower Quechua
Kañiwa	*Chenopodium pallidicaule*	Suni, Puna
Quinua	*Chenopodium quinoa*	Quechua, Suni
Corn, sara	*Zea mays*	Chala, Yungi, Quechua
4. Fruits		
Aguaymanto	*Physalis peruviana*	Yunga, Quechua
Ciruela del fraile	*Bunchosia armeniaca*	Chala, Yunga
Cocona	*Solanum tapiro*	Rupa rupa
Chirimoya	*Annona cherimola*	Yunga
Guanábana	*Annona muricata*	Chala, Lower Yunga
Guayaba	*Psidium guajaba*	Chala, Yunga
Lúcma	*Pouteria obovata*	Yunga, Lower Quechua
Pacae	*Inga feullei*	Chala, Yunga
Cucumber	*Solanum muricatum*	Yunga
Nogal	*Juglans neotropica*	
Sacha tomato	*Cyphomandra betacea*	Yunga, Quechua
Strawberry	*Fragaria chiloensis*	

Table 2.4 Continued

Species	Latin name	Natural region of greatest cultivation
Tumbo	*Passiflora mollisima*	Quechua
Granadilla	*Passiflora ligularis*	
Maracuyá	*Passiflora edulis*	
Tuna	*Opuntia spp.*	Yunga, Lower Quechua
Papayas	*Carica papaya*	
	Carica pubescens	
	Carica candicans	
Lulo, naranjilla	*Solanum quitoense*	
Capulí, guinda	*Prunus americana*	
Zapote	*Matisia cordata*	

5. Legumes

Tarhui, chocho (Cajamarca)	*Lupinus mutabilis*	Yunga, Quechua, Suni
Common beans	*Phaseolus vulgaris*	Chala, Yunga, Quechua
Ñuña, numia, poroto	*Phaseolus vulgaris*	Chala, Yunga, Quechua
Pallar	*Phaseolus lunatus*	Chala, Yunga
Pallar de los gentiles	*Canavalia ensiformis*	
Pajuro, sacha-poroto, basul	*Erythrina edulis*	Yunga, Quechua
Maní	*Arachis hypogaea*	Chala, Yunga, Rupa rupa
Algarrobo	*Prosopis pallida*	Chala, Yunga

7. Cucurbits

Calabaza	*Lagenaria spp.*	Yunga, Quechua
Loche, avinca	*Cucurbita moschata*	Yunga, Quechua
Zapallo	*Cucurbita maxima*	Yunga, Quechua
Caigua	*Ciclanthera pedata*	Chala, Yunga, Quechua

8. Vegetables

Cimarrón tomato	*Lycopersicum spp.*	Yunga, Lower Quechua
Atajo	*Aramanthus spp.*	
Mountain cabbage	*Carica monoica*	
Berros	*Spilontes oleracea*	

8. Condiments

Àjíes	*Capsicum annum*	Chala, Yunga
	Capsicum frutescens	
Rocoto	*Capsicum pubescens*	Yunga, Lower Quechua
Paico	*Chenopodium ambrosoides*	
Huacatay	*Taget es minuta*	

9. Stimulants

Coca	*Erythroxylon coca*	
Tobacco	*Nicotiana tabacum*	

10. Fibres

Cotton	*Gossypium barbadense*	
Cabuya	*Furcrae andina*	

Source: Vavilov 1992; Hawkes 1991; Hernández and León 1992; Tapia 1993.

the peasants. Vavilov, in 1935, considered the Andes the original centre of forty-five species of cultivated plants.

The US National Research Council (1989), using Cook (1925) as a reference, says that in the Andes there have been domesticated seventy cultivated species and adds that when the Europeans invaded the Andes, the number of cultivated species was almost equal to the number cultivated in all of Europe and Asia. These figures illustrate the phytogenetic wealth of the Andes.

The concept of the cultivated plant is cultural. It depends on the conception that a people have of their plants. Since for the Andeans everything is nurtured, everything is useful, the species that modern Western culture calls wild and weeds are also cultivated. (In Andean culture the concept of weeds does not exist.) This causes the number of species of cultivated plants, from the Andean perspective, easily to surpass one thousand. It is worthy of note that each one of these species presents a great diversity of ecotypes, which supports the assertion that the Andean region is to be considered one of the world's richest in vegetal biodiversity.

Even though the most widely cultivated of all these species are potato and maize, the Andean peasant is not a 'specialist' in either potato or maize cultivation. He or she understands that, as foods, tubers and grains complement each other. Don Luis Tomaylla raises 23 potato ecotypes and 21 maize ecotypes in his *chacras* in Quispillaccta and don Juan Mendoza 27 of potato and 14 of maize, aside from diverse ecotypes from 14 other species and, as we mentioned above, the former cultivates 129 different plant ecotypes in total and the latter 111.

Tubers are called *yaku kawsay* (water foods) because they are perishable; they cannot be stored fresh for very long. On the other hand, grains like maize, *quinua* and *achita* are called *chaki kawsay* (dry foods); these can be stored for long periods of time. On this matter a peasant from Quispillaccta says: 'our dry foods (grains) and our *chacra* are our "food stores" ... the water foods (tubers) and animals are only "water foam"' (Asociación Bartolomé Aripaylla 1992).

The peasant, in each one of his or her many and diverse *chacras*, plants a mixture of species, varieties and ecotypes of crops and always in association. For example, in the potato *chacras* in the Suni region, a mixture of potato species, varieties and ecotypes is planted in association with another mixture of *oca*, *olluco* and *mashua* varieties and ecotypes. Some furrows are sown with the potato mixture and others with the *oca*, *olluco* and *mashua* mixture. The same practice is followed with maize. In each *chacra* in the Quechua region, strips of varieties and strains of maize are sown in association with lines of a mixture of *quinua* and/or *achita* varieties and ecotypes.

During the potato's full flowering season, one observes a garden of potato flowers of different colours: dark and light purple, white, pink, cherry, lilac, etc. In the case of the lines of *quinua* in the maize field, diverse colourations of white, green, burgundy, yellow, purple, etc. ears of corn are seen. When the ears of corn are husked during the maize harvest, the diversity in the colour of the grains is obvious. These facts are clear evidence of the cultivation of genetic heterogeneity in these Andean crops. The same thing happens with other cultivated Andean plants.

Among the mixture of varieties and/or ecotypes of potatoes sown there are some that show resistance to drought conditions and others to excess humidity, so that when the mixture is cultivated in a *usyai wata* (a year with little rain, with droughts and frosts) the varieties resistant to these conditions will produce more than those that are not; similarly, in a *para wata* (rainy year, where the incidence and severity of some diseases increase) the varieties resistant to these conditions will produce more than the varieties resistant to droughts and frosts. In other words, in both cases there is an assured stability in food production despite being faced with the variability of the Andean climate (Valladolid et al. 1984).

We note once more that the peasant nurtures genetic heterogeneity in his or her crops in order to broaden their genetic base and thereby better 'attune' him- or herself to the climate's variability. In addition, in order to secure harvests in the diverse and variable Andean climate, the peasant also has a wide repertory of diverse and varied strategies, such as planting each crop in an 'association-mixture', in different places or altitudes, and at different times.

The planting of tubers and grains is carried out in *chacras* situated in different natural regions. Thus the 'association-mixtures' of maize are made mostly in the Quechua region, the 'association-mixtures' of the potato in the high Quechua and Suni regions, but within each region, they are made at different altitudes and at different times.

When hails fall and/or there is a frost, severe damage may be caused in a given *chacra*, for example in those situated in the lower parts of the Quechua region, but not in those situated in the higher parts. Hail and frost follow a 'capricious path' and often contiguous *chacras* are affected unequally. The Andean knows this very well and plants the same crop in various locations and at different altitudes.

The peasants also plant the same crop at different times. In a year with regularly distributed rain (*allin wata*) the peasants of Qasanqay-Ayacucho plants the potato in four planting seasons (Valladolid and Nuñez 1986):

1. *Michka* planting is sowing very early in small plots of soil with irrigation water. The plants used are located in ecological niches that allow plant growth in the cold and dry months of the *usyai uku*.
2. Early planting or *ñawpa tarpuy* is carried out in the potato *chacras* of Qasanqay during the entire month of September and the first half of October and includes 13 per cent of the *chacras* planted with this tuber.

3. Middle planting or *chaupi tarpuy* is done from the middle of October until the third week of November and includes 73 per cent of the *chacras*.
4. Late planting or *qipa tarpuy* occurs from the last week of November until the middle of December, and includes 14 per cent of the *chacras*.

The last three planting periods jointly constitute the *hatun tarpuy* of potato or great planting and include the largest areas planted with this tuber. All are cultivated under rainy conditions, in dry soils without irrigation water, and hence are exposed to the variability of the Andean climate.

When the 'signs' of the climate indicate a year of deficit and irregularly distributed rain, the peasant always plants the *michka* but the great planting or *hatun tarpuy* is done every fifteen days, from September until December, 'ensuring' in this manner a harvest even in these difficult conditions.

Another piece of agricultural wisdom employed by the Andeans is crop rotation, which includes the sequence of crops that are planted in the same *chacra* year after year, until the *chacra* goes into a rest period; following which the planting is reinitiated with a different sequence of crops.

For the Andean, the soil is a living being and therefore it also gets tired and needs rest. This rest period is prolonged – up to ten years – in the *chacras* situated in the high Suni and Puna regions; it is shorter in those situated in the lower high Suni and high Quechua regions, and the *chacras* are planted continuously with maize in the low Quechua. In this last case, maize is planted associated with beans and other wild legumes that, by fixing atmospheric nitrogen, maintain soil fertility.

Crop rotation with a rest period included, apart from restoring soil fertility, is also one of the best ways of lowering the levels of incidence of certain diseases and plagues. The clearest example is found in the case of potato 'nematocyst' caused by the nematode Globodera, whose cysts can survive in the soil for up to ten years. This forces long rotations between host crops.

Broadening the crops' genetic base by means of 'association-mixtures' and through the strategy of planting at diverse altitudes and at different times, the peasant obtains a harvest regardless of the year's climate. But all of this work is not sufficient, help is always needed: the accompaniment and advice of the *Pachamama*, of the *Taita Urqos*, mountain protectors, of the elements of nature and of deceased ancestors, above all those who distinguished themselves as good *chacareros*, as being *yachaq* or *pongo* (those who 'converse with' and receive 'the energy' from the *Urqus*). A peasant from Quispillaccta-Ayacucho says: 'the *runa* (humans), however much physical work they expend, will not obtain harvests without the participation of the rains, of the droughts, of the *Urqus*'.

All activities in the Andes, especially those related to the direct nurturing of the plants and animals, are ritual. Jesús Urbano of Huanta tells us that 'to begin the labours we make the *pagapu* [an offering] to the *Pachamama* ... when we hill ... also when we dig up the first test potatoes afterwards we give thanks for the harvest'. This attitude of profound love and respect in the Andeans is consubstantial with their lives. This is accurately reflected in the following peasant phrases: 'opening the earth (*barbechar*) is like opening the heart of the *Pachamama* ... it must be done very carefully and asking permission' or 'upon opening the *chacra* first some coca leaves are placed into the "mouth" of the *chacra* saying *Pachamama acoycuchun* (*chaccha* [ritually chew] *Pachamama*)' (Machaca, Magdalena 1993). These are expressions that spring from the heart because one 'feels' that the *Pachamama* only lends one the soil so that the *runas* accompanied by the *huacas* and nature obtain food to share among all. The harvest is of all and for all.

The peasant not only nurtures soil, water, microclimate and plants, he or she also raises animals. Part of this nurture takes place in corrals that are called *kanchas* situated near the house where the peasant lives during the cold and dry period of the year (*usyai uku*). In the warm and rainy period the livestock move up to the higher areas where they graze during the day in the natural pasture prairies and at night they 'sleep' in another *kancha* situated in the Puna near the shepherd's hut. Grazing takes place mainly on the natural pastures of the Puna in *puquy uku* and in *usyai uku* mainly on the wild pastures that grow between the planted fields of the lower part and the stubble of the harvest left in the *chacra* after the crop is harvested. It is a vertical grazing, from the Puna region to the Suni and Quechua regions. The moving up and down of the animals is done by communal agreement and there are special authorities in charge of making sure it happens.

Shepherds consider their animals brothers, sisters, sons, daughters, parents. This attitude manifests itself most with llamas and alpacas which are said to be 'sacred animals', and who are sung to in Quechua in the ritual of livestock '*señalacuy*' (branding), expressing their great love and thankfulness to them. In the peasant community of Cotay, Huancavelica, one of these deep-felt songs to the llama says (Espinoza 1996):

> Let's go brothers, let's go fellow countryman
> our maize, our potato have not been enough,
> let's go to the Quechua (to the Quechua region)
> You will enter valiantly,
> You will walk vigorously.
>
> You are my father,
> You are my mother,
> You clothe me,
> You feed me,
> Without you these children of yours would not have life.

The shepherds say llamas and alpacas belong to the *Taita Urqu* who 'only lend them to us ... if we don't take good care of them ... they take them away'. Referring to the *Urqu* (mountain) they say that 'without him they could not live and their animals could not multiply'.

Here also, all of the practices of nurturing such as breeding, curing, branding, birthing and shearing are ritual activities. Before beginning them permission is asked of the *Taita Huamani*, of the *Apu*, of the *Achachila*, and offerings are made – principally in the months of August and February, which are generally the months when llamas and alpacas mate and also give birth.

The llamas and the alpacas are considered by the Aymara family to be life itself because with the production of wool all their needs are satisfied. It is the Aymaras' *chacra* with feet (*Kayuni Yapu*) (Quiso 1991).

Andean culture makes use of diverse processing techniques for the storage, conservation and use of the harvest's products. Since harvested tubers cannot be stored for long periods of time because they 'shrivel' and sprout, if 'sweet' potato production has been abundant, *cocopa* (dried potato) is made. From varieties of bitter potato, *chuño* is made. The method of its preparation is a singular and careful technology of preparation, involving exposing the tubers to the extreme frosts of June nights and the severe insolations of the day in such a way that they dehydrate; they can be stored in this form for years. Something similar is done to the other Andean tubers, so from *oca* one gets *khaya* and from *olluco*, *ligli*. By means of a similar technique *charki* (dehydrated and dried meat generally from the llama and alpaca) is made.

Andean grains – such as corn, *quinua*, *cañiwa* and *achita* and *tarhui* – once harvested can be stored for long periods of time. For this reason they are highly valued and each family tries to secure them, if not by cultivating them directly, then through barter for other products. They say, 'without maize the *runa* cannot pass (cannot live)'.

The grains *quinua* and *tarhui* have certain alkaloids that give them a bitter taste and thus before consumption they must go through a 'de-bittering' process. For example *quinua* is washed, rubbing the grains, while *tarhui* or *chocho* is boiled with ashes and then soaked in running water for several days. All of these technologies demand great effort and dedication from the peasant but he or she does them joyfully accompanied by the coca, 'if there is no coca there is no work' (Urbano and Macera 1992).

Before each labour, coca leaves are ritually masticated (*chacchar*). If they taste 'sweet' work will go well; if the opposite is the case, some kind of difficulty will arise and one must be careful.

The Andean lives communally and considers him- or herself one – and not the most important – member of his or her local *Pacha*. He or she is equivalent to a humble rock or an imposing mountain, which is also son, brother, father of all that forms the *Pacha*. He or she knows that the

Pacha is alive and, therefore, he or she is part of the organicity of this living being.

In order to contribute to the nurturing of harmony in this organicity of the *Pacha*, humans (*runa*) nurture the heterogeneity of life in the *chacra* through varied and flexible forms of interrelation between all elements of the *Pacha*. Conversation and reciprocity are the most evident manifestations of this attitude of respect and love with which everything is nurtured.

One converses continually with everything; proof of this is the conversation with the climate by means of 'signs'. One also reciprocates with everything without demanding immediate return. For example, one reciprocates through *ayni*, *minga* or *uyay*, which is the joint work of various families of the *ayllu*, on one of their *chacras*. The peasant on whose *chacra ayni* takes place provides food and musicians so that the work can be done in an atmosphere of *fiesta*, of joy, where people dance and eat well. 'For all of the chores of the *quechua runa* (those who care for the *chacra*) and *sallqa runas* (those who care for the animals) there are always special songs. There are songs for the potato, there are songs for the maize, there are songs for the *oca* and for the *olluco*' (Urbano and Macera 1992), and there are also songs for the llama and the alpaca (Quiso 1991, Espinoza

Table 2.5 Characteristics of the nurturing of heterogeneity in the Andean *chacra*

---

1.   *Continuous conversation with the climate and the soil through 'signs'*

1.1   Signs of the climate.

1.1.1 Stars: e.g. the sun, the moon, Andean constellations such as the *suchu* (the Pleiades).

1.1.2 Plants: e.g. the time and abundance of the flowering of *sankay* (in Vinchos – Ayacucho), *Oluypiña* (in Conima – Puno), *Tamia tucto* (in Chetilla – *Cajamarca*).

1.1.3 Animals: e.g. change in colour of the skin of the *janpato* (toad), the song of the *chilliku* (cricket), the howl of the *atoq* (fox).

1.1.4 Meteors: e.g. the colour of clouds, the direction and colour of the winds, the presence of the rainbow.

1.1.5 Dreams.

1.2   Signs of the soil: e.g. in the community of Chetilla, the wild plant *Chupika kewa* appears on the *chacra* when the soil asks for rest. When a soil is rested it asks to be cultivated by the appearance of certain wild gramineous plants.

2.   *Diverse forms of growing soil according to a conversation with the climate*

2.1   In a year with little rain, *usyai wata*, the planted area is increased in the higher parts; in other words, 'the crops move up' and the direction of the furrows is diagonal to the direction of the sloping soil.

2.2   In a rainy year, *puquy wata*, the planting area is increased in the lower parts, 'the crops move down' and the direction of the furrows follows the slope of the terrain. In this case the furrows are short and alternate (*huaccho* system).

3. *Diverse ways of growing plants in the chacra*

3.1 By enrichment of the genetic heterogeneity of the plants.

3.1.1 Planting in the same *chacra* a mixture of varieties of each cultivated species, e.g. a mixture of potato varieties, promoting a greater intraspecific genetic variability.

3.1.2 Planting 'associations of crops' in a *chacra*, for example, plant in strips mixtures of varieties of maize, alternating with rows (*shaiguas*) of mixtures of *quinua* ecotypes. This increases interspecific variability.

3.2 Through a broad range of knowledge for planting on multiple and dispersed *chacras* situated at different altitudes and planted at different times.

3.2.1 Planting at different altitudes
(a) In diverse natural regions: e.g. in Qasanqay-Ayacucho and the Suni region associations of mixtures of Andean tubers; and in the Quechua region associations of mixtures of Andean grains.
(b) In different places within one natural region: e.g. in Qasanqay-Ayacucho three *chacras* of maize are planted in the Quechua region, and four potato *chacras* in the Suni region.

3.2.2 Planting at different times
(a) Within one agricultural year: e.g. in Qasanqay-Ayacucho 4 potato plantings take place at intervals:
   (1) Very early planting or *michka* in *chacras* with risk of frost.
   (2) Early planting (*ñaupa tarpuy*).
   (3) Intermediate planting (*chaupi tarpuy*).
   (4) Late planting (*qipa tarpuy*).
(b) In several consecutive years (crop rotation).

4. *Diverse forms of raising animals that go along with the agricultural practices through rotation and vertical grazing in diverse natural regions*

Example: in Qasanqay the livestock 'moves up' from the Quechua region to the natural pasture region or Puna in the hot-rainy season of the year (*puquy uku*) and 'moves down' once again to the Quechua and Suni regions in the *usyai uku* (cold-dry season). Furthermore, the livestock's manure provides the main source of fertilizer for the *chacras*.

5. *Diverse practices for the processing, storage, conservation and use of harvested products*

5.1 Of vegetable origin, for example:

5.1.1 Dehydration of tubers:
(a) From the bitter potato for the elaboration of '*chuño*'.
(b) From the 'sweet' potato for the elaboration of '*cocopa*'.
(c) From the *oca* for obtaining '*khaya*'.
(d) From *olluco* for obtaining '*ligli*'.

5.1.2 De-bitterment of grains such as *tarhui* and *quinua*

5.2 Of animal origin: e.g. dehydration of llama meat for the elaboration of '*Charki*'.

6. *Continuous conversation and reciprocation between the relatives within the Andean Ayllu, confirming an organicity that facilitates the nurturing of the* chacra.

This is achieved through practices of mutual help such as for example *ayni* and *minka*. This help takes place in an atmosphere of *fiesta*, with joy and always asking permission of the *huacas* or Andean deities.

1992). The chores in the *chacra* and the corral are done with song, music and dance.

All parts of the *ayllu* – be they stars, hills, lakes, rivers, wild and cultivated plants and animals, even *runas* and rocks – all nurture and let themselves be nurtured by all, in an environment of happiness and mutual respect.

Table 2.5 aims to sum up and present in sequential order some of the knowledge used by the Andean peasant for the nurturing of diversity in the *chacra* in such a way that this nurturing is attuned with the diversity, density, variability and cyclicity of the Andean climate.

Andean peasant agriculture is thus a continuous conversation between the peasant and nature and this conversation is different in each place, given the diversity and variability of the Andean environment.

The nurturing of the *chacra* by the entire *ayllu*

To grow life's heterogeneity in the *chacra* one converses with everything. Figure 2.5 illustrates the conversation among all members of the *ayllu*, giving a synopsis of pastoral and agricultural activity in the peasant community of Qasanqay-Ayacucho (3,100 to 4,000 metres above sea level). The data supporting this synopsis were obtained during a three-year stay in this community (PISCA 1983), which allowed us, as technicians, to learn Andean agriculture from the peasants rather than teaching some modern agriculture to them.

Qasanqay is a peasant community situated in the Cachi river basin, in Vinchos, Ayacucho. It is home to 117 families (PISCA 1983), each one containing on average five members and, as we have said before, each one with a plot that varies from 0.18 to 0.34 hectares, dispersed and located at diverse altitudes in the three natural regions of the community. The crops that use the most land are maize and potatoes.

In the Quechua region between 3,100 and 3,200 metres one encounters mainly *chacras* with mixtures of maize with lines of mixtures of *quinua* and/or *achita*. Each peasant plants between two and three *chacras* of maize. The High Quechua and Suni regions, at between 3,400 and 3,800 metres above sea level, comprise mainly *chacras* with clone mixtures – an average of seven species or varieties – of potatoes. In this region each community member grows four *chacras* of potato and three of barley. Above 3,800 metres lie the prairies of natural pasture which are the basis for livestock grazing. Mainly bovine and ovine animals are raised.

Lying between 3,200 and 3,400 metres above sea level is Pincullonga, which is another peasant community with which the lower Quechua region is shared for the planting of associations of mixtures of maize and *quinua*.

The *chacras* of the Quechua region are planted with maize at different altitudes and those of the Suni with potatoes, each one during different planting seasons.

The characteristics of the climate are also shown in Figure 2.5 by means of a climatogram which shows the variations in the average monthly maximum and minimum temperatures and accumulated monthly precipitation. On the basis of these characteristics, each month's hydric balance has been calculated. The hydric balance is the difference between each month's rainfall, minus the humidity lost to evapotranspiration in that same time period, so that, theoretically, each vertical bar represents the excess or deficit humidity accumulated in the soil which, according to theory, can support the growth and development of the crops.

In general terms a marked distinction can be made between two seasons: one with little rain and intense cold, in which the temperature can fall to below 0 degrees Centigrade and which the peasants know as *usyai uku*; the other, rainy with higher temperatures (*puquy uku*), which is the season in which the crops grow in the *chacra*. Each season contains two periods of different duration and the following characteristics:

1. In *puquy uku*:
a) hot-dry period, from September to October, which mainly includes multiple planting times; and
b) hot-rainy period, from December to mid-March – the period when the crops grow.

2. In *usyai uku*:
a) cold-rainy period, from the middle of March to the end of April, when the crop's fruits ripen; and
b) Dry-cold period, which includes the months from May to August, time of harvest, processing and storage of the *chacras*' products, followed by a renovating rest period, when the peasants celebrate the community's patron saints' *fiestas* and Andean rites of reciprocation with the mountain protectors or *Taita Huamanis*, through the ritual offerings or '*Pagapus*' to these protectors.

It is clearly noted that there is a close relation between the cycle of the periods of Andean climate and the cycle of the crops; and it could not be any other way, since 90 per cent of the *chacras* are rain-fed (they are *secano* crops).

Figure 2.5 also shows the humidity conditions of the soil, where the soil proves to be dry from June to August; humid from October to December; very humid from January to the middle of March; to become humid again from March to the end of May. In this case one also observes a close correspondence between the periods of the climate and the cycle of the crops.

These conditions of the climate and soil, especially the climate, vary from year to year around the averages shown. It does not surprise Andeans if in a particular year conditions are very far from the average, causing a

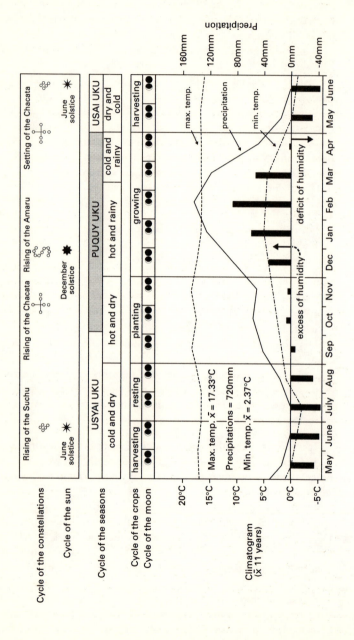

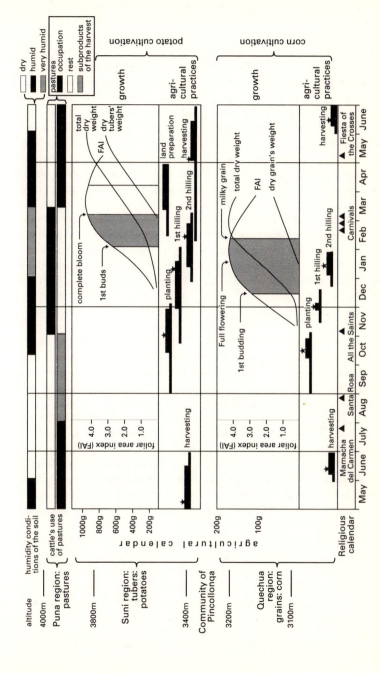

Figure 2.5 Pastoral and agricultural activity in the peasant community of Qasanqay-Ayacucho (3,100–4,000 metres above sea level)

dry year or *usyai wata* or a very rainy year, *para wata*. Thus, the Andean climate walks wherever it wishes just like a wild animal.

In the synopsis in Figure 2.5 the following characteristics are shown: the cycle of the constellations of the southern sky that are observed by the peasant. The cycle of the sun, in other words, the sun's 'walk' as it rises on the eastern horizon each day during a year, from the June solstice near 24 June, *fiesta* of Saint John, until the December solstice near 25 December, *fiesta* of Christmas, and to the June solstice again. The journey of the sun during two consecutive June solstices corresponds to the period of one calendar year.

Furthermore, Figure 2.5 shows the cycle of the seasons and the periods of Andean climate with the characteristics already described, those which are closely related to the cycle of the crops: sowing; growth, which includes the fruit ripening period; and the harvest, which is always followed by a restorative rest period.

Also included in Figure 2.5 is the cycle of the phases of the moon of each lunation of the year, noting the new moon or *quilla wañay*, a time when no work is done on the *chacra* or in the raising of livestock – such as shearing, castration – because it would not come out right. As will be shown below, the peasants live in tune with and 'synchronized' with nature, in this case, with the nurturing of the *chacra*. The phases of the moon mark the rhythm of 'work' in the *chacra*.

Aside from the climatogram, which is the average of eleven years of a meteorologist's readings and the humidity conditions of the soil, two parallel bars are drawn which indicate the livestock's use of the community's pastures and the periods of occupation, rest and use of the subproducts of the harvest (remains, stubble, etc.).

From November onwards, the livestock that are in the Quechua and Suni regions feeding on the remains from the harvest move up to the Puna region to graze in the natural pastures, which by this time have grown again with the first rains. They stay in the Puna until the middle of March, when they come down back to the Quechua and Suni regions to graze in the harvested *chacras*. From August to October they feed mainly on the subproducts of the harvest (chaff, green corn husk) saved by the peasants for these periods of scarcity.

The graphic synopsis also shows the growth curve of the potato and maize crops based on dry weight and foliar area, and shows the correspondent sequence of agricultural activities: land preparation, sowing, first and second hilling-up, and harvest. The duration of each of these activities is shown by a horizontal continuous line that is widest where it includes the periods when the greatest number of peasants are carrying out these activities. The asterisks above the thickest lines indicate the times when the largest percentage of people are engaged in that activity.

A way of expressing the growth of a plant, or of one of its organs, is by drawing curves that represent the accumulation of dry material which is caused by photosynthesis, throughout the crop's life. The graphs within Figure 2.5 show the total dry weight curve, which means the weight of the entire plant, and the dry weight curve of the potato tubers and of grains in the case of maize.

Since there is a close relationship between production and the speed with which the foliar area of a plant grows and the time that this foliar area lasts in the field, there is also an index of foliar area (IFA) curve which indicates the relationship between the leaf area of a plant and the surface area of land that it occupies. For example, an IFA of 1 indicates that the foliar area of the plant is equal to the surface area that it occupies, while an IFA of 2 indicates that the surface area of the leaves is double the surface area of the land in which it is growing. The IFA shows the rate at which the plant's foliar area covers the soil in which it is growing. It also shows the 'critical periods' of the crop's life, in other words the period in which any kind of damage the plant may suffer, especially in its foliar area – be it because of drought, hail, frost, an attack of pathogenic insects or micro-organisms – will cause a significant reduction in production (Tineo 1984, 1988).

The 'critical period' of potato cultivation arises between the beginning of the formation of buds and complete bloom, and that of maize, between the beginning of the formation of buds on the *panoja* (masculine inflorescence) to the stage when the grains of the *mazorca* (feminine inflorescence or ear of corn) look milky. These critical periods correspond to the times when the total dry weight curve begins to increase abruptly and the foliar area of the plant reaches its maximum. The graph (see Figure 2.5) shows that these periods occur at times of highest rainfall and therefore highest soil humidity, and when the minimum temperatures are the highest; in other words, in the most favourable conditions for cultivation.

Meanwhile, in the middle of March, minimum temperatures begin to drop, favouring the growth and filling out of the potato tubers. These blasts of cold air do not favour maize growth, which is a plant less tolerant of cold than the potato. For this reason the peasants plant it before the potato. This accommodation of the crop to the most favourable conditions of the climate and soil humidity undoubtedly is the consequence of the continuous conversation of the peasant with the climate, through the 'signs'.

The nurturing of plants and animals is not done only by man. All of the relatives of the *ayllu* participate in the nurturing of the *chacra*. The stars, the sun, the moon also participate, 'telling' the farmer when, where and what to plant (Valladolid 1993a).

The constellations of stars that are included in Figure 2.5 are those that are conversed with most frequently. The *Suchu* or *Jarampa* (The Pleiades), which rises on the eastern horizon in the early morning of the June solstice, signals the end of one agricultural year and the beginning of a new one. Hours later the sun will rise in the same place. This coincidence of risings 'tells' the peasant that the dry and cold conditions of *usyai uku* will intensify (see Figure 2.5). Furthermore, as was explained above, at this time the brightness of the stars that make up the *Suchu* is another 'sign' that tells about the character of the coming agricultural year.

The *Amaru* (Scorpius), also known in Quispillaccta as the Condor, is another Andean constellation which rises on the eastern horizon in the early morning of the December solstice. Hours later the sun will rise in the same place. As with the *Suchu*, the coincidence in the risings of the *Amaru* and the sun on this date tells the peasants that the rains of *puquy uku* will increase and that the *Taita Inti* (Father Sun) has completed half of his annual journey.

The constellation most related to the growing of the *chacra* is the *Chacata* or Andean cross, which is not the Southern Cross, but rather another, much bigger cross with arms of equal length (square cross). It includes the stars Alpha and Beta of Centaurus, which make the eyes of the llama (*Llamapa ñawin*) and which jointly with others form one of the arms. The other arm of the cross includes, among others, the Alpha and Beta stars of the Southern Cross.

The *Chacata* rises on the southeast horizon in the early morning of the first days of November, the season in which most of the planting takes place. In the early mornings of the first days of the month of May, the *Chacata* disappears from the southwest horizon, indicating the time when the big harvests begin. This beautiful constellation of the Andean sky converses with the peasants at two of the most important times for raising their crops: planting and harvest. Furthermore, it culminates (passes by the meridian reaching its maximum height above the southern horizon) in the early morning of the first days of the month of February – the season in which harvesting of the early planting fruits begins. In other words, from this date the harvests of the first fruits of the *chacra* begin.

At this time the sun's 'walk' and that of the constellations of stars is ritualized. From Figure 2.3 one can see that the dates of most of the *fiestas* correspond with the rise, culmination and setting of the *Chacata*. Thus on the *fiesta* of All Saints, one not only 'converses' for better nurturing of the *chacra* with the deceased ancestors but also with the rising of the *Chacata*. In the month of February, near the time of the *fiesta* of the carnivals, one converses ritually with the first fruits of the *chacra*, even making them participate in the music and the dance. The Andeans also converse with the culmination of the *Chacata* and in the month of May, during the '*Fiesta* of the Crosses', converse with the setting of this same constellation. The *Chacata* could well be considered the constellation of the *chacra* – accompanying the peasant during the planting and growth until the harvesting of the crops in the *chacra*.

Lastly the *fiestas* of the patronesses of the community – *Mamacha del*

Carmen and the *Fiesta de Santa Rosa* – take place during the rest period, the *usyai uku*, and are related to the *Pachamama*.

Thus Andean peasant agriculture is to nurture with love and to let oneself be nurtured by all; always conversing and helping one another among all the relatives of the *ayllu* (stars, rocks, plants, animals, human beings, mountains, deceased ancestors and many others).

This mutual cultivation of the heterogeneity of life based in the *chacra* is the best way to synchronize with the heterogeneity of the diverse, dense and variable Andean environment.

References and suggested reading

AMIDEP. 1988; *La Sierra Peruana: Realidad Poblacional* (*The Peruvian Highlands: Reality of Settlement*), Editions of the Asociación Multidisciplinaria de Investigación y Docencia en Poblaciones.

Asociación Bartolomé Aripaylla. Ayacucho. 1992; 'Diversificación del germoplasma agrícola en Quispillaccta' (Agricultural germplasm diversification in Quispillaccta), *Campaña Agrícola* 1991–1992 Ayacucho. (typewritten report)

Bonavia, D. 1991; 'De la caza a la agricultura' (From hunting to agriculture). In *Peru hombres e historia: De los origenes al siglo XV*, Lima, Peru; EDUBANCO.

Cavero, C. M. 1962; *Aporte a la castellanización del indígena* (*Contribution to the Learning of Spanish by the Indigenous Population*). Bilingual work in Ayacucho.

Chambi, P. N. 1991; 'La Religiosidad Aymara en el Pueblo Andino de Conima' (Aymara religiosity in the Andean peoples of Conima). Thesis. Course on Andean Agriculture. PRATEC/UNSCH.

Chambi, P., Ch. V. Quiso and V. F. Tito 1992; 'Cosmovisión, Conocimiento Campesino y Tecnología Tradicional de los Criadores Aymaras' (Cosmovision, peasant knowledge and traditional technology of the Aymaras husbanders), Study Document 24. PRATEC.

Cook, O. F. 1925; 'Peru as a center of domestication', *Journal of Heredity*, 16: 33–46.

Espinoza, T. 1992; 'Crianza de Alpacas y Llamas en la Comunidad de Cotay, Huancavelica (4,200–5,000 metres above sea level)'. Thesis. Course on Andean Peasant Agriculture. PRATEC/UNSCH.

Espinoza, T. 1996; *Alpacas y Llamas en la Comunidad de Cotay-Huancavelica*. Ayacucho. Universidad Nacional de San Cristobal de Huamanga.

Figueroa, A. 1986; 'El Desarrollo de la Agricultura Campesina de la Sierra del Perú' (The development of peasant agriculture in the Peruvian Highlands). In the Annals 5th International Conference of Andean Farming Systems, 10–14 March, Puno, Peru.

Grillo, E. 1979; 'La Producción y el consumo de alimentos en el Perú' (Production and consumption of food in Peru). Paper presented at a seminar organized by AMIDEP.

Grillo, E. 1988; 'Manejo de Suelos en los Andes (Hacia un Marco Conceptual), (Management of soils in the Andes [Toward a conceptual framework]). In *Consideraciones acerca de agricultura andina* (Remarks about Andean agriculture) January. Lima. (Xerox)

Grillo, E. 1993; 'Cosmovisión Andina de Siempre y Cosmología Occidental Moderna' in *Desarrollo o Descolonizaciomn en los Andes?*, PRATEC, Lima.

Grillo, F. E., J. R. Valladolid, V. A. S. Rodriguez, A. A. De La Torre and L. S. Cuzco 1988; 'Chetilla: Paradigma Cultural Andino'. Multicopied by Proyecto Piloto de Ecosistemas Andinos, Cajamarca, Peru, for the International Seminar on 'Ecología y manejo de recursos en áreas de alta montaña'. 20–27 August.

Hawkes, J. G. 1991; 'Centros de Diversidad Genética Vegetal en Latinoamerica' (Centres of Plant Genetic Diversity in Latin America), *Diversity*, 7 (1 and 2).

Hernández, B. J. and J. León, (eds). 1992; 'Cultivos Marginados, Otra Perspectiva de 1492' (Marginalized crops, another perspective of 1492), FAO collection. Vegetal Production and Protection #26. Rome.

Hocquenghem, A. M. 1982; *Iconografía Mochica*, Lima; Pontificia Universidad Católica del Perú.

Holdridge, L. E. 1978; *Ecología basada en zonas de Vida* (Ecology based in zones of life), San Jose, Costa Rica; Interamerican Institute of Agricultural Sciences.

Huaman, Z. 1991; 'Conservación de recursos Fitogenéticas' (Conservation of phytogenetic resources), *CIP Diversity*, 7, (1 and 2).

Ibarra G. D. E. 1982; *Ciencia astronomica y sociologia Incaica* (Astronomical science and Inca sociology) (1st edn), La Paz-Cochabamba, Bolivia; Editorial Los Amigos del Libro.

INIPA. 1985; 'Programa Nacional de Sistemas Agropecuarios Andinos. Documento de Base' (National Programme of Andean Systems of Agriculture and Pastoralism), Lima; INIPA.

Instituto Nacional de Desarrollo. 1984; 'Propuesta de Estrategia de Desarrollo de la Sierra' (Proposal for a strategy of development in the highlands), Series: 'Documentos de Trabajo'. Proyectos Microregionales en Sierra.

Jimenez Borja, A. 1992; 'Las Huacas', *Revista del Museo de la Nación*, 1, Lima, Peru.

Kaulicke, P. 1985; 'La Agricultura en el Perú Pre-hispánico: Su Origen' (Agriculture in pre-hispanic Peru: its origin), *Boletin de Lima*, 7 (40).

Kusch, R. 1986; *America Profunda* (Deep America), Buenos Aires, Argentina; Editorial Bonum.

Machaca M., Magdalena. 1993; 'Kancha *Chacra* Sunqulla'. 3rd Course on Andean Peasant Agriculture. PRATEC/UNSCH. Bartolomé Aripaylla Association. Ayacucho.

Machaca M., Marcela. 1991; 'Vigencia y Continuidad de la Cultura y Agricultura Andina en Quispillaccta, Ayacucho' (Relevance and continuity of the culture and agriculture in Quispillacta, Ayacucho). Thesis in Agricultural Engineering. Facultad de Ciencias Agrarias, UNSCH. Ayacucho.

Machaca M., Marcela. 1992; 'El Gran Rito al Agua de Riego: Yarqa Aspy' (The great ritual of irrigation water: Yarqa Aspy). Research Essay. 2nd Course on Andean Agriculture. PRATEC/UNSCH.

Machaca M., Marcela. 1993; 'Actividades de crianza en la Comunidad Campesina de Quispillaccta, Ayacucho'. In *Afirmacion Cultural Andina*, PRATEC.

Manrique, Ch. A. n.d.; *El mais en el Peru* (Corn in Peru), Lima, Peru; Fondo del Libro del Banco Agrario.

Ministerio de Agricultura. 1987; 'Plan de Desarrollo Agrario de la Sierra del Perú' (Plan for agrarian development in the highland of Peru). (Proposal for Governmental Aprobation). (Xerox)

National Research Council. 1989; 'Lost Crops of the Incas: Little Known Plants of the Andes with Promise of Worldwide Cultivation'. Washington, DC; National Academy Press.

Ochoa, C. 1972; 'El germoplasma de papa en Sud América' (The potato germplasm in South America). In *Prospects for the Potato in the Developing World*, Lima, Peru; International Potato Center.

ONERN. 1976; *Ecological Map of Peru. Explicative Guide*, Lima; ONERN.

ONERN. 1985; 'Los recursos naturales del Perú'. (Natural resources in Peru) Lima; National Office of the Evaluation of Natural Resources.

PISCA. 1983; 'Diagnóstico técnico agropecuario de las comunidades campesinas de Arizona y Qasanqay' (Technical agricultural and pastoral diagnostic of the peasant communities of Arizona and Qasanqay), UNSCH/IICA/CIID; University of Huamanga.

Pulgar Vidal, J. 1987; 'Las ocho regiones naturales' (The eight natural regions). In *Geografía del Perú* (9th edn), Lima; PEISA.

Quiso, V. 1991; 'Kayuni Yapu o Jakkiri Yapu (Chacra con patas o chacra viviente): Crianza de Alpacas y Llamas en la Comunidad de Ajanani Wajra Kucho – Puno'. Research Essay. Course on Andean Peasant Agriculture. PRATEC/UNSCH.

Rostworowski, M. 1992; *Pachacamac y el Senor der los Milagros: Una trayectoria milenaria* (Pachacamac and the Lord of Miracles: a millenarian trajectory), Lima, Peru; IEP.

Salis, A. 1985; 'Cultivos Andinos ¿Alternativa Alimentaria Popular?' (Andean crops: An alternative popular food?), Cusco; Centro de Estudios Rurales Andinos 'Bartolomé de las Casas'.

Silva-Santisteban, F. 1990; 'El Mundo Andino. De la caza a las Tecnologías Agropercuarias' (The Andean world: from hunting to agricultural and pastoral technologies), Cuadernos de Historia XI, Universidad de Lima, Facultad de Ciencias Humanas. Lima.

Soukup, J. n.d.; *Vocabulario de los nombres vulgares de la flora Peruana y catalogo de los generos* (Vocabulary of the common names of the Peruvian flora and catalogue of genders), Lima; Editorial Salesiana.

Tapia, M. 1993; 'Semillas Andinas' (Andean seeds). *El Banco de Oro* (The gold bank), Lima, Peru; CONCYTEC.

Tapia, M. and N. Mateo 1990; 'Andean Phytogenetic and Zootecnic Resources'. In *Andean Mountain Agriculture and Crop Genetic Resources*, K. W. Riley et al. (eds), New Delhi; Oxford IBH Publishing Co.

Tapia, N. M. 1986; 'Guía Metodológica para la Caracterización de la Agricultura Andina' (Methodological guide for the characterization of Andean agriculture). (La experiencia del Proyecto PISCA), Universities of Ayacucho, Cusco and Puno; IICA/CIID.

Tello, J. C. 1967; 'La Religión en el Antiguo Perú: Wirakocha' (Religion in ancient Peru: Wirakocha). In *Paginas Escogidas*, Lima; UNMSM.

Tineo, C. I. I. 1984; 'Efecto de la Reducción foliar sobre el Rendimiento y Calidad de papa, variedad Merpata bajo condiciones de secano' (Effect of the foliage reduction on the production and quality of potatoes, variety Merpata, under conditions of rain-fed agriculture). Allpachaka (3,500 metres above sea level) Ayacucho. Undergraduate level report in Agrarian Sciences, UNSCH.

Tineo, C. I. I. 1988; 'Efecto de la Reducción Foliar sobre el Rendimiento y Calidad del Maíz: Variedad Morocho 501' (Effect of foliage reduction on the productivity and quality of corn: Variety Morocho 501). Canaan (2,750 metres above sea level) Ayacucho. Agronomical Engineering Thesis. Facultad de Ciencias Agrarias, UNSCH. Ayacucho.

Urbano Rojas, J. and P. Macera 1992; *Santero y Caminante: Santoruraj-Nanpurej* (Craft-
man and itinerant: Santoruraj-Nanpurej), Lima; Editorial Apoyo..

Urbina M., C. 1987; 'Condiciones Agrometeorológicas de Allpachaka (3,500 m.s.
n.m.) promedio de once campañas agrícolas y la relación de las fases de la luna
con la precipitación pluvial'. (Agrometerological conditions of Allpachaka [3,500
m.a.s.l.] average of eleven agricultural seasons and the relationship of the phases
of the moon with rainfall), Field Report. Facultad de Ciencias Agrarias, University of Huamanga, Ayacucho.

Valladolid, R. J. 1989a; 'Concepción Holística de la Agricultura Andina' (Holistic
conception of Andean agriculture), *Boletín de Lima*, 11 (63).

Valladolid, R. J. 1989b; 'Cultivos Andinos: Importancia y Posibilidades de su Re-
cuperación y Desarrollo' (Andean crops: importance and possibilities for their
recuperation and development), *Boletín de Lima*, 8 (48).

Valladolid, R. J. 1989c; 'Agricultura Alto Andina' (Highland Andean agriculture),
Boletín de Lima, 5 (28).

Valladolid, R. J. 1990; 'Visión Andina del Clima' (Andean vision of the weather).
Study Document 14; PRATEC.

Valladolid, R. J. 1993a; 'Agroastronomía Andina'. (Andean agroastronomy). In
¿Desarrollo o Descolonización en los Andes? (Development or Decolonization in the
Andes?) (2nd edn), Lima, Peru; PRATEC.

Valladolid, R. J. 1993b; 'Las Plantas en la Cultura Andina y en Occidente Moderno'.
(Plants in Andean culture and in the modern West). In *¿Desarrollo o Descolonización
en los Andes?* (Development or Decolonization in the Andes?), Lima, Peru;
PRATEC.

Valladolid, R. J. and A. E. Nuñez 1986; 'Investigación de los Sistemas Agropecuarios
Alto Andino (3000–4000 m.s.n.m.) en Comunidades Campesinas de Ayacucho'
(Inquiry into the agro-pastoralist systems in the Andean highlands [3000–4000
m.a.s.l.] in peasant communities of Ayacucho), Annals of the 5th International
Conference on Andean Agricultural Systems, 10–14 March. Puno.

Valladolid, R. J., H. Salvatierra and A. E. Nuñez 1984; 'Agricultura Alto Andina:
Rendimiento de Papa en una Comunidad Campesina de Aycucho' (Highland
Andean agriculture: productivity of potatoes in a peasant community of Aya-
cucho), *Boletín de Lima*, 6 (34): 59–66.

Vallejos, M. 1978; 'Origen y Desarrollo de la Agricultura en el Perú Prehispánico'
(Origin and development of agriculture in pre-hispanic Peru), *Revista Ciencia
Interamericana*, 19(1): 21–4. Washington DC; Secretary General of the OAS.

Vásquez, A. V. 1988; *Mejoramiento Genético de la papa* (Genetic improvement of the
potato), Lima; Amaru Editores.

Vavilov, N. I. 1992; 'The Phyto-geographical basis for plant breeding studies of the
original material used for plant breeding'. In *Origin and Geography of Cultivated
Plants*. Departmental Ed. V.F.

CHAPTER 3

The *Ayllu*

Grimaldo Rengifo Vasquez

This chapter discusses the community of relatives which is the *ayllu*. I shall not be concerned here simply with the structure and function of human kinship in the Andean peasant communities; rather the focus of this chapter will be to show the elasticity of this notion – the *ayllu* –which cannot be reduced to what is commonly known as social organization. At the same time, I shall argue that the Quechua word *'runa'* does not, nor does it have to, match the Western concept of man. Man in the West is not just another species; 'man' is a category that radically separates that species from all others. These aspects are addressed in the first part of the chapter.

The second part of the chapter discusses the way of being of all the components of the *ayllu*, and how their physiology is synchronized with the natural movements of expansion and contraction which happen in an 'annual' cycle or *wata*. In the *ayllu* the activity of its members is not modelled from the outside, it is not the product of a planning act that transcends it, but rather it is a result of the conversations that take place between the community of humans (*runas*), the communities of *huacas* (deities), and the natural communities (*sallqa*), in a brotherly atmosphere of profound equivalency.[1]

Activity, in this sense, emerges from dialogue, conversation and according to what the circumstances indicate; it does not derive from an imposition by man over nature. Each of these points is presented in turn throughout the second part of this chapter, which is dedicated to the theme 'regeneration in the *ayllu*'. This section shows that the relationships between humans, nature and the deities is one of nurturance in this space of regeneration of life which is the *chacra*.

The *chacra* is understood not only as an agricultural space, but as the scene of the nurturance and flowering of all forms of life. In the Andes the peasants say: 'The llamas are my *chacra*', the '*chacra* of salt', etc. Similarly, the vicuñas are understood as the *chacra* of the *Apus*, just as certain geese are considered as being the *chacra* of the fox. We are thus dealing with a world in which all are *chacareros* (makers of the *chacra*).

In the *chacra* all converse, and this conversing is a sort of 'revealing', of making the life contained in each one of us, whether *runas*, *allpas* (a type of soil) or potatoes, issue forth. Such revealing was expressed better than anyone else by an artisan from Cajamarca, who said, 'In its interior is its form', when he was asked about the model from which the forms of his stonecraft originated. He did not claim to 'carve' or mould the stone according to a pre-set image of it, rather he understood the stone to have its own form just like any living being – a form that would emerge due to the reciprocal nurturance between the human community and the stone.

These aspects and others, such as those related to authority and the peasant community, are dealt with in the final two parts of this chapter. The overall aim is to try and show that the *ayllu* is a community of relatives made up of human persons, the members of nature and the members of the community of *huacas* or deities. The application of the concept of man as a 'rational animal' to the notion of *runa* is discussed. An attempt is made to illuminate the notion of *runa* – that it includes what the West considers as man but also incorporates 'within it' the notions of *sallqa* or nature and of *huacas* or deities. The *runa* is thus also nature and deity, and can present him/herself in these forms in certain circumstances, a presentation which is not a representation, but rather a showing oneself, revealing the form that corresponds to the circumstances.

'Form of life' is used in this text to mean not the exterior aspect or the customs of a person or a collectivity, but rather the distinctive singularity with which each one of the living beings that inhabit the Andean *Pacha* present themselves in any particular circumstance. Similarly, each form of life, be it a llama, the chulpi corn or don Juan Quispe, has its cycle of life, its manners of being, its attributes which differentiate it from other *runas*, potatoes or corn.

Once in a while I shall use the term 'culture'. This usage should be understood in its Latin sense of *cultus*, participle of *colere*, which means: to cultivate, to nurture (to raise). In the Andes, as we shall see, to cultivate, to nurture is not only a human activity but also one that nature engages in.

The *ayllu*

A first notion of *ayllu*, and the most well known, is the one that refers to relations of kinship and descent which exist among a human group related consanguineously and living in a particular territory. Consanguineous kinship refers to ties among blood kin and affines related in varying degrees to the same person (Lambert 1980: 13). Thus it is commonly affirmed that: 'The *ayllu* is the social unit that gathers several families, often having kinship ties, inside a fixed territory' (Preiswerk 1995: 67).

However, in the Andes the family includes not only the relatives, whether from the same branch or from an affinal branch, but also relatives who are not necessarily affines or consanguines. Whether they are consanguines, affines or not, it is a common way of communicating in the Andes to call people of our father's generation or of our own, father, uncle or brother. On the other hand there is what is called spiritual kinship, such as *compadrazgo* (god-parenting), that relates persons who are not necessarily consanguines or affines. The elasticity of the term is such and its boundaries so fluid that in Lamas, San Martin, for example, the *runas* call the group of people who at festivals get together to eat around a table *ayllu*.

In a world of equivalents – that is not hierarchized – where the notion of person is lived as an attribute of whatever exists and not only characteristic of the members of the human community, the word 'relatives' is extended also to the cultivated plants – to the *chacra*. The peasants consider the potatoes of their *chacra* to be their daughters, and when they are newly incorporated they are called daughters-in-law.

The Aymaras in Puno call the new potato which is being incorporated into the *chacra* '*yoqch'a*' (daughter-in-law). In Conima, Puno, the water that is brought from the Mamacocha or from some spring for the ritual to the water is called son-in-law (*tollqa*) (Chambi 1989: 63–9). This son-in-law is married with a young woman of the community in a special ceremony asking for rain. In another locality, the community of Quispillaccta, Ayacucho, the hail is considered as 'our godfather'. So our relatives are also the members of nature or *sallqa*.

Additionally, the deity mountains called Apus, Wamanis or Achachilas – whether the people are Quechua from Cusco, from Ayacucho or Aymara from Puno – are considered to be our grandfathers, thus extending kinship to the collectivity of the *huacas*. Thus, the Apus, since there is no separation between the *runas* and the *huacas*, and the *sallqa*, all become our relatives. So the *ayllu* is lived as a grouping of relatives *runas*, relatives *chacras*, relatives *sallqa* and relatives *huacas* who all live in one 'house' or *Pacha* which protects them.

This extension of the members of the *ayllu* beyond the borders of human consanguinity springs from the Andean attribute of not separating man from nature. By all being members of my *Pacha* or house of my *ayllu*, all those who live in it are experienced as my relatives. The very activity of regeneration among the *runas* is not only lived as a product of the union of beings of the same species, but also as an expression of the nurturing activity of *Pachamama*. Additionally, the *runas* like to nurture and augment the diversity not only of potatoes and maize but also of human relatives. It is not a matter of nurturing relatives – as some want to see it – for utilitarian purposes such as being able to rely on people able to help a family in given tasks, a help that would oblige it to return the favour in a similar circumstance. Andean reciprocity is the 'pleasure of giving and nurturing with affection' and is not a constraining 'obligation' within the framework of a certain traditional 'right' or 'responsibility' to return what has been given. In the Andes, all nurture relatives and all are nurtured by others simultaneously; it is not an act of giving and returning, not a 'bartering of nurture'.

José Isabel Ayay, from the hamlet of Chilimpampa, district of Porcon, province of Cajamarca, eloquently shows the breadth of the notion of *ayllu*:

> There in my hamlet we speak thus: for family we say *ayllu*. It consists of a family, for example, the young and older animals. That is called a group of families, it is called *ayllu*.
>
> The father and the mother, the children, form part of a family, well of humans. It is just there, within that that is the *ayllu*. And within the *ayllus* are also the grandchildren, the sons-in-law, the daughters-in-law, the marriage. The seeds, the *pirkas* also are part of the family. We call it an *ayllu*.
>
> When one is freshly getting ready to live in a new house, there we need what one needs in the country; for example a *batán* (stone grinder), some stone that is called *palagon* to feed the dog, and some little thing to collect water for the chickens. That is called *ayllu*; 'he is preparing an *ayllu*'. Sometimes something is missing, sometimes it is complete. (Enciclopedia Campesina 1992: 15–16)

Also, the maize crops have their mother, the *Saramama*; the rivers have their mother, the *Yacumama*; the lakes, their *Mamacocha* and the *Pacha* its *Pachamama*. In this sense the notion of *ayllu* is shared among all the collectivities. The peasants call the maize and the beans brothers because they grow together without 'sticking together', that is without harming each other (as the peasants in San Miguel of the rio Mayo, Tarapoto put it).

In the Andes we all live as relatives. A relative is someone close to us with whom we live in harmony and whom we protect and who protects us; someone with whom a life-giving conversation flows that brings about health and makes life fruitful. The *ayllu* is not only a consanguineous relation, rather it is a community of people tied by affection, from whom grows an affectionate and healthy living solidarity . That must be why the peasants in Chamis, Cajamarca, comment that: 'The potato and the quinua are relatives because pests do not affect them' (De Zutter 1990: 4)

Relatives – the family – are all those with whom our caring and affection is most intense and our solidarity is such that pests do not emerge or prosper. Rather one sees love and 'full hands' that – as an Aymara peasant woman said – make it so that there is enough of everything: 'When families let themselves be loved, they take care of each other affectionately, with calm, then nothing is lacking; with full hands they help us, everything is enough.' (Jimenez 1995: 139). As Ayay says, relatives are nurtured and we are nurtured by them; the *ayllu* is made ready, it is nurtured, it is not a given. To be family, to live pleasantly and fully within a place implies that harmony and the generative atmosphere that encourages and creates family affection is nurtured. In this sense, the *ayllu* is the *chacra* that makes possible the nurturance of affection and care.

Since all are relatives being permanently nurtured, the notions of loneliness and orphanhood do not exist; instead there is caring. The Andeans live accompanied by the deities and they shelter, care and protect nature. When someone's mother or father dies, there is always somebody who fulfils that function since the notion of progenitor, as it is conceived in Western culture, is different in the Andean understanding. Rodrigo Montoya (1986) indicates that in the Andean world:

> The biological father does not have the importance that he has in the West, since the mother's brother (uncle) or the grandfather has the affective relation of elder to younger ... What is important in the Andean world is the social father, who is either the mother's brother or the grandfather ... who the father was who conceived the child has little or no importance because in its development and socialization, the mother's brother or the grandfather assumes the function of father.

The *ayllu* also does not have fixed physical borders. In certain circumstances, my *ayllu* is my community or *ayllu* of *ayllus*. But if I am in the community I can say that I belong to the *ayllu* of my paternal name, or to the *ayllu* of my Apu of reference, or to the *ayllu* of the sector in which I live. In other contexts, for example if I am in the provincial capital and if I am asked about my *ayllu*, I can answer referring to the name of the district to which my community belongs and with whose Apus I feel familiar, and thus the *ayllu* also can be my province and one is always in the *ayllu*. In this sense kinship is fairly malleable and kin can expand or contract according to the circumstances a group experiences at a particular point in time.

Such fluidity of borders is also found in each of the forms of life of the *ayllu* (be it *runa*, *huaca*, or *sallqa*). In each *runa* live the forms of life of the *huacas* and the *sallqa*, just as in every Apu live the forms of the *sallqa* and *runas*, and in every tree of the *sallqa* live forms of *runas* and *huacas*. An attribute of the *ayllu* is interpenetrability and an absence of exclusion among the various forms of life.

From this it follows that a member of the community of *runas* can present him- or herself in a particular circumstance with the life form of a *huaca*, and in other circumstances with that of the *sallqa* or nature. On 30 August, at the feast of Santa Rosa in Lamas (Tarapoto), the day of the *carachupa* (armadillo) is celebrated. The members of the community, dressed in dried banana leaves, dance and play as *carachupas*. Those who participate in these events experience themselves as members of the community of *carachupas* – which as we know belong to the wild or *sallqa* (*sacha* in the local Quechua of Lamas) – not as members of the human community. Dancing as *carachupas*, the peasants are not acting in a play or representation, that is they do not symbolize *carachupas*. They experience these circumstances as if they were *carachupas*; they not only say this but they 'believe' it to be so (personal communication from Ruth Escudero).

On 19 January (Saint Sebastian) in Tilali, Puno, the ceremony of offerings to the deities of hail, frost, wind and snow takes place. On that day the deities of the agricultural products are made present by members of the human community. The *Marani* is the authority of the *chacra* and directs the ceremony with his twelve councilmen and -women who, in this situation, are the *huacas* of the crops. The males are the deities of the grain crops (*Muchu*) and the women are the *ispalla walla* (deities of root crops). The deity of the potato is the *Ispalla*, the *Phurija* is the deity of the early potato, the *Muchu* is the deity of bearded barley, the *Qarachili* is the deity of bald barley, the deity of the *oca* is *Lampaya*, the *Chocopa* is the deity of the lima bean, *Nolberto* is the deity of the *isañu*, the deity of the pasture is *Pastia*, *Chukima* is the deity of the lake grass boat, *Pachamama* is the deity of the holy earth (personal communication from Jorge Apaza Ticona, April 1996).

This helps in understanding the ease with which an Andean nurtures and also lives being nurtured by a llama or a potato, because in him or her nest the other forms of life, just as in the other forms of life nests the human form. It is not that a member of the human community in certain circumstances 'represents' the *oca*, the *carachupa* or the maize, but rather that in that moment he or she and the community experience the circumstances as the *oca*, *carachupa* or maize itself. Andeans do not represent forms of life because they have neither separated nor disaffected themselves from nature and from the *huacas*. In them the *sallqa* and the *huacas* dwell; they are at once *sallqa* and *huaca*.

When that particular circumstance has passed, which normally occurs during accentuated ceremonial intensity, the *runa* form once again emerges. This same way of life is expressed when the alpacas or the waters are married. It is not a matter of the male and female alpacas or the male and female waters representing human beings, nor are they humanized; rather they do what they need to do in particular moments of their life as any member of the *Pacha* does. In the *ayllu* all share the same attributes; man is not the measure of things.

Representation exists when in the relationship between the human community and nature an image of the world mediates, a rational construction of the world with which the thinking subject dialogues. This implies the division of the world into subjects and objects, that is the separation and hierarchization of the beings who inhabit the world. In that case, man is not embedded in nature but rather is outside and above her. Representation also occurs when all that exists, exists only as a functionary of the subject – man.

For Andeans, the manner of living together takes various forms according to the way circumstances advise. In whichever of these forms, their manner of being is one of conversing directly, face to face and without intermediaries, because they are dealing with relatives such as the *oca* and the wind – who also converse since they possess similar attributes. To live in the Andes, one does not need representations. In this mode of being, *Pachamama* is not only the mother of the land, but this person is also experienced as our mother. When we say it like that, in the circumstances in which we allude to her we are not using a symbolic language – a language that personifies – nor are we using a metaphor, but rather (as don Jesus Urbano tells us) it is experienced like that:

> *Pachamama* makes the pasture grow for its cattle. Some say that the mountain is more powerful and that because of that it is above, his wife is *Pachamama* and he, Taita Orcco, as husband, as male, commands. I don't know; *Pachamama* is very great, she is everywhere. Below Mama Ccocha there is also *Pachamama*. There has never been conflict between *Pachamama* and the Orcco, nor among the mountains, but not all mountains are the same. For example, Rasuwilca is the father of all, the richest, the most powerful, the one who leads the others. All of them try to seduce *Pachamama* and the lady chooses according to her desire.
>
> Who are their children, you ask? All, everyone are the children. I myself am the child of my parents, may they rest in peace, but I am also the son of *Pachamama*. (Urbano and Macera 1992)

From this one sees that the notion of *runa* (Quechua for human) or *jaque* (Aymara for human) in the Andes cannot simply be compared with the Western notion of man. The notion of *runa* does not imply a trans-cendance of that which is not human, a liberation from nature, but rather the most intimate and affectionate shared life between the forms of life of nature and of the *huacas* in the very internal centre of the *runa*.

In addition, to be richer and more powerful in a given situation must not be interpreted as synonymous with hierarchy and in opposition to others; rather they are the attributes of the charismatic authority, of the person who assumes the responsibility (*cargo*) in a given moment and who possesses the greatest vigour and wealth needed to redistribute and to harmonize everyone in regenerating life. This *cargo*, furthermore, is rotating. We are thus dealing with a world very different from the Western world which, as Goldschmidt says (1974: 25), has a different form.

It must be due to this complicated situation that many authors have difficulties in finding a univocal idea of the *ayllu* on the basis of human kinship. Fuenzalida (1976: 235), citing the Quechua dictionary of Gonzales Holguin (1952), finds that the *ayllu*, in different contexts, means: 'genealogy, lineage, kinship group, nation, gender, species or class'.

Furthermore, since there is no linear notion of time – that is a historical, progressive and evolutionary sense of time – Andean kinship, just like the climatic seasons of the *wata*, regenerates itself cyclically and is, as we say, perennial. It would not occur to anyone in the Andes to be considered civilized today and call their ancestors barbarians or savages, and thus discover a non-civilized type of human kinship. The ancestors are also relatives, they are one's contemporary grandparents (*achachilas* in Aymara), and are considered equivalent to any *runas* living today.

Regeneration in the *ayllu*

In the *ayllu*, life is regenerated cyclically and through conversations that nurture harmony which flourish in this field of equivalents that is the *chacra*. The activity does not arise from arranged contracts, from obligatory arrangements between the members of the human community. What is done is the expression of the participation of all in the regenerating flux of nature.

We use the notion of regeneration as the re-creative and cyclical renewal of the different forms of life and to differentiate it from the notion of production in which man becomes independent from the cycles of nature and creates his own productive cycles within a historical sense of life. In the Andean *Pacha* everything is regenerated, everything comes back, everything returns to the rhythms and cadences of nature. It is a matter of a return (*muyuy* in Quechua), constant re-creation – a continual renovation of the cycles of life. Regeneration is not generating again something from nothing, rather it is the emergence of new forms of life already contained in the existing ones, a making visible which results from the united participation of the communities of the *runas*, of the *sallqa* and of the *huacas*.

In regeneration, the cycles of the communities of the *runas*, the *sallqa* and the *huacas* are synchronized and in symbiosis; and the regeneration of each member of the world is intimately tied to that of all the others. In a modern production system, man intervenes in nature in order to produce goods independently of the manner in which nature regenerates herself.

In the *ayllu* the *runas* do not feel themselves to be superior to and distant from the members of nature or inferior to the deities or *huacas*. One could say that the *runas* are just one more member of nature; they are, as we have noted, nature itself. We are dealing with a pan-natural world made up of equivalent beings. In this context to speak of regeneration is to refer to the conversation between the members of the community of humans, of the *sallqa* and of the *huacas* to help the re-creation of the forms of life nested in the *Pacha* during an annual cycle or *wata*. Because of this, in regeneration the natural forms of life are not only reproduced but their diversity is increased. With the Andean *chacra*, in contrast to what is produced in the modernagricultural enterprise, nature has not diminished the forms of life, rather it has increased them without producing waste or by-products which clog and devalue the normal physiology of nature. The Andean region is one of the centres of biological mega-diversity in the world. Regeneration implies not only the re-creation of each one of the members that participate in the regenerative act (which could be interpreted as repetition) but also the amplification of forms of life.

One characteristic of every regenerative act is the equivalence and affection between the members of nature and not the separation and hierarchy between the natural and the human communities. I consider this to be one of the implicit arguments in the dynamic of regenerative variability, since behind a homogenizing impetus one finds power per-petuating hierarchy which is contrary to equivalency.

Equivalency In the Andean world everything is alive and important; nothing is inert and nothing is superfluous. The very stone is alive, it speaks and the peasant converses with it as person to person. It is not that the peasant extends the notion of person to the stone (which is generally understood as 'personification') but rather that, for the peasant, the stone is alive – possessing the attributes of the *runa* and vice versa.

In the Andean context we cannot speak either of the inanimate as opposed to the animate, or of the essential as opposed to the contingent. The whole *Pacha* is a community of interconnected living beings, in which man and water are as important and alive as are the *huacas* and the wind in terms of the regeneration of life. A few brief sentences on how stones are alive will help us understand what we are affirming; in the words of don Carlos Olivares and don Javier Huaman Lara, peasants from Caja-marca:

> Our ancestors said that the *chungo* (from the Quechua *chunku* meaning stone) has life, it grows, and is our idol. And yes, it is true. Five or six years ago, my old man found a *chungo* and we all told him that he should re-bury it where he found it. After a while we dug it out again and it was bigger ... When we took the *chungo* out again and put it in a different place, it no longer grew. (Enciclo-pedia Campesina 1992: 21)

> If we find a snake and we take a stone to kill it, it is difficult and sometimes we can't even reach it ... That is why they say that the stones are the relatives of the snake and the lizards. (ibid.: 32)

In the Andes we are all people and we are all related, and the life of each does not obey mandates from supernatural beings which transcend us (as is the case with the Judaeo-Christian God); rather it emerges from conversations between similar and equivalent beings. Since there is no separate reality – no supernatural world – the Andean deities or *huacas* are manifest – they dwell here, they are evident, they can be seen, they are accessible to our senses – since they are within the world and are, like any other being, treated like persons. For Andeans the saints, for example, do not dwell in the sky but are part of the *ayllu*. Marcela Machaca, an agronomist and member of an Andean community, says that Mamacha Carmen (the Virgin of Carmen) in her *ayllu* of Quispillaccta is considered like another shepherdess (Machaca 1992: 30).

Furthermore, we are dealing with a world which – as we Andeans say – is one of equivalent beings in which there is no hierarchy of origin or one based on biological make-up; that is we are not in the world of biological evolution and of history, where the monkey is more advanced or evolved than the fishes and where man occupies the highest level in the hierarchy. Concepts such as 'primitive' or 'advanced' are foreign to that world. Andeans do not perceive themselves as more evolved than the Amaru, nor do they perceive the activities they engage in as being the product of a mandate or order originating in the will of a deity that transcends them. The *huacas* are relatives with whom one converses, one reciprocates, with affection and respect.

This feeling of equivalency finds its roots in the interpenetrability of the various forms of life. Within each form of life (for example in the form of *runa*) live also other forms (*sallqa* and *huacas*), so that all share similar attributes and perceive each other as similar. In this way of life, the presence of the 'Other' does not make its appearance as something distant and different from oneself.

Regenerative cyclicity   Linear and progressive time, as we know, is a Western construction which has one of its roots in Judaeo-Christianity. As Mircea Eliade says:

> Thus, for the first time, the prophets placed a value on history, succeeding in transcending the traditional vision of the cycle (the conception that ensures all things will be repeated forever), and discovered a one-way time. (Eliade 1959: 104)

In the regeneration of the *ayllu* there is neither origin nor end, no irreversible linear time; even the very concepts of time and space – which are abstractions for the purpose of intellectualizing and thinking reality – do not exist since life is lived inside the *Pacha*, an animated landscape re-created cyclically each year and for whose regeneration no one makes distance from another in order to think and act upon it.

The world is full of forms of life without the mediation between them of 'space' or 'emptiness'. (The wind, for example, is considered to be another person just like the *oca*. The notion of the *Pacha* as a woven cloth where there is no emptiness at all between each knot is a manner of visualizing what we Andeans call the world.) The members of the *ayllu* live as if their world, their *Pacha*, as they experience it today, has always been like that, and in it there is a continuous and renewed regenerative dynamic, a continual cyclical happening. There is no notion of progress which is intrinsic to nature's own designs that might be applied to the evolution from simple to more complex forms of life.

The annual cycle or *wata* can be understood as the aggregate of events that happen to the different forms of life during one year. The year or *wata* has its moments of birth, growth, maturation, weariness and death. The one who leads and orients life in the *Pacha* is the Sun and its *wata* goes from the June solstice (around 21 June) to the December solstice (around 21 December). At the end of June a Sun emerges (*Waman Poma* draws it small compared to the December sun), in December it is in the middle of its life journey and begins its return journey or *muyuy* in order to rest and to 'die' in June, the point at which the feast of the Sun or *Inti Raymi* is celebrated. This feast propitiates the renewal of the Sun's life and of all the forms of life in the *Pacha*.

This renewal of the forms of life such as the emergence and flowering of others is circular and does not follow a defined model. One knows that there will be a return but one does not know the circumstances or the manner in which the Sun, the rains, the maize, the *runas* and the winds will present themselves in their re-created form. That is why here an archetype does not repeat itself. Referring herself to the *wata*, Marcela Machaca says:

> For the person from Quispillaccta, the year or *wata* is a living being which flows in a circular manner (cyclically), and because of that, it is often said that: 'the planting (season) comes back', 'the rains come back'. There is always a *muyuy* (return) of the months and the seasons, but they return always renewed and thus there are no years or seasons that are the same in their passing. (Machaca 1992: 31)

In this cyclical life there is no notion of a created world, of a life-giving flame that breathes life into a world situated outside of it, nor of a creating nature that evolves by itself in progressive stages from the savage to the civilized. For the Andeans the idea of a world created from nothingness is alien, as is the idea of an evolution of species. The world is lived as a conjunction of cyclical regenerations which happen to each and every form of life, these life forms being interconnected as if they were members of another living being. I shall now look at some aspects of this regenerative cyclicity.

The generation of forms of life In the world of cyclic regeneration there are moments in which the forms of life prepare themselves to generate. These moments are synchronized with the condition of nature in its entirety. There are signs or indicators that tell us about the opportune moment and circumstances, such as the number of eggs a bird lays, or the number of vicuñas there are in a herd, and so on. These signs indicate the moment and likelihood of success for union and conception. In this fashion the multiplication of forms of life stays in conformity and harmony with the others. Harmonizing means to follow the signs that other living beings show. Each living being is a sign for the others. There is no cyclical regeneration independent from the cyclicity of other forms of life.

In the Andes it is not conceivable that any of its members can be asexual; all are sexed since all renew themselves. There are male rains and female rains (*warmi lluvia* as they say in Tarapoto); male and female mountains; male and female plants; male and female stars; there is male water and female water and the child is the product of a heterosexual relation between persons of the same species. The notion of parthenogenesis does not exist and, in general, it is believed that a person comes from the successful relationship between a couple of the same species – that is an alpaca comes from the relation between a male and a female alpaca and the same is true for the *runas*. Jorge Montoya Maquin says the following on this issue:

> The child of a couple is not a mixture, but the fruit of a successful and fruitful relationship between both in which each member of the couple retains its own personality. The fruit is another person who assimilates the vitality of its progenitors, but who also has its own personality; it is a person from persons. (1991: 5)

In the Andean world one cannot conceive of a world of separated genders. Something incomplete is called *chuya* in the Quechua from Cajamarca, which means 'the one who is missing its other'. In order to become whole, one has to pair up. *Juk* in Quechua is not the exclusive number one of the decimal system; instead it is the way of referring to the couple: one with its complement(s). In the Andes one lives and one nurtures the couple. That is why, in the Andean and Amazonian communities, the presence of an adult without a partner or without family is strange. It is not that they cannot exist, but what is encouraged and promoted is the couple rather than the single state, since life itself would be truncated if that were not so. There is a diverse range of ceremonies that promote heterosexual relations.

It is not only a question of there being animals, *Apus* and *runas* of different sexes; for the relationship to be successful, that is for a person to be brought forth, there has to be an accord with the climate, the soils, the constellations, etc. – that is, an accord with the whole world of people which is the *ayllu*. An Aymara woman peasant tells about these pre-marital ritual ceremonies conducted by Andean priests:

> He asked everyone to protect us, so that we could live beautifully, with respect … with understanding, with determination … He called us both, and we too lifted hot coals, asking permission, praying to everyone, to the ancestors, to

Pachamama, to the 'Qullu Achachilas', to the Virgin of Rosario ... giving our word to live well, beautifully ... in accord with everyone, helping each other, supporting everyone. (Jimenez Sardon 1995: 35)

This 'accord' is sanctioned ritually in the wedding which is an affirmation of the re-creation of life and of the increase of its diversity. As we know, in the Andes the wedding is not an exclusively human event. The alpacas, the *quinuas*, the waters, the Apus, etc. marry when the propitious moment in the cycle advises it.

The ways of being in the cycle of a person The cycle of each person (of a potato, maize, Juana or the Mantaro river) has its moments, its seminal points and circumstances: germination, growth, maturation and 'death'. The regeneration in this cycle is not experienced as the qualitative transformation of a moment or circumstance into another considered superior which cancels the 'old order', but rather as a periodic and dynamic actualization of a cyclical renewal in which a circumstance is born from the previous ones, without those being the backward past of superior moments. The other moments 'live' in each moment of the cycle.

A *runa*, as any other member of the natural community, has in its form of *runa* its manner or manners of being that keep changing throughout one cycle of life – for example it goes from being a *wawa* (infant), to a *maqta* (youth) before becoming *runa*. The change through which a way of being is born or through which a non-*runa* form is born, does not cancel the previous manners or other forms; rather the cycle is experienced as the successive appearance of forms and manners of being that each form involves. What is noticed in the Andes is a re-creative change by which one renews oneself periodically – that is, one presents oneself in different ways according to the manner suggested by circumstances. In many instances the 'passage' or change from one way to another is marked by ceremonies such as the *rutuchiy* (tonsure). The child is not considered – for example through arguments about its mental development – to be in an inferior phase in the development of man, but instead to be a way of being typical and specific in the life of a *runa*.

The cyclical succession of forms of life Far from a concept of death as the cessation of life, in the Andes a person who 'dies' goes to live according to another form of life: that of 'departed or soul'. In this state of life, such a person has a *chacra*, favourite crops, and a special day when his or her presence is felt, lived and seen by his or her closest relatives. This 'soul' form, which is how Andeans call those who have passed to another form of life, is not akin to the Christian concept of the soul separated from the body (the notion of the separation of body and soul is incomprehensible to Andeans). This 'soul' is a person like any other, it is also another *chacarero* (maker of *chacra*), it is someone who is present but in his or her own way. A person 'dies' after having made his or her journey, passing to another form of life. Nothing disappears since there is no sense of finitude, of a cessation of life. Within each person there is embedded a multiplicity of forms of life and one lives a particular form without erasing the former ones. The anthropologist Luis Millones says that one has to understand that:

> death lacks the terminal meaning it has in the West. Instead of disappearing, humans reach another dimension of reality which they share with the Andean deities, whose existence, if very different, is not disconnected from ours. (Millones 1989: 110)

This does not mean that each member of the *Pacha* does not have a definite form in which it is present in life. But this particularity (as the form of *runa* or maize can be) does not mean the transformation and exclusion 'inside itself' of the other forms of life that inhabit the *Pacha* or even of those forms of life that could be considered 'invisible' to common eyes.

The multiplicity of forms of life that are embedded in a person excludes any possibility of enclosing that person in one gender or species. The analytical categories of identity and of the excluded middle by which each object is 'identical to itself' alone, excluding any other inside of that one – such as, that 'no object can be at once P and not P' (Ferrater Mora 1981: 3,226–7) – are alien notions to the Andean way of life. It is only by standing outside of the Western framework that it is possible to understand the wedding of a young woman of a community with the water which the families of the community bring from another place during the festivals for propitiating the rains. In this circumstance, and because that is how the *ayllu* desires it, the person that is water makes visible the *runa* form contained within itself.

In brief, each member of the *Pacha* not only hosts and nurtures a multiplicity of forms of life within themselves but also a diversity of ways of being in each form. In this way, each form of life (alpaca, maize, water or *runa*) has in its cycle of life many 'ways of being', manners of behaving which become explicit in certain circumstances; when these circumstances pass, another way of being appears, and so it goes on. Each way of being has, in its turn, its own *wata* or 'time'. Thus the *wata* cannot be confused with a year of 365 days.

When an Andean speaks of *muyuy*, of return, he or she does so because there is no erasure of any form of life. In the seed is the forthcoming fruit, and in that fruit the future harvest. One way of being of a person 'dies' to give way to another which contains the former, as an Aymara peasant woman says referring to her ancestors:

> When the children arrive, everyone must receive them with joy, with great

happiness; just as *Pachamama* who loves the laughter of her children, the children are seeds, seeds of their mother, since infancy they are the seeds of all their ancestors. (Jimenez Sardon 1995: 50)

The regenerative increase of new forms of life Each form of life has a great diversity, for example, there are more than 3,000 varieties of potatoes alone. The cultivators of potatoes do not exclude the old potatoes, the parent generation, in order to retain only the new ones. In a progressivist and evolutionist world – such as the modern West – the new is considered to be superior due to some particular characteristic and it is the one that survives while the previous forms are eliminated. What is advanced and modern replaces and eliminates what is considered backward and traditional; it does not contain it or add to it. From this it follows that the range of variability in the West becomes increasingly narrow. In contrast, the Andes harbour one of the greatest levels of biodiversity on the planet. We are dealing with a complicated world: incommensurable life forms exist together, precisely because each form of life that is born does not erase the previous ones.

In the West, the construction of society had, almost as a precondition, the liquidation of whatever form of nature that could have been embedded in Western man. So the concept of 'man', 'purified' of all nature, is an inclusive one and this happened fairly early in the history of the West. The Aristotelian concept of man as a 'rational animal' was already a way of differentiating, distancing and hierarchizing the relations between man and nature. On this concept of man, one that becomes the Judaeo-Christian standard of a man created in the image of God and whose task is to subdue nature, is constructed the modern concept of society. As the concept of man is born, so is that of nature.

Society is a concept which modern social theory uses to refer to human groups organized according to certain ends, and whose members are conscious of living and interacting with other individuals in the process of transforming nature. On this subject Auguste Comte says the following:

> Whatever system of society, whether constituted by a handful of men or by millions, has as a definite objective to direct all its particular forces toward a general goal, since only where a general and combined action is carried out, do we have a society. In any other hypothesis there exist only agglomerations of a determinate number of individuals on the same soil. That is what distinguishes human society from other animals who live in herds. (Comte 1979: 63)

The end to be aimed for or general and combined action is, for the founder of sociology, nothing more than 'the action over nature to benefit man or production' (Comte 1979: 64). This last sentence implies not only that one should differentiate and distance oneself from nature – that is to know oneself as a social subject different and superior to what is natural: all 'who live in herds' – but also to know oneself to be recognized as distinct from the other subjects.

In this sense explanatory notions such as 'society' can be relevant to show one form of the world but not to show all forms. To universalize is to sacrifice diversity for the sake of a belief in 'a single world'. To show what is Andean cannot be done in the explanatory mode or in terms of society, because that leads us to a reality constructed in other contexts and that is explained conceptually.[2] This is why I have opted in this chapter about *lo Andino* for a narrative language which is able to reveal lived experience instead of representing it conceptually and with quantitative criteria.

To explain the Andean world in terms of a concept such as society would lead to distorting it. This is why there is a dissonance between the lived experience and the attempts of those who try to explain analytically what is lived by Andeans as the *ayllu*.[3]

Conversation and circumstance   Like any animal, like any living organism, the Andean *Pacha* has its moments of contraction and others of expansion; of relaxation and of tension; of systoles and diastoles. Nothing is static, since everything is in a continual regenerative change. Referring to such changes, Marcela Machaca says:

> The month of June is characterized by the presence of excessive cold, with frequent frosts, reducing life to a minimum in the Sallqa and High Suni region; that is the grasses yellow, the springs dry up, the strongest frosts happen and the vegetation ends ... the only thing left are the seeds, the bulbs and roots under the earth, and that is why it is said that 'life is reduced to its minimum' ... In the month of November the agricultural activities become more intense in the villages with the planting of potatoes and other crops of the Suni and low Sallqa region. The early planting of potatoes is associated with the feast of All Souls (*Alma punchaw*) or Day of the Dead, which corresponds to the second of November, after All Saints Day. It is a feast at the level of the whole *ayllu* whose importance is due to the 'encounter with the Dead' in order to plant potatoes. In the Quispillactan vision the 'dead' continue the *chacarero* life just like the other members of the living community. (Machaca 1992: 31, 32)

There are circumstances of generation, of birth and of flowering, as there are those of rest and 'death'. There are hot times and others that are cold, as there are humid and dry times. In each of those times every living being continues its vital flux, readjusting and synchronizing itself with the particular organic circumstances. 'Andean organicity (and not social organization), is that capacity of the living Andean world to converse with the peculiarities of the *wata* and of periods of *watas*, in such a way that the life of the *ayllu* does not suffer impairment' (Grillo; intervention during the first unit of the 7th course of Formation in Andean Agriculture; Lima, April 1996).

In order to live at ease in such a world one needs to love the world 'just as it is', otherwise one lives in constant frustration, looking for a world 'as it should be', and on that journey one does not learn to converse with variability. The Andean person neither lives in nor seeks an ideal world, instead he or she lives life as it is; accompanying it without aspiring to transform it, unlike the Westerner. The members of the community do not impose themselves on any form of life as someone superior who plans and directs his or her activities according to a utopian vision. If everything is regenerating continuously and if what is at issue is to accompany this flow, the lives of animals, *runas* and rivers do not follow a pre-established plan but instead re-create themselves in each changing circumstance of life.

To live in this unpredictable and capricious 'animal world', as Rodolfo Kusch (1962) calls it, means constantly to nurture the capacity to attune oneself, to make adjustments, to accompany and understand what each one is saying to us, the sign that each one expresses in a given circumstance – in brief, to converse, that is to share similar 'verses' with the others.

This is particularly important in an unpredictable world since, although we may be in the rainy season, no one knows exactly what will happen tomorrow. It is not a predictable world, one susceptible to being planned for. From this it follows that what one does depends on the conversations that take place in each particular circumstance.

We are dealing with a complicated world, complicated because of a dense variability of forms of life which reside either in the *chacra* or in the wild and whose classification as part of the homogenizing process is non-viable due to the changing nature of the circumstances and because the variability of ways of being does not allow itself to be reduced to a given number of normalized categories. Each form of life is *sui generis*, unique and, being of its own kind, does not bear comparison. Comparisons always make reference to a unit of measurement, which is taken as a model in order to classify the rest. In this sense the understanding of the particular and of the way in which the *sui generis* life form expresses itself is what makes conversation and the regeneration of the Andean world possible.

For we Andeans, the Andes is a world of affectionate conversationalists because it is love for the world which allows life to flow. It is what makes the actions in life – such as eating, drinking, dancing, making *chacra*, raising potatoes and *ollucos* – continue and multiply.

Conversation requires, as everything in life, to be nurtured and stimulated, in order for life to be re-created. A prerequisite in this nurturance is that we all be disposed to listen perpetually and in each circumstance to the 'speaking', to the sign of each one. Since Andean life does not repeat an archetype but is instead capricious, it is necessary that everyone be attentive to the often unpredictable signs that emanate from all the others – signs that will not be 'spoken' again in the way expressed in a particular moment. (One of the most capricious people is the climate, in particular the presence and intensity of the rains, the frosts, the hail and the winds.)

Each one in every moment is saying something, and one has to converse with this 'sign' that indicates something to us and says something at the same time that it invites us to give an answer. The colour, the taste and smell of the wind on a specific afternoon is speaking and alerting us about the weather now and that which is to come. The gestures of a *runa*, the cry of an infant, the cloud formations or the way a fox is howling also tell us something about life now and that is to come. In order for regeneration to flow, one has to converse in each moment with everyone and everything; one has to 'follow' what one is being told, advised, as they also 'follow' what we are telling them.

An article on herding in the *altiplano* of Puno, written by the group Chuyma Aru, informs us about that conversation between *runas* and vicuñas. There one reads that:

> the members of the natural community inform the shepherds in various ways [...] When a herd of vicuñas is made up of 10, 11, 12 or 15 vicuñas, it is showing that a fertile male *jaynachu* can alone mount as many females as there are in the herd. (Chambi, Quiso and Tito 1992: 19)

Don Jesus Urbano Rojas, a maker of saints' images and an itinerant vendor, native of Huanta, Ayacucho, tells us the following about similar signs:

> For all the branding ceremonies one has to see the time when they are born. Everything begins with the vicuñas (that nobody brands), daughters of the sun and of the *illa* [an object or being that brings the presence of the sun in it] of the sun; they are born in the month of February in the middle of torrential rains, storms, and if they are born well with many who do not die, people say that we are going to have a good year; the animals of Taita Orcco [grandfather Orcco] are being born and the cattle of the *runa* will follow. (Urbano and Macera 1992: 60)

To follow is to attune oneself, to 'adjust' oneself to the signs of the forms of life of the *sallqa*. When that happens, life flows, the cattle of the *runas* – as don Jesus says – will follow. And that is because the cattle of the *huacas* have also attuned themselves with the life of the communities of the waters, the pasture lands and the weather. What the human community does is to follow, to join with this circumstance that is telling it the manner of nurturing that has to happen at that moment. If there is attunement, life 'runs' and flows, but if one wants to contradict the life signs, regeneration does not follow – it gets stuck.

If each one listens and converses, 'follows' what the signs in that circumstance are saying, life continues its regenerative course; if the listeners are not alert and the conversation becomes a monologue, it does not flow – it is interrupted, producing obstructions, anger, restrictions, accumulations, which prevent and make difficult the regeneration of life. These conflicts produce encumbrances which necessitate ritual encounters or *tinkuy* in order to dissolve them so that life can once again follow its course.

In a world of sensibilities, conversation makes itself evident also in the wisdom of knowing how to 'see', in the sensitivity of touching, of tasting, smelling and hearing the sign of the other (be they members of the community of humans, of the Apus or of the *sallqa*). Those who 'see' and 'touch' best are those that are in the best conditions to attune themselves, to converse with the other; and in that way life continues, goes and follows with harmony in its respective cycle or *wata*.

In the conversation each member of the *Pacha* is recognized as a sensible organism in constant speech. Here language is not only a human attribute but one belonging to all the members of the *pacha* and communication takes place through the senses – which are like the 'windows' of life. It is through them that one converses with everyone. The common senses are amplified in rituals; the person who participates in them sees 'more'. The profound and intense moments of the organicity of the *Pacha* are expressed in the intimacy of ceremonies. In these moments one can and does know and live with plenitude the life of the other members of the *Pacha*, relate intimately with nature, be 'an animal oneself' as don Juanito Lozano of the community of San Antonio, Lamas, San Martin, expresses it.

Conversation is thus an attitude, a mode of being in unison with life, a knowing how to listen and knowing how to say things at the appropriate moment. The symbiosis that life in common is, in which each one is enriched by the life of the others, is the form in which conversation flourishes between the different forms of life. The form which in the Andes lives this symbiosis and in which each one follows the other is the *ayni*.

The pleasure of giving   *Ayni*, *minga*, *humaraqa*, *waykanacuy*, etc. are modalities of the 'pleasure of giving' and are sites of solidarity and cooperation between the *runas*, nature and the *huacas* so that life can flow. In Cajamarca, the peasants say: 'everything is *minga*', referring to the fact that there are no activities that are not done with solidarity and the conversation that pleases the group. The group involved in conversation is called *minga* or *ayni*, depending on the region. It is not to be understood as an activity done by someone called a subject and that acts on an object-*chacra* in order to transform it according to its own will. Those concepts do not accord with the Andean conversation. The conversation in the Andes presents itself in the form of *ayni*.

Since life is consubstantial with *ayni*, the *ayni* has to be re-created daily in order for life to regenerate itself. It is not a loan that one is obligated to return, although it has that appearance to foreigners. The *ayni* – like the *chacra*s in the *muyuy* which always rotate – is a consubstantial part of the life of the *ayllu*; it is a constant and dynamic weaving that ceremonially threads the relationships between all the living beings; it is the concrete form that Andean communitarian life takes. It is not possible to understand Andean life outside of *ayni*. Life itself is *ayni*. The invitation, the very activity and the thanksgiving are all moments in the *ayni* which are done ceremonially and with great joy.

Ayni and its various modalities does not only refer to agricultural activity, but also to herding; to the building of houses, of irrigation canals; of roads; to the patron feasts; to funerals; etc. All activity is done in *ayni*. Everyone is prepared to give their support in everything. There is no division of labour as in industry. There are no specialists; the Andeans are 'generalists', they do everything and because of that they are ready to accompany anyone in any activity. In this way of life technicians do not make their appearance and it makes no sense to classify the human community by the type of work or activity it does – something which is central in the institutionalization found in the modern West.

Another aspect of *ayni* is its festive character. The *fiesta*, like ritual life, is not separated from life. About the patron day *fiestas*, we can only say that they are an amplification and intensification of daily life. The *fiesta* is not separated from daily activity, instead the activity itself is carried out festively, and *fiesta* and activity are joined and identical. In the Andes nature and the *chacras* sing. There is music in the cornfield, in the water, in the trees. What the community of *runas* does when working in the field, hilling the potato plants, in the harvest and in any other activity is to attune themselves with this music. Dance and *fiesta* are, so to speak, in the very heart of nature so that the executed activity does nothing more than attune itself with the natural festivity.

Ayni makes evident the conversation between the different communities. There is *ayni* between the human community and the weather, there is *ayni* between *runas* and *huacas*, between human communities and the community of the *sallqa*. Life itself is – to re-emphasize – an *ayni*.

Ramon Conde, an Aymara Catholic catechist, says the following about *ayni*:

> Let me try to be clear about what many say, namely that we worship stones and the like. With our *huacas* we act reciprocally; in Aymara this is called doing *ayni*, doing *minka*. I can do *ayni* or *minka* with my brother here or with anyone else. We do not worship stones; it only looks that way from a Western point of view, that we worship stones, *Pachamama* (The Earth Mother), the *Achachillas* (Grand-parent Mountains); this is a wrong way to see it. What we do, what our elders do, is to do *ayni* or *minka* with the stones, *Pachamama* etc. We do this because they give us the fruits of the earth and we have to reciprocate those gifts. (Van den Berg 1989: 217)

These *aynis* and *mingas* can at any given moment involve only a few members, and at other times congregations of hundreds. There are times in which life is more intense, for example the moments in which *chacu* is done, the periods of harvest, of making a road or an irrigation canal, and when many *ayllus* get together. Then *ayni* achieves its moment of greatest flowering. At other times, according to the rhythms of life, just the most immediate family will be enough. The *ayni* takes the modality that accords best with the conversation of the *telluric* cycles.

Nurturance In many Andean settlements it is common to hear the members of the community say: 'Just as we nurture the alpacas, they nurture us' or 'as we nurture potatoes, they nurture us'. Nurturance is lived as an activity which commits one to: 'nurture and let oneself be nurtured' and in this *runas*, *huacas* and *sallqa* find themselves on an equivalent plane.

In Quechua, 'to nurture' is *uyway*, and it means the affective attunement achieved between the members of the Andean community (which includes *runas*, maize, alpacas, winds, water, etc.) in the regeneration of their *Pacha* (which can be understood as the 'lived world', the house that shelters us and of which we are members).

In the Andes we all nurture and nurturance is not an attribute limited to the *runas*. In the ceremonies of first fruits offered to the *huacas*, that is to the Ispallas, one hears from the mouth of the Aymara priest that the old potatoes from the barn say to the newly harvested potatoes: 'Nurture these men (*jaqes*) as we have nurtured them'. There also exists an Aymara version which says: 'the day that the alpacas disappear, the world will disappear'. The alpacas were given by the *Apus* to the human community to be nurtured. The human community considers that the alpacas are people, who also nurture them, while the alpacas consider that the human community is its nurturer. Since we all nurture, we are all in turn nurtured by all. If there is no nurturance, regeneration will cease and without regeneration life ceases. Nurturance for Andeans thus takes place in the way of being of each one of the members of the *ayllu*. The *ayllu*, in this sense, is a community of nurturers.

The *chacu* and the *chacra* are human modalities of nurturing nature. In the *chacu* (Quechua for rounding up; to intercept; to take in group) the members of the human community in a dynamic and rhythmical way have access to the products of the *sallqa*. This happens when the *sallqa* 'tells' them that it is the time to converse, to do *chacu* and to have access to its products (fishes, trees, boars, deer, vicuñas, foxes, etc.) because it is then appropriate to the flow of life. The *runas* converse ritually, they speak to the forest (the *sallqa*), they make their offerings (*pago*) at the same time that the *sallqa* allows itself to be 'harvested', 'pruned', 'thinned' – that is, at a point when it is cultivated in order to allow the emergence of new growth and so that the symbiosis which it harbours may flow with greater vitality.

The agricultural *chacra* is another modality of nurturing life. The *chacra* is made in the place where one makes *chacra*; not all places 'ask' for *chacra*. When and how to make *chacra* emerges from a ritual conversation with the *Apus*, the forest and *Pachamama*. Certain plants and animals from the *sallqa* are nurtured by *runas* in a special context – the *chacra* – which makes the emergence of new attributes contained in these plants and animals of the *sallqa* possible. In this fashion the diversity of plants is increased. With the crops and animals nurtured by the *runas*, the waters are also re-created with the growth of irrigation; the weather also, with the appearance of microclimate, is also nurtured as is the landscape as a whole. The agricultural landscape emerges that gladdens and does not contradict the natural landscape.

In re-creating new plants and new animals the *chacra* 'fills' nature with more forms of life and accompanies it in the regeneration of life. In order to make maize grow all the communities have to agree, they have to be in symbiosis, they have to converse harmoniously. The capacity for empathy and symbiosis flowers in the *chacra* according to the way life is multiplied. In the *chacra* all speak; the plants tell the *runas*, speak to the *runas* all the time, just as the *runas* speak to the plants:

> On the day of the seed fair they gave me two kilograms of maize, I planted it, but the common maize that I planted beside it was better [...] I speak to this improved maize and it does not answer. For example, the other day I was passing by the maize that they gave me and I ask it: What's the matter, skinny corn, are you a dwarf or do you want me to hit you? (Rengifo, Panduro and Grillo 1993: 33)

When the plant germinates, flowers or bears fruit, all of life fills with jubilation, with songs and dances, and that is so because one has known how to converse with the multiplicity of circumstances that accompany *Pachamama* in the regeneration of life. It must be remembered that the *chacra* is not only an agricultural site. The *comuneros* (members of the human community) always say things such as: 'The llama is my *chacra*', 'my *chacra* of salt', 'the *chacra* of *totora* (grass-made boat)', 'the *chacra* of gold', etc. In this sense the *chacra* extends beyond the boundaries of agriculture, being any context of conversation that renews the multiplicity of forms of life.

The *chacra* of the human community is a re-creation of the *sallqa* or nature, while the *sallqa* regenerates itself in the *chacra* of the human community. In the *chacras* of the Lamistas (people from Lamas) in the valley of the Mayo river in Tarapoto, there are many creatures of the forest called *sachas* (which means forest in the Quechua of Lamas) that are nurtured and are members of the *chacra*: wild cucumber (*sachapepino*), wild peanut (*sachamani*), wild potato (*sachapapa*), wild coriander (*sachaculantro*), etc. as well as many trees of nature (which in Cochabamba are known by the name of *sachas*).

Furthermore, in the Andean world-view, the *runas* and the members of the *sallqa* or nature are the '*chacra*' of the *huacas*. The Aymaras of the *altiplano* of Iquique, Chile, as part of a longer narrative, explain that the ritual of flower bedecking is not exclusive to the *runas* since the *Mallcos* also do it:

> this bedecking with flowers was not done by human persons, it belonged to the mountains which have from time immemorial been called Mallco, these mountains bedecked its herds of vicuñas with flowers. (Flores et al. 1990: 169)

These activities are experienced as a commitment of the *huacas* in the nurturance of the *sallqa* since in that way they contribute ritually in each circumstance to the harmonious renewal of the cycle of life of the *sallqa*.

Just as the notion of consanguinity turns out to be too narrow to understand what the *ayllu* is, the definition of *chacra* as an expanse of land within a given territory also requires revision. The *chacras* of an *ayllu* are also dispersed in contiguous *ayllus*. One of the ways of dialoguing with the diversity of circumstances in life is to nurture dispersed *chacras* in other *ayllus*. Such a distribution converses well with the creatures and crops, with the variability of the Andean landscape and weather, and with the way of being of the *runas*.

This is what actually happens: for example, in the *ayllus* of Conima, Puno, families of the Sullcata *ayllu* have *chacras* in other *ayllus* of the district and in the *Yunga* (warm valley) of San Juan del Oro (Nestor Chambi, personal communication). This situation is found everywhere in the Andes, and is typical of the Andean way of being; in spite of the forced relocations (*reducciones*) of the Viceroy of Toledo, in many places people continue to live like this. Cook Carrasco, in an ethnohistorical work of the different Collagas settlements (in what is today the department of Arequipa, Peru), writes:

> Within the seat of Yanque-Collagas, we found Indians from the village of Tisco who were relocated (*reducidos*) in the settlement of Callalli (1617) and Indians from the village of Tina resettled in Achoma (1616); still today, the inhabitants of Callalli have lands in Achoma [...]. The presence of those resettled *ayllus* outside of their territory, either from the village or the seat to which they belong, is due to the fact that they have to continue to maintain control over these lands in order to obtain greater satisfaction of their needs. Nevertheless, one has to note, at least within our conception, that we must assume that we are dealing with a different notion of territoriality. (Cook Carrasco 1989: 35–51)

Each *ayllu*, each ethnic group, nurtures in diverse and dispersed zones. Due to this it is difficult, for people used to the separation of territory by defined borders, to perceive where the territory of an *ayllu* begins and ends. Such dispersion adjusts itself to the particular mode of being of the *ayllu*, which as we saw is a family without fixed borders. With the re-settlements (*reducciones*) of Toledo this way of being was distorted with the borders of the *encomiendas* and *haciendas* and with the republican territorial delimitations of departments, provinces and districts. The *ayllu* gave way officially to jurisdiction, that is to say to a space over which power is exercised. This is a concept that is alien to the Andean way of being and provokes too many conflicts between the actual communities.

As we have said, in the vital cycle of the *ayllu* there exist periods of increased intensity. In these times the activity in the *chacra* and the dialogical and reciprocal relations between its members become deeper and stronger. When such a period happens, the communities rework their relationships in order to converse with the new circumstances.

Speaking of the ethnic groups from the coast, before the European invasion, Maria Rostworowski says the following in an ethnohistorical work referring to Canta:

> The most surprising particularity of the economic organization of Canta was the existence of 18 temporary settlements inhabited only in order to accomplish certain communal tasks. When the work was finished, the hamlets remained deserted, their occupation rotating according to a previously arranged plan. (1989: 8–13)

Another example of long-term malleability is one noted by Grillo (1990), and which refers to the movements of various *ayllus* which left a region due to climactic changes of long duration. We know of the existence of long periods of colder weather in the Andes (Pan Andino Wari, Tiawanacu and Inca) that covered vast zones in the high parts of the Andes with ice. In those cold and dry periods, agriculture was not possible at all altitudes, particularly in the high parts. Many peoples were thus forced by the conditions to migrate to zones propitious to agricultural activity. This meant the construction of an infrastructure (for example terraces [*andenes*]) in the areas to which they migrated so as to increase the quantity of food that could be grown in order to maintain both the local population and the migrants.

The population that was displaced took along its seeds and its plants. The 'receiving' *ayllus* established relations of reciprocity and conviviality with the displaced ones. When the availability of cultivable land becomes a problem for the peasants, the *ayllus* cooperate among themselves, especi-ally when the climate affects one of them. In the *altiplano* of Juliaca this relation is known as 'help':

> In years of low productivity, the owners of the *chacra* cannot deny the help offered by those who, not having had any harvest, come to cooperate with

them in order to receive at least the portion of produce that the owners are obligated to give. (CEPIA 1989: 177)

In such circumstances, the conversation and the reciprocity intensifies with the *ayllus* of neighbouring or distant regions with whom there could or could not have been relations in the past, so that agricultural life can be re-created in those zones. Grillo (1990) suggests the formation of alliances between *ayllus* of different zones under the leadership of a charismatic authority, with the creation of regional and pan-Andean federations. When the cold and dry epoch had passed, the *ayllus* would return to their zones of origin, to their *chacras* and their regional space protected by their *Apus* of reference.

Such malleability is consubstantial to the *ayllu* and contrary to institutionalization, to the notion of a fixed territory with defined borders, and to the creation of a structured framework that freezes life. It allows adjustments to the entirety of Andean life circumstances, even though many years can pass between one event and another.

Authority

Authority in the Andes is not an abstract notion. When Andeans speak of authority they usually refer to the person in charge of a *cargo* (responsibility), known as the *carguyoc*. There are *cargos* for all activities – an agricultural festival, a liquid offering to the deities of the crops, the holding of the festival of the *huaca* or deity of the *ayllu* and so on. The *cargo* is not a political administrative function with ritual trimmings, it is rather a rotating ceremony in which all the communities participate led by the *Apu* or *huaca* whose turn it is and who celebrates the feasts of one of the *huacas* whose 'saint' or name – if one may put it that way – coincides with it or is related to an agro-astronomic event.

A *cargo* is assumed not only by those among the human community whose turn it is, but also by the *Apu* or *Achachillas* whose turn it is, who is the great facilitator of life and who in the feasts plays a primary role in the harmonization of life in the *ayllu*.[4] The one who names or confirms the members of the human community who take a *cargo* is the *Apu*, in agreement with the other *huacas*, and a ritual *mesa* (literally this means a table but it is in actuality a kind of altar) is made. It is the *mesa* which 'tells' who is to be chosen and which *huaca* will be in charge of the feast in that particular circumstance of the *wata* (ritual year). The ceremonial *mesa*, presided over by the *Apu* and led by the *paqo* or *yatiri* (Andean priest), is a great assembly in which the three collectivities are present in order to orient the realization of the activities. Thus the *cargo* is not a regulated exercise with a political administrative character carrried out by the members of the human collectivity in order ritually to synchronize the agricultural activities with the climactic, astronomical and social conditions of the *ayllu*. Such an assessment is the product of an anthropocentric perspective. The event of the *cargo* is an emotionally forceful and complex ceremony, in the realization of which the members of the three collectivities whose turn it is participate as *huacas*. The *huaca* within the *ayllu* is the person who is most experienced and who deserves the greatest respect, affection and consideration on the part of the whole *ayllu*.

The community of the *sallqa* participates in the feast, being present in some cases with animals (foxes, bears, etc.), or with flowers and plants of the *sallqa* which are there as responsible for the *cargo*. At particular feasts it will be specific plants or animals that participate, while others present themselves in the next *cargos*. The animal or plant who has the *cargo* does so in its capacity of *huaca*. In certain feasts one observes *runas* that wear the skin of a bear or the flower of a plant who has the *cargo*, participating in the feast as members of the *sallqa*. It is not – as we have said – that they represent this or that plant or animal, but that in those circumstances they *are* that plant or animal. It is true that in other cases the members of the community of *runas* make this or that plant or animal 'dance' and do not embody them. It may also be the case that the *huaca* whose day one is observing is a member of the community of the *sallqa* – for example, the feast of the water – and during the feast it is accompanied by the other collectivities.

Viewed from the perspective of the community of *huacas*, what is noticeable in the feasts of the *carguyoc* are the Christian saints that participate in the *cargo* in their role as *huacas*. In other cases one can see that the saint embodies in that moment a given Andean *huaca* as, for example, in the case of Mamacha Candelaria embodying *Pachamama*. In this case, from the Andean perspective, the manner in which the ceremonial feast is carried out has little do to with the way the Virgin of Candelaria is celebrated in the Christian faith, but rather with the way in which the *ayllu* celebrates the feast of *Pachamama*. The feast may be, and more often that not is, for an Andean *huaca* whose turn it is, such as *Pachamama*, *Mamacocha*, the *Apu* or *Achachilla*; the *Chacata* (constellation of the Andean cross); the Sun; or the Moon.

Viewed from the *chacra*, the feast is performed for the crops or the animals in one of the agricultural and pastoral cycles such as the coupling, planting, hilling, marriage, branding or harvest. The crops as well as the animals responsible for the *cargo* are in their condition of *huacas* and are decorated accordingly. There are certain crops in the *chacra* that are the authorities of the *chacra* at a given point in the *wata*.

Viewed from the human community, the authority that embodies the *cargo* in the feast is what has been most focused upon in the studies of Andean culture, and it is from that perspective that they have been seen as a political activity and as a 'tool' of social organization and for managing resources. The roles of other collectivities in the Andean *cargos*, such as the *huacas* and the *sallqa*, have not been understood and have remained largely invisible; for the external institutions, what stands out are the official *cargos*.

In terms of the official authorities, the situation is similar to that of the Christian saints. Just as the saints have been incorporated into the feasts as *huacas*, something similar has happened with the colonial and republican systems of authority which have been imposed on the communities. The *ayllu* has digested the extension of political authority in its territory and has assimilated it, making these authorities part of the office of *carguyoc*. The Deputy Governor and the Municipal Agent that exist in the *ayllus* are just one more *cargo*.

These official institutions have not politically institutionalized the community or *ayllu*; instead they have been incorporated in diverse modalities of carrying out the *cargo*. In certain cases they function with the tasks assigned to them by the governmental authorities of the country and they are elected according to the imposed norms; in other cases, they have official tasks but besides those they also carry out the responsibilities of the ancient '*varas*'. But in both cases the new systems have not eliminated the Andean modality of carrying out a *cargo*. The agents and deputies are there, as are the members and directors of cooperatives, but they have not displaced the authorities that lead the ceremonies for *Pachamama*, the *Apus*, the Hail, the Winds. It is even true that many of the new authorities also carry out *cargos* in the feasts of the virgins, saints, water and crops.

The *cargo* implies the realization of a series of activities that normally involves a group who has a head or *uma* and arms. It is not an individual activity; instead it is viewed as a living person within which lives a micro-collectivity of *huacas* of the *ayllu* whose task is to make life flow in this particular circumstance. Within this micro-collectivity, leadership rotates between the different *huacas*, whatever the origin of its community might be (*runa*, *huaca* or *sallqa*). In a particular circumstance it can be carried out by a member of the community of *runas*, in another by a member of the community of *huacas* or of the *sallqa*. Since in the *cargo* all are *huacas*, whatever their community of origin, it may be that one of the leader *huacas* that is carrying out the authority becomes tired; it is then replaced by that *huaca* which, at that moment, has the greatest vigour. Some call this vigour that animates and gives strength *kamaq* (Araujo 1989: 237).

Rotation also takes place among the members of the same community. The *cargo* is taken at a given moment by a member who has charisma for that community, but the next *wata* it can pass to another. Since the *cargo* is not individual but collective, any member of, for example, the *runas* is prepared to carry it out and modes of accompanying the one who leads exist. The leader who has the main *cargo* is usually accompanied by others who, according to their ages and abilities, carry out certain tasks – rather like an arm does for a body. This rotation does not apply exclusively to the human community but characterizes all the communities, including that of the crops.

The authorities are re-created and they accompany rhythmically the regeneration of the *Pacha*. It may be that the circumstances require the growth of new authorities – as happens, for example, in periods of drought in the *altiplano*, when the authority of the nettle or the *tola* (an asteroidal plant) appears, that is the plants that replace crops in periods of scarcity. The *cargo* thus emerges in order to coordinate the distribution of the harvest of these plants and thus permit the flowing of life. The order that emerges is to facilitate the life of all the members of the *Pacha*.

The authority thus emerges in order to lead the adjustment of each of the collectivities that inhabit the *ayllu* through the different circumstances of the *wata*. It is an authority without institutionality since the order that appears is only for that particular circumstance (Ortiz Rescaniere 1933).[5] Once the drought is gone a new mode of being of life emerges and a new authority will rise to correspond to that new mode. Thus there is no room for institutionality. By definition, an institution is something regulated, normalized and useful for a time beyond that of any given circumstance. Institution is part of life in society and becomes a means to achieve a given end; for that it has its own activities, personnel and materials needed by the people who compose it in order to achieve the prefigured norm. Here nature and *huacas* have no place.

In contrast, the tasks and obligations of a *cargo* are carried out according to the rhythm of the life of the *ayllu* and have different durations according to the specific *cargo*. A *cargo* can last one week, one lunar month, one *wata*, and so on, and is carried out according to the conversation between the different collectivities. The mesa 'says' what has to be done, but this activity is reconfigured in each circumstance. We are not dealing here with a plan along the lines of development planning, where the plan is part of a project, of organizing the means in order to achieve an end. What the mesa 'says', it says for a particular set of circumstances, and what is done is what is indicated by the conversation of the moment. So if the *cargo* indicates that one has to do the pruning of trees, but the moon indicates that one should not prune, one simply leaves that activity for another time.

Harmony in Andean life is not something given but something constantly in the process of happening; that is why we speak of harmonizing. In this process of finding harmony in each circumstance, the *huacas* whose turn it is to have the *cargo* have an important role. Thus there can be obstacles, disorders in the harmony, moments of conflicts and disequilibrium in the conversation between the members of the *Pacha*. These situations are experienced as inattentions and mistakes in the responsibilities that have been ceremonially assigned to each one. It is then necessary to re-establish conversation and harmony through ceremonies of *tinkuy* or encounters between collectivities which want to remake their relationships of conversation and thus allow life to flow. These ceremonies to untie the knots of disequilibrium can take violent forms of punishment and fights among those who have not known how to converse. One can even punish not only the *runas* but also the *huacas* who have not known how to carry out their tasks. After the ceremony of *tinkuy*, everything regains its equilibrium until a new set of circumstances obliges one to do it again. In these ceremonies the *paqos* and *yatiris* (Andean priests) play a decisive role because, due to their capacity to 'see', they are able to fathom the intimacy of the unstable Andean order and to know the way to re-establish harmony so that life regains its flow. Disequilibrium is not seen analytically as if it were only a matter of a difficulty with a diseased organ. What is viewed instead, is the totality of the local order within which the organ lives. In the process of curing, not only is it important that the organ return to its harmony but also that the affected *Pacha* recover. From this it follows that, in each cure brought about by the *paqos* or healers, the healing is part of the ceremony of conversation with all the *huacas* of the different collectivities that are in charge of the *cargo*.

The peasant community

The peasant community with its territory and its rules is a colonial creation, an instance of the nuclearization of the Andean population – what is called 'the community of Indians' (*comun de indios*), created to organize and control the Andeans in the exploitation of natural resources. Some of these communities were created on the basis of the original *ayllus* and these are known as 'original communities' (*comunidades originarias*). However, the majority were the result of the transfer of people to territories away from their original ones.

Once installed in these, the Andeans had to observe the regulations imposed by the colonial administration, beginning a difficult process of assimilation of the new institution. This was especially difficult since with the new communities came the notion of the communal property of a territory with defined borders. The *ayllu* and its *Pacha* was modified and constrained to the imposed territory, with the emergence of something never before experienced: the competition between communities and *haciendas* for the right to use resources. The 'ritual border' of the *Pacha*, this space of sheltering, was replaced by the judicial border of the communal property. The craftsman of this process was the Viceroy of Toledo.

What characterized life in the Indian communities and in the *haciendas* (with the exception of the plantations) was the type of agriculture practised there. Homogenous cropping did not dominate the agricultural landscape;

instead what dominated was Andean agriculture characterized by the creation of small *chacras* and of polycropping carried out by the re-constituted *ayllus*. Heterogeneity was, and is, the characteristic of the creation/nurturance of Andean space. Nevertheless, and as one can still see today, the *chacras* of the communities, which make up 90 per cent of the agricultural and pastoral units in the whole of the Peruvian Andean territory, are made not only in reduced space compared to the middle-sized and large landholdings – which occupy more than 85 per cent of the available cultivable space – but are located on mountainous slopes without significant access to the full range of ecological levels, in particular to the irrigated lands of the low zones. The colonization drastically reduced the *Pacha* of the *ayllu*.

Since then the struggle for the recuperation of the *Pacha*, torn by the colonizer, has been a constant in the relations between the Andeans and the *haciendas* and plantations. The number of indigenous rebellions during the colony and the republic was very high, and conflict characterized the relations between the owners of the *haciendas* and the Andeans. Some of these, such as those by Tupac Amaru, Tupac Katari and Atusparia, were the longest lasting, the largest and most intense in this decolonizing dynamic of the reclamation of the *Pacha*. In that sense, decolonization began the day after the European invasion and has lasted until today. Its sign is not the appropriation of lands, but rather the recuperation of the harmony of the *ayllu* disturbed by the invasion. That must be why some use the term 'return' for the peasant mobilizations – a return to the harmony of the *Pacha*.

It is this harmonizing desire on the part of the Andean peasant that has ensured that there are no owners of *haciendas* in the greater part of the territory of Peru. The agrarian reform of the Velasco regime in Peru in 1969 and the peasant insurrections led by the MNR in Bolivia in 1952 were important steps in this dynamic. Today in Peru we are in a process of recuperation of the lands of the cooperative enterprises – not in order to create peasant enterprises, but in order to re-establish the *ayllu*. The number of communities in Peru has increased significantly. Today there are almost 5,000; in 1977 there were fewer than 2,837 (Flores Galindo 1988). The communities' state-drawn territorial borders are often ignored since for numerous activities groups organize themselves among members belonging to different communities (Cotler 1959).[6] Andean organicity thus allows for the adoption of a variety of forms, according to the circum-stances, but always keeping its own way of being.

One habitual form of being in the *ayllu* is what is called *custom* (*costumbre*). When one asks Andean people the meaning of any activity, almost always the answer is 'this is our custom', a phrase which is not followed by explanations that give the rationale for what is being done. The *runas* do not interrogate nature in order thus to obtain an analytical explanation of its daily life. In the Andes, rationalizations of what one does do not exist. As Eduardo Grillo would say, 'one just lives'. This phrase seems to encapsulate the secret of the perennial continuity of Andean regenerative activities, since the custom one hears about today in the communities is the same as it has been since time immemorial – the same response of 'it is our custom' from a people who have always lived feeling themselves part of the rhythms of nature. These customs renew themselves yet do not repeat themselves since, in a heterogeneous world such as the Andean world, each one lives custom according to their own circumstances.

Customs disappear when the homogenizing institutionality converts customs into the repetitive habits of 'rational people' that guarantee institutional continuity. The official community (which successive state powers have tried to impose) in that sense has not succeeded in normalizing the life of the *runas*, which is now a mode in which the *ayllu* has re-created itself. It is not the case that with the introduction of the community the *ayllus* have not disappeared; on the contrary, since to utter the word 'community' is now a way of naming a series of *ayllus* enclosed in that collectivity.

Adherence to custom is typical of those who experience life cyclically. The Andeans know that there will be a new period of rain within the climatic cycle, but its particular nature and the precise moment it will fall is unknown even with the most accurate of predictions. That is why the ceremonies associated with custom are not repetitive; instead they attune themselves to the particular situation and take different forms. A ritual to the rain performed one year is never the same as that of the previous *wata*. To be repetitive is to nullify the daily re-creation of life. Thus the concept of archetype is alien to the Andes since an archetype implies that there exists a preconceived model.

For someone who repeats a ritual or an activity it is indispensable to have an archetype and institutions that preserve the rules and norms associated with its reproduction. Memory for the Andean is – as the Mexican Carlos Fuentes puts it – 'the strength of the past in the present'. It helps to keep alive what has happened, to guide one in the execution of an activity, to make present what has happened, but it does not indicate the precise manner of doing so. What is done accords with the conversation that takes place in the present circumstances. This is contrary to the attitude of modern Western man, for whom utopia – the conceived reality, the longed-for future, the 'should be' – is what guides his behaviour and is the aim of his life.

The Andeans say: 'just as the grandparents did it, so do we do it'. Such respectful remembrance of the ancestors (*runas*, *huacas* and *sallqa*) does not lead them into reiterative activities but into re-creative ones. Memory, this 'human faculty to preserve ideas previously acquired', is indicative –

although for Andeans what is 'preserved', if one can phrase it that way, is not ideas or representations, but lived experiences of occurrences that are made present when circumstances call for them.

The custom that is lived today in the communities emerges from its own heterogeneity. There is nothing homogeneous in the Andes which would lead Andeans to the practice of habits – to the slavish conforming to archetypes. The same *chacra* is not cultivated the same way from one year to the next. Habit is characteristic of society that regulates its life normatively. In custom, decisions are taken ritually in daily conversation, just as conflicts are resolved in the *tinkuy*. In a people who have norms, life and conflicts are resolved through the mediation of institutions regulated by human laws which become, by virtue of repetition, coercive measures since they stifle the flexibility of life by capturing it within systematic regulations.

A normalized people lives in society that is resistant to diversity and to complication because the unusual disturbs the mechanisms that regulate its functioning; a people of custom re-creates heterogeneity and is prepared for the new and even the uncertain. The Andean pantheon has been re-created and amplified with the incorporation of the Catholic saints and is ready to receive others. A similar situation arises, as we have said, with the carrying out of *cargos*. Custom has absorbed institutionality. When the communities were incorporated into the official system of democracy and the constitution gave the vote to the unlettered, who were mostly Andeans, the *ayllu* began experiencing it as a widening of the variability of the ways in which to carry out the *cargos* – its 'political pantheon' became wider in its diversity. To elect a President of the Republic or the representatives of the fatherland becomes part of the ritual of electing the *carguyoc* – the election of a distant *ayllu* for a *cargo* called 'Mister Government'.

Notes

1. When in PRATEC we speak of these three communities we only make visible what is perceived in an obvious way in the *Pacha*: the deity mountains or Apus; the community of the *runas*; and the wild (called in Quechua *sallqa*) – that is, what is not cultivated by the *runas*.

2. For Hegel, for example, society emerges with the French Revolution, by abolishing the distinction between master and slave and establishing the principles of popular sovereignty and the governance of the law (Fukuyama 1992: 18).

3. About this lack of attunement Augusto Salazar Bondy (1981: 112) said (referring to philosophy, but it could be applied to other areas of intellectual activity) that: 'It is not possible for the community to recognize itself in the philosophies spread among the educated people in our countries, precisely because we are dealing with transplanted thinking, installed, so to speak, in a void of reflexive tradition, and because they can be considered as spiritual products expressive of other peoples and cultures, which a refined minority arduously tries to understand and share in our milieu.'

4. 'The Marani, as an authority, had always existed in all the *ayllus*, but nowadays there is only one in the *ayllu* Kupisaya-Mililaya, and has disappeared in the other *ayllus*. But the Luwaranis (*Apus*) have not done away with the Marani as we have; among themselves they continue to select a Marani. For the current year the Marani is Wila Wit'o of the community of Aynacha Huat'asani; the Luwaranis say that they converse just like the human communities in order to elect an authority.' Words of don Erasmo Larico and his wife dona Rosa Trinidad Pilco, of Mililaya, Puno. In Chambi et al. 1992; *The Nurturance of the Yoqch'as in the Districts of Conima, Tilali and Ilave*, Puno.

5. The men of the Andes – says Alejandro Ortiz Rescaniere (1933: 254) – give circumstantial evaluations, they do not seek the essence of things so much as the being of them; they perceive and define themselves in the circumstances, they are in things, they are not in front of things.

6. An example of this Andean malleability and constant adjusting to change is illustrated by the work of Cotler on the communities of San Lorenzo, Huarochiri Lima. He tells us: 'even until the end of the nineteenth century the communities of this zone took charge of organizing mutual help, of the distribution of water, of the collective tasks, etc. At the beginning of this century, on the basis of the privatization of agricultural land and later of pasture land, they lost their ability to organize the population. That is why the so-called "work societies" were formed for mutual help, which obviously, continued to be necessary. These groups could also be organized inter-communally, thus traversing the borders of individual communities.'

References

Araujo, Hilda. 1989; 'Organizacion social andina y manejo de los recursos naturales en la sierra' (Andean social organization and management of natural resources in the highlands). In *Ecologia, Agricultura y Autonomia Campesina en los Andes* (*Ecology, Agriculture and Peasant Autonomy in the Andes*) Fundacion Alemana para el Desarrollo Internacional and Instituto Nacional de Planificatión. Feldafing, Lima and Hohenheim.

CEPIA. 1989; *Credito Campesino: Experiencias y Evaluacion* (*Peasant Credit: Experiences and Evaluation*) 2do. Seminario Taller. Lima; Editorial Horizonte.

Chambi, N., V. Quiso and F. Tito. 1992; *Estudio sobre cosmovision y conocimiento campesino y technologia tradicional de los criadores aymaras* (*Study of peasant cosmovision and knowledge and traditional technology of the Aymara herders*), Doc. de estudio No. 24. Lima; PRATEC.

Chambi Pacoricona, Nestor. 1989; 'Proceso de integracion de nuevos cultivos o variedades a la celula de cultivos familiares' (Processes of integration of new crops or varieties in the family field). In *Manejo Campesino de Semillas en los Andes* (*Peasant Management of Seeds in the Andes*), Lima; PPEA, PRATEC: 63–9.

Comte, Auguste. 1979; *Ensayo de un sistema de politica positiva: Estudio preliminar* (*Essay of a positive political system*), Estudio Prelimar de Raul Cardiel Reyes. Universidad Autonoma de Mexico. Mexico.

Cook Carrasco, G. 1989; 'Allyu, territorio y frontera en los Collaguas' (*Ayllu, territory and frontier in the Collaguas*). In *Organizacion Economica en los Andes* (*Economic Organization in the Andes*) La Paz. Bolivia; Hisbol.

Cotler, Julio. 1959; *Los Cambios en la Propriedad, la Familia y la Comunidad en San Lorenzo de Quinti*, Lima; Universidad de San Marcos.

De Zutter. 1990; *El paisaje de la salud ambiental de ecosistemas andinos* (*The landscape of environmental health of the Andean ecosystems*), Proyecto Pilote de Ecosistemas Andinos. Cajamarca.

Eliade, Mircea. 1959; *Cosmos and History: The myth of the eternal return*, New York; Harper and Row.

Enciclopedia Campesina Piedra Adentro. 1992; 'Nosotros los Cajamarquinos' (Us from Cajamarca), Tomo 13. Cajamarca.

Ferrater Mora, J. 1981; *Diccionario de Filosofia* (*Dictionary of Philosophy*), Barcelona, España; Alianza Editorial.

Flores, Rucio et al. 1990; *Uybirmallco: Cerros que nos dan la vida* (*Uybirmallco: Mountains that give us life*) Iquique, Chile; Crear.

Flores Galindo, Alberto (ed.). 1988; *Comunidades Campesinas: Cambios y Permanencias*, Chiclayo, Peru; Centros de Estudios Sociales SOLIDARIDAD.

Fuenzalida, Fernando. 1976; 'Estructura de la comunidad de indigenas tradicional: una hipotesis de trabajo' (Structure of the traditional indigenous community: A working hypothesis). In: *Hacienda, comunidad y campesinado en el Peru* (*Hacienda, community and peasantry in Peru*) Problema 3. Jose Matos Mar (comp) IEP. Lima.

Fukuyama, Francis. 1992; *El fin de la historia y el ultimo hombre* (*The end of history and the last man*) (4th edn), Colombia; Planeta.

Goldschmidt, Walter. 1974; 'Prologo'. In *Carlos Castaneda: Las enseñanzas de Don Juan; una forma Yaqui de conocimiento* (Carlos Castaneda: The teachings of Don Juan: a Yaqui form of knowing), Mexico; Fondo de Cultura Economica.

Gonzales Holguin, Diego. 1952 (1608) *Vocabulario de la lengua general de todo el Peru llamada Quechua* (*Vocabulary of the general language of the whole of Peru, called Quechua*), Lima; Instituto de Historia, UNMSM.

Grillo, E. 1990; 'Vision andina del paisaje' (Andean vision of the landscape). In: *Sociedad y Naturaleza en los Andes* (*Society and Nature in the Andes*), Tomos I. Lima; PRATEC, PPEA-NUMA.

Jimenez Sardon, Greta. 1995; *Rituales de vida en la cosmovision andina* (*Rituals for life in Andean cosmovision*) Convenio Editorial. Secretariado Rural Peru-Bolivia; Centro de Informacion para el Desarrollo. La Paz, Bolivia.

Kusch, Rodolfo. 1962; *America Profunda* (*Deep America*), Buenos Aires; Hachette.

Lambert, Berndt. 1980; 'Bilateralidad en los Andes' (Bilaterality in the Andes). In: *Parentesco y Matrimonio en los Andes* (*Kinship and Alliance in the Andes*), Mayer, E. and R. Bolton (eds), Lima; Fondo Editorial, PUCP: 11–54.

Machaca, Marcela. 1992; 'El agua y los quispillactinos' (Water and the people of Quispillaccta). Thesis; Pratec. Asociacion Bartolome Aripaylla. Ayacucho. Peru.

Millones, Luis. 1989; 'Que es el mito para un antropólogo' (*What is myth for an anthropologist?*). In *Mitos universales americanos y contemporaneos* (*Universal American and contemporaneous myths*), Sociedad Peruana de Psicoanalisis. Universidad Nacional San Antonio Abad del Cusco. Vol. I. Lima.

Montoya, Rodrigo. 1986; 'La cultura quechua hoy' (*Quechua culture today*). In *Hueso Humero* No. 21. Diciembre 1986.

Montoya Maquin, Jorge. 1991; 'Mestizaje: Un mito para aculturar runas' (Mestizaje: a myth to acculturate *runas*), *Diablada*, 1(2).

Ortiz Rescaniere, Alejandro. 1993; *La pareja y el mito: Estudios sobre las concepciones de la pareja en los Andes* (*The couple and myth: studies on the concepts of the couple in the Andes*), Lima; PUC.

Preiswerk, Matthias. 1995; *Educacion popular y teologia de la liberacion* (*Popular education and theology of liberation*), Argentina; Celadec.

Rengifo, G., R. Panduro and E. Grillo. 1993; *Chacra y chacareros: Ecologia demografia y sistemas de cultivos en San Martin* (*Chacra and chacareros: Ecology, demography and crop systems in San Martin*), Lima; CEDISA Fondo de Contravalor Peru Canada.

Rostworoski, Maria. 1989; 'Canta: Un caso de organizacion economica andina' (Canta: a case of Andean economic organization). In: *Organizacion economica Andina*, La Paz; Hisbol.

Salazar Bondy, A. 1981; *Existe una filosofia de nuestra America* (*A Philosophy of our America exists*), Siglo XXI (7th edn), Mexico.

Thompson, Lonnie. 1985; 'A 1,500 year record of tropical precipitation in ice cores from the Quelcaya ice cap, Peru', in *Science* 299: 971–3.

Urbano, J. and P. Macera. 1992; *Santero y Caminante: Santoruraj-Nampurej* (*Craftsman and Itinerant*) Lima; Apoyo.

Van den Berg, Hans. 1989; *La tierra no da asi nomas: Los ritos agricolas en la religion de los aymara-cristianos* (*The earth doesn't give just like that: the agricultural rituals in the religion of the Christian-Aymaras*), La Paz; Hisbol, UCB, ISET.

CHAPTER 4

Development or Cultural Affirmation in the Andes?[1]

Eduardo Grillo Fernandez

Western powers are used to presenting their dominant, expansionist and voracious mode of proceeding as if it were a cause for celebration, a catalogue of heroic deeds that reaffirm the excellence of their virtues. Such virtues logically entitle them to subjugate the rest of the world. Having done so, they aspire to impose on others this mode of evaluating their own actions as the only correct one.

Such arrogance fully accords with the colonialist character of the West. It is part of the West's strategy of cultural colonization of the rest of the world. However, colonization will succeed only if it finds people disposed to subordinate themselves – people willing to admire, follow and support Western domination. Let us be clear: those who are colonized are so because they allow it or accept it. Colonization is a form of bond, a form of union, and thus it is not and cannot be unilateral; it is necessary that the colonized voluntarily give up their intimacy to the colonizer. The colonizer and the colonized are complementary.

With five hundred years of effort, the colonizing state in the Andes has succeeded in forming, within the Andean peoples, a small group of colonized-colonizers. They make up the official apparatus of our Andean countries, that is of our colonized portion. They are the climbers ready to subordinate themselves to an order imposed from outside so as to gain personal credit in their official careers. They are the agents of colonization among us.

The official system of education, with its schools, high schools and universities, tries to subject the Andean peoples to the order that the West wants to impose, arguing that such an order is the highest attainment of 'humanity' and that it is necessary to the process of self-development in the Andes since it has 'universal' relevance.

But let us see what education is in the Andes. We realize that it is an accretion – an alien addition to the Andean way of being – imported from Europe or the US by the colonizing state, which the education system installs, in greater or lesser measure, in the Andean people who pass through it. Once this installation is achieved, we can note two types of behaviour among educated peoples: first there are those who have great pride in wearing such an accretion and they adjust their behaviour accordingly, as a way of fulfilling a duty that would make them deserving of the rewards and the rights that accrue to the agents of colonization. They are enraptured by the precepts that education has taught them; they are devoted admirers of the successes of the West. Secondly, there are those – and they are the vast majority – who in spite of having passed through the education system and being subjected to the education accretion, know very well what it is all about. They use it only when, due to life circumstances, they need to relate with the apparatus of officialdom. This second group keep alive their Andean culture and their spontaneity, both in everyday life and in the great ceremonies. They continue to be fully Andean; they have not been seduced by the West but rather have studied it, and they know it and how to converse with it. They understand the West but they do not adhere to it, and they do not share its colonizing ambitions.

We Andeans do not concede any 'cognitive authority' to the West. It is an authority that the West gives itself. Anxious to be recognized as authoritative, it has no faith that the merits it attributes to itself will be recognized by the peoples of the world. Neither does it have the patience necessary to gain the recognition of the peoples of the world. The West declares itself, based only on its own evaluation, to be the paradigm of 'humanity'. It has invented the comparative method in order to justify itself. Since the West declares itself to be the paradigm, if there is something that we do not have and that it posseses, we are assessed as being deficient or lacking. But this is due to the bias inherent in the comparison; if the situation were reversed and we were the paradigm, the West would be the deficient one. But, clearly, this game does not interest us.

Westerners are said to be competitive but they are only self-promoting. They are prisoners of a vanity which prevents them from accepting the possibility of losing. They abhor risk. They run races in which we do not participate and they declare themselves the winners. One example of Western self-promotion based on the comparative method is the classification of countries according to their GNP (Gross National Product). Westerners have destroyed their own indigenous communities and have built on their ruins 'society' – that is, an aggregation of uprooted individuals, each of whom struggles against the others in order to secure their own interests. In these circumstances, society, in order to function, requires the regulation of both the state and the market – institutions that are now indispensable to, and encompass everything in, the Western world. It is in the West that GNP has some meaning since, by definition, it is the sum of the expenses undergone in a country to acquire in the market the final products – that is, the goods and services ready to be consumed. We here in the Andes, from time immemorial and for all times, are communitarian. Here the state and the market are alien to us. They are frameworks that colonialism has installed in our countries but that are of no account for most of us. In the Andes we are not economic units dependent on a system of production regulated by the exigencies of economic efficiency; here the GNP has no meaning.

This chapter is concerned with showing that in the Andean world we have our own way of living and feeling, far removed from that of the modern West. The difference between our worlds explains why the West's version of our experience, its manner of recounting events, says nothing to us and says nothing of us.

Despite what they in the West say, here in the Andes we have never been conquered by European invaders; we are neither poor nor malnourished nor underdeveloped; we are not victims, we have not been subjugated, and we demand nothing. It is our view that – just as the frost, the hail or insects sometimes visit our *chacras* – five centuries ago a very virulent plague appeared here suddenly that has gravely damaged the life and happiness of our Andean world – that of the *huacas* (deities), of the *sallqas* (those of the wild) and of the *runas* (people). But this happened because we deserved it – just like when frost, hail or insects visit our *chacras* – because at that time our world did not know how to be sufficiently harmonized, because we were careless in the daily nurturance of harmony. Since we Andeans love the world as it is – with humility and with vigour, without fear, laments, resentments, or anger – we have gradually found the way in which to reharmonize ourselves, the manner in which to cure ourselves of this terrible plague. Each day we are recovering something of the lost harmony; each day we are closer to our completeness. We will be fully healthy when we have harmonized ourselves again with all those who configure the Andean world: the *huacas*, the *sallqas* and the *runas*. It is among all of us that we nurture harmony and, in turn, that harmony nurtures all of us. We nurture harmony when each and every one of us adjusts with joy and goodwill to the circumstances of each moment; and harmony in its turn nurtures us, making us feel at ease and cared for in each moment, full of the joy of living in community.

The virulent plague emerged here from among us because we had lost our harmony, because we had harmed ourselves to the point of opening a wound which even began to fester. And it is among ourselves that we are healing the wound. We are nurturing with what is ours the harmony that we need. Here in the Andes everything emerges from within – both the plague and its cure. We are an immanent world in which one day we were careless and became seriously ill but we are close to regaining our health. We will emerge renewed and enriched from that illness due to the experience of living with and recuperating from it. Here health (that is harmony) and illness (that is the disturbing of harmony) are not opposed;

rather they are complementary in the living Andean world, and both renew and strengthen the happenings and diversification of life.

Well then, when we have fully recuperated our health this plague will disappear from life in the Andes in the same way it appeared, that plague which throughout five centuries has accompanied us, like the frost, the hail or the insects that only pay temporary visits to our *chacras*. Obviously it could come back, but only if we are careless, if we disharmonize ourselves. In any case, if it came back, it would be because we deserved it. Harmony in the world is not given; rather it has to be nurtured day by day, by all together – that is what the sun repeats to us with every dawn.

I want it to be very clear that here I am only trying to summarize, with reference to the theme that occupies us, my experience forged very slowly during many years of living the Andean (*lo andino*)[2] in my own way; trying to understand the Andean from within itself; using as a base my own experiences, what has been revealed to me during Andean ritual ceremonies, or what I have seen during my long and numerous work trips and research, and the many conversations I have had with Andean peasants in many different places in Peru: on the coast, in the highlands and lowlands, in the country and in the city. Now an internal imperative pushes me to blend and combine my experiences – my sensations, visions, feelings, reflections and memories – in this *general presentation*, in this conviction that grows inevitably from within me and which would not find sufficient sustenance in one particular experience of mine nor in the totality of my experiences. This general synthesis emerges simply and directly, I repeat, from the fusion and combination of what I have lived, of the singular path of my life, from the conviction that it has formed in the ripeness of my life. This synthesis empowers what I have been able to perceive directly allowing me to reach *a general vision of 'lo andino'*. This is why I do not include in the text peasants' voices, because by themselves they would not support what I am presenting. It is clear that this chapter does not purport to be a reasoned and coherent explanation of the mode of being of Andean culture. Nor do I want to convince the reader. I only want to bring to the reader something of myself. I only want to show how I see development and Andean cultural affirmation in the immanent world typical of the Andes. I only want to articulate my own personal convictions on this topic. That is all I intend: to show my Andean manner of feeling and living my Andean world, to whoever wants to draw close to it.

The living Andean world

I began by saying that there is not only one world. Every great people, each culture, each form of life has its own world. In this way the Andean world has its own peculiar mode of being and therefore experiences, in its own way, the events of its life. It is necessary to spell this out because intellectuals, technicians and artists in general consider that the terminology of modern Western culture is the only valid one. That is how imperialism has made them think. Academia has taught them that there is a single world and that it is the modern Western world; and they have taken pains to learn it well. But the reality is not like that; there are as many worlds as there are cultures. Therefore, whatever evaluation that can be made of the Andean world in terms that are foreign to it, simply does not concern it. That is why there exists in the Andes a great mismatch between Western or Westernized intellectuals and the Andean people. The Andean world and the modern Western world are incommensurable.

Here in the Andes we are our living and life-giving world; we ourselves are our Andean world. We are all living and we all engender life. We are all relatives. We all belong to our community which we nurture and which nurtures us in turn. The contribution of each one of us is indispensable in the daily nurturance of our harmony and our harmony nurtures each one with the same love. Here there is no world in itself differentiated from ourselves – unlike in the West where the whole is distinguished from the parts, or the contents from the container, and humans from nature – and about which one could speak in the third person: the world is this or it is that thing. No, here the world is ourselves.

In our living Andean world all of us who exist are alive: not only humans, animals and plants but also the stones, the mountains, the rivers, the gorges, the sun, the moon, the stars and so on. In our world we live the equivalence of the diverse, the heterogeneous, because here the mosquito, the frog, the frost, the hail, the fox, the human, the mountain, the river, the stars are all indispensable in the delicate nurturance of our harmony; because only this, our exhuberant diversity, knows how to nurture our harmony, the one that belongs here, the one which knows how to nurture us.

Our community is not something in itself; it is not an institution, it is not something given or established. Our community is our way collectively to accommodate ourselves among ourselves, according to what is fitting to each moment of the continuous conversation which we sustain with the circumstances of life in order to continue living and generating. This is our form of life. Our community is not simply a human environment, rather it is all of us who live together in a locality: humans, plants, animals, rivers, mountains, stars, moon, sun. Similarly, our *ayllu*, our family, is not only the people of our blood lineage; rather we are the whole of the human community of the locality (*runas*) and also our natural community (*sallqas*) and our community of the sustainers of life (*huacas*) with whom we share life in our locality (*Pacha*) in the annual telluric-sidereal rhythm (*wata*). We, the Andeans, reach the full delight of our lives in contributing to nurture our *ayllu* and in letting ourselves be nurtured by our *ayllu*. We live in symbiosis, that is, facilitating the life of our community brothers and letting them facilitate our lives. Our nurturance consists in the un-conditional affirmation of our communitarian life and in the affirmation of our love in our communitarian life. Our manner of living, nurturing – that is facilitating – our communitarian life, is delightful for those who nurture as well as for those who let themselves be nurtured, a situation where the roles are reversed from moment to moment. This is our way of participating in the wholeness of the daily *fiesta* of our life. This is our attitude in life. Here we know how to enjoy everything a little without attachment, which damages. This exaltation of sensibility opens us to the enjoyment of very diversified pleasures. The communitarian feeling is rooted in the conviction that only in our belonging to the community can we be who we are, feel what we feel, enjoy what we enjoy. In such a world, solitude does not exist. Here we all know each other, we all accompany each other, we all always see each other. Here life is only possible in the symbiosis of the community. From this arises a feeling of incompleteness on the part of each one, because we well know that our life is only possible inside this energetic flowing of life which is the Andean communitarian world.

This manner of being of the Andean world, communitarian and nurturer, is completely different from that of the modern Western world, where there is an absolute distinction between the Judaeo-Christian creator and all-powerful God and the world created by Him. Similarly, man (created 'in the image and semblance of God') is separated and distinguished from nature, which is seen as having been created for man's service. We are dealing there with a very hierarchized world. The West is the habitat of the individual – a human being specialized in competitive struggle to open his own road to success. The individual does not nurture or allow himself to be nurtured since that would lead him to form bonds and he needs to be as independent as possible in order to play more efficiently and win the struggle to secure his interests, rejecting others' attempts to impose their interests on him. Even the reduced nuclear family is a heavy burden for the individual.

Plague or conquest?

Our Andean world is an animal world (Kusch 1962). It is like ourselves; it needs to nourish itself and to rest. It is highly sensitive, changeable according to the circumstances, susceptible of becoming a prisoner of its own preferences, desires, appetites, passions, joys, sadnesses and angers, and, of course, of its sensuality. Like any other animal it is mysterious, unpredictable and even capricious. The Andean people who live in a world with such a temperament know what they are contending with and because of this they interact with it all with spontaneity and familiarity. The Andean people are at ease with the unexpected, the unstable and the contradictory,

and face them without repugnance or apprehension. They are seen simply
as things that sometimes happen in life, and so do not surprise or frighten
anyone in our living world. And so the frost, the hail, the drought, the
floods, the exaggerated abundance of insects or fungi 'happen' in the
Andes in close relations with the harmony of our world. Their severe
presence reveals a more pertinent alteration of harmony in our living
animal world. They are opportune warnings – signs – to help us if we
want to regain the lost harmony. We are always implicated in the alteration
of the harmony of our world since, as we know, harmony is not a given
and has to be nurtured day by day. If we are careless, if we are lazy in
its nurturance, an alteration happens. It is necessary that we nurture our
harmony with more care, with more love if we want the conditions we
like the most to maintain themselves. The frost, hail, drought, floods,
insects, fungi, etc., make us feel with the force of their presence that we
did not nurture the harmony that was agreeable to us with the required
care or the necessary love, and indicate that we were not sensitive enough
to less drastic, earlier symptoms that our animal world has lived through
due to our carelessness. That is why we are grateful to its kindness in
alerting us and we try to be more attentive to the circumstances of life
in order to nurture harmony more diligently, with more love; a harmony
that befits this great festival which is our life. Here in the Andes, everything
can be remedied, nothing is definitive, nothing is fatal.

Well now, the harmony that fits best our plenitude is the one that
allows our health to flourish; the alteration of this harmony, which our
body experiences like a disharmony, is what makes us ill. But here, in the
living Andean world, in contrast to what occurs in the modern Western
world, health and illness are not opposed to each other, rather they
complement each other in the nurturance of life. When we have cured
ourselves of a disease, our life becomes richer – becomes stronger out of
that lived experience. This is because, with the help of our community,
we have been capable of re-establishing within ourselves the harmony we
had lost, we have been capable of re-encountering harmony and now we
know how to nurture it better, both for our own benefit and for that of
our community.

But this is not all. It is not only an issue of re-encountering the
harmony that we already know well and that we like. Here, in the Andes,
we also know how to nurture in each case new harmonies that fit life
when conditions have changed drastically. We have experienced various
long-term drastic changes in climate and each time we have known how
to nurture, in the most extreme of conditions, the harmony that was
most suitable for our life so that it was not diminished. Andean peoples
have lived those experiences and with them we have learned that here
nothing is irreversible, that here nothing is fatal. Over the last ten thousand
years (Cardich 1958, 1974, 1975, 1980a, 1980b; Absy 1980; Thompson

1985; Guillet 1990), extreme periods of colder and drier weather occurred that lasted several centuries, in which the perpetual snow line was lowered to around five hundred metres below the present level. In those times, we have known how to let ourselves be nurtured by the existing conditions and the different Andean peoples have concentrated themselves in the middle and lower levels of altitude and have abandoned the highest altitudes. In order to facilitate this human concentration without damaging the occupied territory, we have known how to nurture the irrigated terraces and other forms of irrigation related to the snowmelt of the great snow-covered mountains of those times. We are referring to the Pan-Andean periods: Chavin, Tiawanaku and Tahuantinsuyo. And there have also been periods of heat and humidity in which we have known how to converse with all the great diversity of conditions of life which the verticality of the Andes offers us when the line of 'eternal' snows climbed five hundred metres. In response our Andean peoples have dispersed throughout the territory because that is what was appropriate in such circumstances of life. Thus has our Andean world lived rhythms of systoles and diastoles, of concentration and dispersion, of the Pan-Andean and of the Regional, because that was the heartbeat of our life which continued to flourish.

And that is how we were – here in the Andes, with our mode of being, with our experiential baggage – when five centuries ago there arose among us a terrible plague from whose impact we have not totally re-covered, although we are very near a complete cure.

The plague is a living being which appeared suddenly in our Andean world just as sometimes a strange plant will appear in our *chacras* – a plant we have not planted and do not know, that we do not like but that we cannot easily eliminate. In our living world, because the plague is a living being it has to live, it has to eat and one cannot kill it with impunity because if it is there it is because the *Apus* have wanted it. Otherwise it would not be there. We are dealing, certainly, with a very strange being in our world. Whereas all Andean beings try to contribute to the nurturance of the harmony of our world, with greater or lesser ability, the plague, in an obvious and impudent way, tries to disturb the Andean world, to disharmonize us. Its attitude challenges us and makes it evident that our capacity to harmonize ourselves is not sufficient, because if it were, the plague could not bother us. The plague makes us feel our weaknesses and this helps us because it motivates us to become stronger. The plague is a being who, if it does not deserve our love because of its behaviour, does deserve our respect because it makes us see our defects.

We Andeans have become directly aware of the disturbing capacity of the plague and have also realized that its appearance among us must be due to our carelessness and negligence in the nurturance of harmony, giving rise to the presence of this strange and aggressive being. But this realization has also led us to redouble our harmonizing efforts now so that the conditions that made the plague appear could not repeat themselves. Thus, though we could not kill this plague with impunity, it is not punishable to prevent its regeneration by changing the conditions that make its growth possible. It is completely correct that we nurture with care our harmony and that is precisely what prevents the regeneration of the plague. The plague makes our carelessness in the nurturing of harmony visible, and at the same time, it orients us towards a better and more vigorous nurturing of harmony which will bring us back to the plenitude of Andean life.

This plague erupted suddenly and in a very virulent way. First a series of illnesses appeared which gave rise to a very high mortality among us since they were totally unknown to us and we did not know how to deal with them – that is, first the 'pathological viruses' appeared among us. Only after some twenty years did we actually see the 'carriers' of such viruses, that is the boats and their crew members: a small group of mangy Europeans, horses, rats, flies, mosquitoes, lice, fleas, bedbugs – all of them unknown here until then (Patino 1972).

This plague, which without doubt we deserved, has certainly damaged our Andean world. All members of our *ayllu* – the *runas* (humans), the *sallqas* ('nature') and the *huacas* (those who protect life in the living world) – have suffered due to the mortality of humans, animals and plants; the plunder of our mineral wealth; and the alteration of many aspects of life such as the great spread of the Spanish language and the installation in our world of the state, the church, the market and an estate of intellectuals, professionals and functionaries. But all of this has not been able fundamentally to alter the harmony characteristic of the Andean world to the extreme of changing it, to the extreme of making it different from what it had always been. In the Andes we continue being what we have always been. The plague has not changed us. We live and feel the way we have always done from time immemorial. We are ill but we are not someone else. And we are constantly becoming less sick.

We continue living in our living animal world, we continue living in *ayllu* and in community, we continue nurturing and letting ourselves be nurtured; the Andean *chacra* continues to be as immeasurably diversified as it has always been, we continue celebrating our *huacas* in the agricultural and pastoral festivals, we continue to reciprocate because we continue wanting to give.

The plague has taken neither our world nor our convictions away from us; it has not changed our way of being. Even though we often speak in Spanish we continue to say the same things as always because our world and our way of being continue being the same. One becomes aware of this each time one records the words of Andean people, whether in the country or even in the city. In that sense the publications of the Peasant Encyclopedia Project directed by Alfredo Mires Ortiz in Cajamarca, Peru, are an excellent contribution, as are the theses of the graduates of the Course in Andean Peasant Agriculture that PRATEC offers (with the accreditation of the National University San Cristobal of Huamanga from 1990 to 1993 and of the National University of Cajamarca since 1994). As far as the intellectuals, professionals and functionaries that are now in the Andes are concerned, it is well known that when they need a career advancement, have some serious illness or some serious problem – that is, when the life of the official world oppresses them – they secretly have recourse to the 'sorcerers', which is what they call our wise Andeans. It is thus evident that, despite their lengthy school and university training and their long years of professional activity, at bottom they continue to be Andean because they have not changed their deepest convictions regardless of their apparent daily behaviour trying to imitate their foreign colleagues. Dr Victor Antonio Rodriguez Suy Suy has anthropologically documented this matter.

Well now, all that we have just referred to and we ourselves have lived and felt as the Andeans that we are, at the same time is appreciated and experienced in a different way by the modern Western world. This is natural because their world is totally different from ours, because its manner of being and feeling what is happening is radically at variance with ours. But theirs is only one way of perceiving, just as ours is a different way. Their claim that the ways of the West are the only valid ones is just a presumption.

They say that, armed with and following the mandate of their all-powerful creator God, they have spent five centuries pursuing what they call the expansion of the West to all the corners of the earth, covering in that adventure Asia, Africa, America and Oceania. They maintain that in quests of unequalled heroism, they discovered America, arrived in the Andes, and conquered and colonized us until we had been totally transformed. They say that we are no longer the Andeans that we were; they say they have converted us into citizens of the West and into Christians. They believe that they have accomplished successfully the task that Thomas Babington Macaulay, British governor of colonial India, considered to belong to education, namely to form 'types of persons that by their blood and colour of skin were Indian, but British in their taste, in their opinions, morality and intellect'. They cannot accept or even imagine that we continue to be as we always were because that would mean their admitting they had failed in their 'civilizing' and Christianizing mission with which their God entrusted them.

All these claims of the West do not concern us in the least. We have lived and continue to live here in the Andes in our own way; we have absorbed Christianity by assimilating Christ as a *huaca*, the Virgin, certain Saints, as well as the Church and even the priest. We have also assimilated the market by making of it one more arena for reciprocity – that is, to exercise the desire to give that is so typical of us – and for Andean interpersonal relations.

The modern Western world has its way of living and feeling; we have ours. For the Andean world there has been no discovery, no conquest, no colonization, no Westernization. We continue being the same as always. What has happened to us is an alteration in the harmony of our world due to our own carelessness; that is why we have become ill with the plague that we let emerge among ourselves. But we have been learning to heal ourselves and we are already very much better – on the eve of a total recuperation.

Healing ourselves of the plague

We Andeans have not run away from the plague. We have not segregated ourselves nor have we let ourselves be segregated from anything that has happened here in the Andes over the last five hundred years. We know about this plague in detail because we have lived through each one of its symptoms and, by knowing it, we have been learning to cure ourselves from it. Here in the Andes, to learn is to live. We have also not been in a hurry. Here in the living Andean world all is alive and it has its cycle of life, including the plague, which seems to have a life-cycle of five centuries' duration. This plague will not be able to regenerate itself among us because to do so it would require the same conditions of serious imbalance of harmony in the Andean world in which it was first generated. These conditions no longer exist because since the very moment that the plague appeared we have been healing ourselves, that is we have been nurturing the re-establishment of harmony in our world.

The appearance of this plague at the beginning of the sixteenth century has brought with it a high death rate, not only among humans but also in the fauna and flora, due to the virulence of the epidemics that were let loose among us. In human terms alone it has been calculated that the plague has killed at least nine out of ten people (Cook 1984), although there are those who maintain that in Mexico and Brazil only one person in twenty-five has survived (Ribeiro 1991). The plague brought then a human demographic collapse. Our wise ones have been painstakingly studying these epidemics and now know how to cure us from them. Our Andean world has absorbed or 'digested' them. Nevertheless, until 1945 we have been recuperating very slowly from that collapse in population. More recently the so-called 'demographic explosion' has allowed us rapidly to increase our population so that demographic levels are now comparable to those before the plague. (Seen in this light, the 'demographic explosion' has been useful in the nurturance of our harmony.) However, although human population is now as high here as in the early sixteenth century, what is new is the concentration of population in the cities – before we were very dispersed throughout the whole Andean territory. But I shall return to this subject later.

With the plague there also appeared here priests, churches, Christ, the Virgin, the Saints, and the very angry and excluding biblical God who orders: 'This is how you must deal with them [those who do not recognize Him as the unique true God]; you will destroy their altars and break their statues and cut down their groves and burn their images' (Deuteronomy 7: 5–6). And in truth the priests tried to execute perfectly the mandate of their God and to be the most pathogenic symptoms of the plague in order to terminate our world as soon as possible. As early as 1545 Hieronimo de Loayza, Bishop of Lima, ordered that the priests and catechists locate the *huacas*, destroy them and place crosses in their place (Vargas 1952: 140, cited by Van Den Berg 1989: 149). This priest confused our *huacas* with the Christian temples which are tiny and precarious sacred islands in the sea of profanity which is the modern Western world. Our *huacas* are the earth, the mountains, the rivers, the lakes, the sun, the moon, the stars, and so on; they are all those who at one time or another in each year facilitate life in the living Andean world; they are all those who contribute to the sustaining of life in the Andes. But if in one moment the *huaca* nurtures us, in another moment it needs to be nurtured by us. The *huacas* are like ourselves, they have the same incompleteness we have. Due to the way of being of our Andean world it happens that Christ, the Virgin, certain Saints, the local church itself and even the priests have become *huacas* in the Andes. Here they are not worshipped as divine beings, rather people converse with them and reciprocate with them as between equals, as with any other person in the Andean world. Here there is no Andean Christianism nor any syncretism. Here there is only an Andean world; Christianity has been assimilated into the Andean world, the Andean way. Pope John Paul II, faced with the evident failure of his institution over the past five centuries, is currently trying for a second evangelization in the Andes. It is already evident that it is a vain attempt.

The commons of Indians (the land assigned to the indigenous community) and the *hacienda* appeared here among us as further symptoms of the plague. The Viceroy of Toledo, who without doubt was a powerful force of the plague, established the reduction of Indians – that is, the concentration of various Andean *ayllus* on territory that previously was inhabited by only one of them. This was facilitated by the demographic collapse. Once relocated, the Andean *ayllus* were considered to be an Indian common or an indigenous community, and they were given a title of ownership and a plan of their territory. Thus, formally, at the margins of the indigenous Andean property vast territories were left that were adjudicated to be *hacienda* land, so that they could become the places where the plague could flourish unhindered. The *hacienda* was created to be the ultimate expression of the power of the plague in the Andes. But the Andean world, in spite of its sickness, has enough vitality to overcome the plague. The Andean world has lived in the colonial artefact of the indigenous community and it has also lived in the colonial creation that is the *hacienda*, despite its being formally foreign territory. In the *hacienda* all agricultural labour and the raising of animals was carried out by the Andean population. It is thus clear that the *hacienda* was totally dependent on the Andean people. Although the *hacendado* (owner of the *hacienda*) appropriated an important part of the production, production was achieved entirely by the Andeans and was carried out in an Andean way – even in the case of the imported plants and animals, which soon became part of the baggage of the indigenous communities. From the very first, we Andeans were beginning to regain *hacienda* territory for the Andeans, even though it was ostensibly *hacendado* land. The timeless Andean ceremonies continued to be celebrated inside the *haciendas*, often with the personal participation of the owners. Likewise the landscape of the *hacienda* remained very similar to that of the indigenous community. It is evident that the whole of Andean life has been lived inside the *haciendas*. For the last century and a half the *hacienda* has been in crisis. Due to the agrarian policy in force during that time coupled with the non-existent entrepreneurial capacity of the *hacendados*, a great many of the *haciendas* were economically broken, bankrupt. Their territories became once more the property of the Andeans, who either bought them out or took them over through direct action – basically, taking back what was theirs. They organized themselves into indigenous communities, whether they took this name officially or not. In this way the *hacienda* – this greatest expression of the power of the plague – was also digested by the Andean world. The government agrarian reforms of 1969 finished the liquidation of the *haciendas* in Peru; however, they did not return the land to the peasants; instead they imposed trials of foreign models such as the cooperatives and the SAIS (Agricultural Societies of Social Interest). It is interesting to note that the studies that were done motivated by the agrarian reform showed that even in the *haciendas* of the Cattle Division of the mining enterprise Cerro de Pasco Copper Corporation, which were the most capitalized and technologized in the country, 20 per cent of the cattle that lived on them were the property of the shepherds that worked there (Martinez Alier 1973). Not even these *haciendas* were able to escape the strong presence of the Andean culture within their boundaries. Only twenty years after the agrarian reforms the crisis and disappearance of the cooperatives and the SAIS were witnessed; in their place, however, indigenous communities continue to be formed. These indigenous communities are shaking off their origins as a symptom of the plague in order to reinstall the authentically Andean *ayllus* which were once reduced to 'state-created' indigenous communities. In this way the population is dispersing itself and the conversation with the *Pacha* is facilitated in each locality. Here in the Andes we have digested the *hacienda* and we are in the process of digesting the indigenous community and re-establishing the original *ayllus*.

Finally, I shall discuss that other symptom of the plague: the cities in the Andes. As we have already shown, the human population in the Andes before the plague was similar in size to that of today but it was dispersed throughout the Andean territory. As dispersed groups we conversed very well with the great diversity that our *Pachas* present us with. But the plague had as one of its symptoms the appearance of some cancerous tumours called cities where the population was piled up and where the plague concentrated its most virulent pathogenic germs, with the intent of making the system's control more efficient and thus its impact more drastic. However, over the last fifty years, concurrently with the 'demographic explosion', the cities in the Andes have also seen an enormous growth due to the influx of a great number of people of Andean culture – Andeans who have made themselves present in order directly to experience what was happening there. We Andeans do not marginalize ourselves nor do we let ourselves be marginalized by anything happening in our territory. In the same way as we dealt with the *haciendas*, we Andeans are now appropriating the city; and as happened with the *haciendas*, we are not preserving but digesting it. We do not come to the city in order to live there according to the norms of the city – as individualists and so-called 'universal' citizens, neither do we come to subjugate ourselves to an order already established; rather we come to the city to live according to our own perennial communitarian customs. If in those moments and with a transitory character, the dance of Andean life goes through the city, it is because we know that we have to know the city well, as we do all symptoms of the plague that affect us. We know that only thus will we cure ourselves fully of the city; only thus will we come nearer to the complete re-establishment of our own Andean harmony. The conviction that led us to saturate the city with 'andinicity' is that in the living Andean world all that is opposed to life is reversible. In the Andes we will deactivate the city just as we have deactivated the *hacienda* and the other symptoms of the plague – and thus we will affirm Andean culture here in the Andes.

Development: senile symptom of the plague

Here in the Andes we feel that development is a symptom of the senile dementia – which presented itself forty years ago – of the plague that has infected us for five hundred years and that now finds itself in the last stages of its vital cycle. It is a matter of an acute alienation since the plague in its ravings is led to affirm that we must stop being what we are, that we must develop, that is that we must change, that we must exert ourselves to become as similar as possible to the United States of North America which sees itself as the model of a developed country. In this demented game, from the start it was assumed that we are underdeveloped and that is why, when we are compared with the model, each difference encountered is automatically classified as a lack in us. Because we are different, because we are ourselves, we are classified as underdeveloped. In this madness which is development, it is forbidden to be different. The plague says that we live in 'one world' which each day is more integrated by the market and by telecommunications – a 'universal' world in which there is only one correct order possible that fully corresponds with economic globalization. That unique order is precisely the order character-istic of the postulated Western model. In its insanity the plague also says that development is a quality inherent in each people and that all peoples have been endowed with identical capacities for development. So, if we have been 'left behind', if we are seen as lacking, it is exclusively because we have not known how to overcome the obstacles and the restrictions that have presented themselves in our path – because we have not known how to administer and take full advantage of our capacities for develop-ment. Due to this situation, so the story goes, it is evident that we require science, technology and the experts of the developed countries. But to have access to them we must submit ourselves to the advice and accompanying rigours of the International Monetary Fund, the World Bank, the Inter-American Bank for Development, and the United Nations. Only then would we be in a condition to solicit 'international help for development', which supposedly would help us approximate the model.

We are indubitably dealing with a form of madness. Over the last forty years, in the name of development, there has been a frenzy of construction activity in the Andes and, in the process, the country has contracted an enormous external debt. The result of all this expensive 'development' work has been what Palao and Garaycochea (1989) have accurately called the 'archaeology of development': that is an accumulation of ruined vestiges that the infrastructures built by development planners rapidly become because they are totally alien to the Andean way and Andeans have no use for them. Not surprisingly, 'development' structures are left to the mercies of the weather, which destroys them quickly and reduces them to the 'garbage of development' which dirties the Andean landscape.

But this senile madness of the plague has only been able to infect in the Andes the brothers of the plague, those who accompanied it here: the state, the church, the market, and the estate of the intellectuals, pro-fessionals and functionaries. It is in them that development has been embodied – and they are an insignificant minority. But the Andean people do not accept development; they reject this foolish game. They treat these 'brothers of the plague' with pity and with tolerance, as one would a mad man, but they do not accept their development game which does not respect Andean customs. For example, in the name of development irrigation canals are built without asking permission either from *Pachamama* or from the *Apus*, without asking the lands that will supposedly be irrigated if they want to be irrigated, without asking the river if it wants its waters to irrigate those lands, and without asking the places that the canal will traverse whether they give their permission. Of course, in such a case it fails. If we ask the peasants about these canals, they answer that those canals are not theirs – they belong to that engineer or to that NGO or to that project – and they are not disposed to accept them. That is why the weather destroys them: because they are not cradled in the protection of the Andean people. In spite of all this, next to these expensive new canals of development, we find Andean canals thousands of years old in full use because they have been nurtured according to Andean customs, and because they are protected and ceremonial offerings are made to them with love and respect by the Andean community.

Here in the Andes, we appreciate the value of diversity. We know that there are as many different worlds, forms of life, as there are cultures. We do not accept that any culture propose itself as the paradigm. Each people knows how to nurture the harmony that suits its *Pacha* and these harmonies, corresponding to their particular locality, in turn harmonize themselves in harmonies salutary to the earth. The diversity of the harmonies proper to the different brother people enrich *Pachamama*. Homogeneity brings with it weakness and fragility. That is why we do not accept the senile madness of the plague that is development, a development proposed as a solution for the Andes.

Andean cultural affirmation

We call Andean cultural affirmation the nurturance of the harmony that is most suited to the plenitude of the living world that we are. All of us who are the living Andean world live according to the nurturance of harmony. But, due to a carelessness in this nurturance a terrible plague appeared among us five centuries ago. We know that this plague is immanent to us and that we deserve it but we have not accepted it for all that. Immediately we began to cure ourselves of it and soon we will have regained our health completely. And we are not disposed to allow such a monstrosity to repeat itself. Andean cultural affirmation is our way of re-harmonizing ourselves with the plenitude of Andean life; it is our manner of curing ourselves of the plague which has damaged the vitality of our living world.

We are close to our complete recovery because at no point has our love for the plenitude of the form of Andean life lessened; we have never vacillated in our conviction of Andean cultural affirmation, be it in the indigenous community, the *hacienda*, the tunnels of the mines or even in the city. The *runas*, we have never ceased our ceremonies of offerings to the *huacas*. Never have we failed in our love and respect to the *sallqa*. The destruction that one observes has been done exclusively by the plague.

We Andeans have lived each one of the symptoms of the plague in our living world. That is how we have learned its manner of being, its character, its intentions, its behaviour. The plague cannot fool us. We have never confused what befits the nurturance of harmony in the Andean world with the requirements of the plague, however their appearance may have been masked. That is why we have made the *hacienda* disappear; because of that we have 'andinized' the city as a first step to the return of its population to the country where *Pachamama* awaits them tenderly to give them its protection, to facilitate the re-encounter with the delightful regeneration of life which is typical of the countryside. It is because the plague does not fool us that the 'archaeology of development' has occurred in the Andes. What the plague builds without respecting the *huacas* and in its attempts to confuse us, we, the *runas*, do not accept – and the weather of the *sallqa* destroys it.

Once we have recovered and eradicated the plague, Andean cultural affirmation – in nurturing the harmony that is most congenial to our living world – will remain a health cure allowing us to maintain our wholeness. Then our climate, being as diverse as it is now, will nevertheless be even more harmonious. The droughts, the floods, the erosion of soils and of germplasm will drastically diminish. The *sallqas*, in re-establishing themselves, will regain their role in the harmonization of the Andean world. The *huacas* will augment their facilitation of the life of the *sallqas* and of the *runas*. We, the *runas*, will once more harmonize ourselves with those of the *sallqas* and with the *huacas*, acting with the love and respect characteristic of nurturance.

Let it be clear that although we do not want that the plague repeat itself, that is not a reason to consider it a fatality or a curse. We well know that the plague has, in some senses, been helpful to the living Andean world because it made clear to us our grave carelessness in the nurturance of harmony. It gives us the opportunity, through curing ourselves of it, to learn how to nurture harmony better than we did before. This will make our living world healthier and more vital.

Andean cultural affirmation is the attitude of vitality characteristic of those of us who are the living Andean world (*huacas, sallqas, runas*). In continuous and animated conversation, charismatically led in each moment and in turn by those among us who have the best aptitude for it, we come to an agreement, with the participation of all and of each, in the nurturance of the harmony that is most congenial to the world that we are, according to the circumstances that each moment requires of us.

The living Andean world is a world giving of itself, an unquenchable source of living beings continuously being generated, in which everything renews itself continuously. Here nothing remains static. This is why a theory of the world or a methodology do not belong here. Here the only thing that belongs is an open and continuous conversation, with the active participation of all those of us who are the Andean world, so that no circumstance goes unnoticed by us and we are able to nurture the harmony most congenial for everyone without hurting anyone.

From time immemorial and for always, this mode of life of the Andean world endures, always being renewed, without arthritic stiffening.

Andean cultural affirmation is neither a theoretical position nor a principled position, rather it is a daily living of the Andean people. Therefore here there is no room for fundamentalism or essentialism. We are the world of love and nurturance, of exuberance, of voluptuousness, of exultation. There is here no manner of substratum that would sustain any intellectualism or dogmatism. This is no context for moralism or puritanism. Here the one truth cannot live.

Andean cultural affirmation is not a political position. Our living world of nurturance is ignorant of power or of struggles for power. Here authority is charismatic and transitory; it emerges spontaneously to facilitate the flow of life, to help harmonize our world. Here we love the world as it is. We cannot even imagine having the presumption to impose a 'must be'. In our Andean world, utopias do not belong.

Andean cultural affirmation is not a position of violence. Nurturance knows nothing of confrontations, only of caresses, of murmurs and of conversations. This is not a land of voluntarism but of revelations. Here there is no desire to homogenize behaviour, appearance, opinions, emotions, passions. Here we are all equivalent persons and indispensable in the nurturance of harmony. We know that the harmony of the world is not given and that it is precisely the revelation of diversity – the exaltation of the distinct sensibilities – that facilitates for us the best conversation with the richness of circumstances, that facilitates for us the nurturance of the harmony most befitting the living Andean world.

Here in the Andes, as we always have, we live in an Andean manner. Never, during the whole time that we lived together with the plague, have we confused the harmony that is characteristic of us with the requirements of the plague. As has been said, with the plague there appeared among us strange beings whom we call 'brothers of the plague' who do not repulse us but with whom we do not confuse ourselves; rather we consider them different from ourselves. However, we are capable of involving ourselves in their activities so that nothing that happens in the Andes remains foreign to us. That is what happened in the *hacienda*, in the mine, in the city, and so on. But we have never identified with those strange beings or with their activities. When we involve ourselves we know that we are 'in their business'. This had never happened before in the Andes and it will end when we will have completely recovered from the plague. Cultural affirmation in the Andes includes the digestion of 'them' and of 'theirs' by the Andean. Playing, we learn 'their business'; their activities are simply toys which attract some of us.

Here in the Andes, we do not learn formally, seriously. We do not learn with instruction manuals or submit to didactic methods. Here we do everything our way. We learn to play the guitar familiarizing ourselves with the sounds of its chords and 'taking out' little by little the songs that we like. We learn chess by watching it being played until we know each piece's move, and then we just play. We do not take guitar lessons or buy chess manuals – we go directly to the toy we like and play with it.

In a similar way we Andeans make ourselves into engineers, physicians, mathematicians, businessmen, machinists, mechanics, electricians or cobblers; we go to the toy and we play. Sometimes the toy includes the university. That is how we make our professional careers. But we do not take them terribly seriously. For us, to learn 'their thing' is a matter of assuming a certain behaviour, it is simply a process – a requirement of the game. This does not engage in the least our form of life; we do not incorporate ourselves into the world of the toys with which we play. We do not accept that world, but we do know it. Our professional career is one more game in our life. We do not take on board the basic assumption that underlies our professions, that is that the world is a machine. For us, as Andeans that we are, the world is a living and life-giving animal. Even the toys with which we play are alive for us. What appears in the Andes with the plague and its brothers we contextualize in terms of our Andean vision of the world. In this way we are digesting the plague – a mode of Andean cultural affirmation.

But one should not confuse this mode of ours of taking 'their things' as a game with the notion that we are incapable or mediocre in those contexts. Nothing could be further from the truth. We know where the game is, we know how to play and we do play – very well. It is precisely in this that our ability to digest the plague and its brothers lies. Let us look at some examples.

I was walking and conversing with some peasants of mature years in the valley of Mantaro, the most commercial in the Peruvian Andes, and they were showing me the *chacras* they were cultivating 'for their families' and those they cultivated 'for the market'. I asked them why they made this distinction and they told me that the 'potato for the market' injured health and they mentioned to me in detail the names and the symptoms of some of the peasants who had been affected. That is why they cultivated separately a *chacra* in the Andean way, with native varieties of potatoes without chemical fertilizers and pesticides for family consumption and reciprocity with friends. In contrast, for the market they cultivated potatoes according to the instructions of the extension agent: improved varieties that the extension agent gave them and the technological package that the extension agent indicated to them, including pesticides and chemical fertilizers. When I asked them why they cultivated like that for the market since they knew that it was damaging, they answered: 'because that is what the market asks for'. So they produce precisely what the extension agent, promoter of production for the market, asks for and what the consuming public buys. The peasants enter to play in the market according to the rules of the market. And they are very clear that they are dealing with something that is very different from the Andean way of life.

In the summer of 1961, when I was doing my pre-professional practice in the *hacienda* Cartavio, I had an experience very relevant to the issue of the relationship of the Andean peasant with the handling of complex machinery. The enterprise had decided very recently to change its system of transport of sugar cane from the country to the factory, moving from rail to road transportation. For that purpose they built the necessary tarred roads and bought a flotilla of trucks with complex '12 speed' handling. A previous decision of the enterprise prevented them from hiring new workers which meant that in order to get the necessary drivers they had to ask for trainee drivers from among their current workers. The super-intendent in those days, Ingeniero Carlos Pinella, told me a year later that those who came forward to fill the new jobs were the peons of the countryside who had never driven a machine before and were mostly unlettered – the wages were not attractive enough for any other groups. With the flotilla of trucks they had bought came an instructor to train the drivers. Normally, the time of instruction was six months but the contract provided for an extended period of another six months. However, within three months all the candidates had learned perfectly how to drive such complex trucks and the instructor left Cartavio. This is evidence of the ability of the Andeans to deal with difficult machinery; they simply familiarized themselves with the commands, with the instructions, with the motor and with the truck, establishing a flowing conversation.

Similarly, in Peru the ability of Andean mechanics to perform well-nigh impossible repairs on motors and transmissions is well known. For us, engines are living beings with whom one establishes a friendly and cordial conversation. That is why between them – the mechanic and the engine – they achieve adjustments not foreseen in the repair manuals of cars. It is thus clear that here in the Andes we do not need the so-called prerequisites of formal education in order to manage with ease in the market, in the handling of complex machinery or in mechanics; rather, in our way, we deal directly with the situation at hand and find a way to converse with it.

Andean cultural affirmation is the eagerness that we display day by day, all those here in the Andes who live contented, nurturing our harmony which is inseparable from our exuberant diversity. That is how we recuperate daily the plenitude of our Andean vigour. This is neither an intellectual nor a dogmatic attitude; it is a matter neither of politics nor of violence. Andean cultural affirmation is the vital attitude of our living world.

Andean cultural affirmation is not separating or letting oneself be separated from the plague; quite the contrary, it is to experience each one of its symptoms in order to know it in detail and thus learn to recover from it. Nothing that happens in the Andes is foreign to us. Because of this we have even learned the activities of the brothers of the plague, not to accept them but to know them and thus to digest them in our Andean way – as we have digested the *hacienda*, Christianity and diseases, and are now digesting the city.

Notes

1. This is Eduardo Grillo's last essay, written and revised in the months before his death.
2. The Spanish '*lo andino*' does not translate accurately as 'the Andean'; there is no corresponding English term. I will henceforth use the Spanish '*lo andino*'.

References

Absy, Maria Lucia. 1980; 'Dados sobre as Mudanças do clima e vegetaçao de Amazonia durante o Quaternario' (Data about the changes in climate in the Amazon during the Quaternary), *Acta Amazonica*, 10 (4): 920–30.

Cardich, Augusto. 1958; 'Los yacimientos de Lauricocha: Nuevas interpretaciones de la prehistoria Peruana' (The remains of Lauricocha: New interpretations of the Peruvian prehistory), *Acta Prehistorica*, Vol. 2, Buenos Aires.

Cardich, Augusto. 1974; 'Los yacimientos de la etapa agricola de Lauricocha, Peru y los limites superiores del cultivo' (The remains of the agricultural stage of Lauricocha, Peru and the upper limits for cultivation), *Relaciones, Sociedad Argentina de Antropologia*, Vol. 7, Buenos Aires.

Cardich, Augusto. 1975; 'Agricultores y pastores en Lauricocha y limites superiores del cultivo' (Agriculturalists and pastoralists in Lauricocha and the upper limits for cultivation), *Revista del Museo Nacional*, Vol. 41, Lima.

Cardich, Augusto. 1980a; 'Origen del hombre y cultura andinos' (Origins of man and Andean culture) *Historia del Peru*, Vol. 1. Lima; Juan Mejia Baca.

Cardich, Augusto. 1980b; 'El fenomeno de las fluctuaciones de los limites superiores del cultivo en los Andes: su importancia' (The phenomenon of the fluctuation of the upper limits of cultivation in the Andes: its importance), *Relaciones, Sociedad Argentina de Antropologia*, Vol. 19, Buenos Aires.

Cook, N. D. 1984; *Demographic Collapse: Indian Peru*, Cambridge; Cambridge University Press.

Guillet, David. 1990; *Andenes y riego en Lauri: Valle del Colca* (*Terraces and irrigation in Lauri: The valley of Colca*), Arequipa, Peru; CAPRODA, Centro de Apoyo y Promocion al Desarrollo Agrario.

Kusch, Rodolfo. 1962; *America Profunda (Deep America)*, Buenos Aires; Editorial Hachette.

Martinez Alier, Juan. 1973; *Los Huacchilleros del Peru*, Ruedo Iberico; Instituto de Estudios Peruanos.

Palao, Juan and Ignacio Garaycochea. 1989; 'Proyecto de desarrollo rural en Puno: Un avance descriptivo y apreciaciones 1950–1985' (Rural development project in Puno: a descriptive and evaluative advance 1950–1985). In Alberto Giesecke (ed.) *Burocracia, Dermocratizacion y Sociedad (Bureaucracy, Democratization and Society)*, Lima; Fomciencias Centro: 175–202.

Patino, Victor Manuel. 1972; *Factores inhibitores de la produccion agropecuaria (Inhibiting factors of agro-pastoralist production)* Vol. 1, Factores Fisicos y Biologicos. Cali, Colombia; Imprenta Departamental.

Ribeiro, Darcy. 1991; 'Los Indios y el Estado Nacional' (The Indians and the National State). In Instituto Nacional Indigenista (ed.) *Seminario Internacional: Amerindia hacia el Tercer Milenio* (International Seminar: Amerindia towards the third millennium), Mexico; Instituto Nacional Indigenista: 69–82.

Thompson, Lonnie. 1985; 'A 1500 year record of tropical precipitation in ice cores from the Quelcaya ice cap, Peru', *Science*, 299: 971–3.

Van Den Berg, Hans. 1989; *'La Tierra no da asi nomas': Los ritos agricolas en la region de los aymara-cristianos de los Andes* ('The earth does not give just like that': the agricultural rituals in the region of the Christian-Aymaras of the Andes) Amsterdam, The Netherlands; Center for Latin-American Research & Documentation.

Vargas Ugarte, R. 1952; *Concillos Limensis (1551–1772)*, Vol. II; Lima: 139–48.

CHAPTER 5

The Aymara Couple in the Community

Greta Jimenez Sardon

Foreword

This chapter is an attempt to show the affective world of the Aymara couple through the spontaneous accounts of many women who conversed with me.

I am interested in offering an inside account of the intensely ritual life of the Aymara women and men. For my purpose I did not find a better way than presenting directly the liveliness of their conversation, so tender and sincere – the open gate to the wisdom of an ancient culture which maintains its wholeness in spite of five hundred years of colonization.

In these conversations it can be perceived that in the Aymara world families include the animals and plants that are nurtured, as much as the plains and the slopes, the mountains and rivers, the lakes and lagoons, the birds and clouds, *Pachamama* (Mother Earth), the *Apus* (mountain deities), the ancestors, Mamita del Carmen (Little Mother del Carmen) and the Saints, in such a way that there is no distinction, classificatory or hierarchical, between man and woman, humans and nature, the deities, nature and man. Love and respect among these forms of relations and life of the Andean world constitute its intense rituality.

I am satisfied with having motivated these accounts of some Aymara women who narrate the life cycle rituals of their culture in the daily nurturing of the *chacra*, in the falling in love of the couple, in the gestation and birth of their children, in marriage and in the chastening of the violence against life. With feeling and spontaneity they tell us that they are not individual deeds but collective experiences in which all beings of the Andean world dutifully participate in nurturing life.

I have been able to have these conversations because during my whole life, I have cultivated the friendship of peasant families, especially of the Aymara women of the countryside who are the ones who preserve tradition in its most beautiful forms. Only in this way has it been possible for such beautiful conversations to unfold.

To deal with such intimate subjects, the Aymara women prefer to speak in their own language though they also speak an Aymarized Spanish which I have used to render conversations which were originally recorded on tape. My familiarity with these friends allows me to know how they would say in Spanish what they told me in Aymara.

I must declare that to share this part of my work with you, I had to exercise much patience and care. It was difficult to obtain the authorization of the peasant women in order 'to narrate to other people'. They had to approve the translation (into Spanish) and consult, by means of coca leaves, all the families: the *Pachamama*, the *Apus*, Little Mother del Rosario, Mama Q'ota (Lake Titicaca), the Saints, the ancestors, the deceased, and so on. In their communities, '*loj'tañas*' (offerings) were made so that their words could be 'received with a good heart' and that those who receive them could 'think with their hearts'.

This is an initial effort in my aim to achieve and pass on a better understanding of the Andean world. To these efforts I continue to be devoted.

My sincere thanks to the peasants and their relatives, particularly Juana Nina, Sonia Ortís Callomamani, Rosa Poma Quispe, Teresa Calderón, Evangelina Gómez, Luisa Turpo Mamani, Tomasa Charaja and Maria Aruwata Apaza. All of them have helped me in my immersion in the Aymara world, accompanying me during the last three years.

At the same time, I give thanks to the five hundred Aymara women who with their testimonies have nurtured me in my work of more than twenty-five years in the different peasant communities of the Peru-Bolivia high plateau and in the inter-Andean valleys of Moquegua and Tacna.

They have answered questions that were certainly impertinent, they accepted deductions and conceptualizations that were at times hasty, at times incoherent with the conception of a world completely different from mine. Little by little I learned to familiarize myself with subjects that go far beyond recording the needs, problems and hopes of daily life, as is usually done in most public and private institutions. To these peasant women who made possible the nurturance of friendship and the sharing of their marvellous Andean vision, I offer my gratitude and admiration.

I wish to thank Grimaldo Rengifo, Eduardo Grillo, Enrique Moya, Julio Valladolid, and my friends at PRATEC for their patience in listening and for their unfailing encouragement.

Finally, I thank the Consejo Andino de Manejo Ecológico (CAME) (the Andean Council for Ecological Management) for shelter within its institutional framework.

The couple is raised by all the families ... and is also chastised by them

I had twenty-five little pieces of cheese and now only three remain. I sell to my *caseros* [favoured clients] in Ilo [a booming town in southern Peru], they are honest people, they are *rescatistas* [resellers/retailers]; they then resell the little cheeses among the miners in Cuajone [mines in the department of Tacna in southern Peru]. Every fifteen days I come down from Carumas [a town in an inter-Andean valley in the department of Moquegua], I visit some relatives in Moquegua [a department of Peru neighbouring Tacna]. Sometimes I stay overnight and then, as I am doing now, I come directly to Ilo.

We, Carumas women, like to dress prettily; we like flowers very much, so we decorate our hats with flowers of all colours. Flowers are our companions; we also decorate our blouses with thin coloured ribbons. Other blouses we like to embroider with multi-coloured yarn: we sew flowers, little birds, seeds, stars, rainbows, rain, clouds. All this is embroidered on the blouse's front, on the cuffs and, according to taste, all over the sleeve too. Other blouses are also made with coloured cloth with flowers. Over the blouse we put on a kind of jacket.

We like strong colours that can be seen from afar; thus the skirts that we use have colours according to the season. I like the yellow colour of the flowers of the broom [*retama*]; the green of the leaves of the shrubs of fava beans, the colour of the '*ayrampu*' [*Opuntia haenquiamus*. The fruits are deep red and have medicinal properties], the red of the geranium. The skirts are also decorated with ribbons and embroideries; we wear three to five long skirts.

We fasten our skirts with a waistband woven with sheep's wool dyed in many colours, embroidered with diverse motifs, like stars, people, birds, flowers, llamas, and so on.

In times of feasts it's very nice to look at the women, because they then wear the clothes they'll use for working during the whole coming year.

I am from the community of Parina in the district of Chucuito [peasant community located in the Chucuito peninsula in the department of Puno]. When I was ten I came accompanying my aunt Eugenia, so that I could help her in caring for her house, her *chacras*, and her little herd.

My aunt Eugenia is my father's younger sister; she came by way of Moquegua and stayed. Sometime later, she met a Carumas man and formed a family. My uncle's name is Quintin; he's already an old man, full of perseverance, ingenious and honest. They raised me as their eldest daughter; they have treated me as such with their inheritance. They have not left me out.

With them I learned to care for the household, to cook, to wash clothes; to breed the cows, to milk them, to make cheese, to heal them when they fall sick, to take them for a walk, to give them water and food in their time. Every cow is different, like ourselves: some are quiet, obedient, affectionate; others are *cariches* [pampered], conceited, annoying – they get stubborn even suckling their brood, and they make milking difficult. One has to beg them.

My uncle says that they are like '*wawas*' [little children in Quechua], that you have to nurse them with a lot of affection and care; that way their number increases, they give good broods, have milk, do not get sick, do not fall down and break their legs and fatten prettily when their time comes to be sold. In August the family gathers to make the '*misa dulce*' [sweet mass: offering to the *Pachamama*[1]], to take care of the *Pachamama*, to ask for protection to the *Qullu achachila* [mountain deity]. To them they also commend each little cow, each little sheep, and also give thanks for them.

In the months of February or March, in the time of carnivals, when branding and the 'wedding of the cows' take place, there is a nice feast. The wedding pair is feasted, adorned with paper streamers, they are given *chicha* [slightly fermented corn beverage] of maize with blessed water brought from the chapel. The *tata yatiri* [he is the master, like the priest who conducts the ceremony] while ringing the little bell, walks around the couple, caressing them, conversing and recommending with these words:

Nicely you will live.
Your children nicely you will bear.
Very carefully you must walk by the *bofedales* [moist places], by the hills.
Nicely, well, you will protect and care for the people who are taking care of you.

This celebration must be done with much affection and much care must be taken because the land, the water, plants, the pastures, the rains, the winds, the prickly pear fields, the flowers, the men and women must enter into an agreement lasting the whole year. Everyone asks and gives out the responsibilities and must keep them well – and in no month, in no day or night must they forget them.

If there is neglect on the part of any of the families, something bad happens to them. Sometimes a person gets sick or gets angry; for instance the wind gets angry. Without the help of the wind the mosquitoes which are lodged in the leaves of the plants remain and begin to multiply so much that they gather as a cloud. To prevent this, the wind with its strength must carry them to other places so that they will not annoy any of us and thus we all remain in peace.

---

1. Mother Earth: an act of reciprocity made with a set of vegetal, animal, mineral, food elements. There are different classes: *alta misa, chiwchi misa, ch'iara misa, insinshu misa, janq'u misa, K'uti misa, llampu misa, muj'sa misa*, presented according to the circumstances and intent.

The Carumas valley [inter-Andean valley located in the department of Moquegua, with deep gorges, high and rugged mountains between 2,300 and 3,400 metres above sea level, presenting a diversity of ecological floors and climates] is beautiful; there is a big river also called Carumas, and it has other streams, little brothers, which come down from very high up, passing from *patapatas* to *patapatas* [terraces]; laughing happily they walk; they hide within the bushes, and look so clean and bright, that seen falling from afar they look like mirrors which reflect silver sparks. The streams play, hide themselves within the big roots of the eucalyptuses and *molles* [*Schimus molle L.*]; flirt with the *lluqui y chujo* [*Kageneckia lanceolata R.et.P.* The bark is used for dyeing; the wood is good for the fabrication of diverse domestic utensils], with the sweet grass, the *chilliwua* [*Festuca dolichophilla Presl.*], the *yareta* [*Azorella yarita.*]; water springs [*ojos de agua*: underground springs] surge close to the land that is well kept. It is born among the rocks, the stones and, around it, the *uq'ururu* [watercress: Nasturtium fontanun. It grows in the borders of the springs and is used to cure liver diseases], the *layos* [*Lupinus ananeanus Ulb*], the pastures grow bright green.

When at night one goes for a walk or sits by the groves, among the trees, or on a rock, one hears the conversation of all the brothers and sisters who like walking at night; the toads and frogs on one side sing competing with each other, the trees talk with the wind moving their branches and leaves, the birds send their messages to the *j'aquis* [human beings] who sleep. Far away you also hear a *pinquillo* [a wind instrument made from a reed with four to seven holes] or a bugle rehearsing for the next feast.

In Carumas, if one walks from the *pampa* to the heights, one finds little parrots, *chinchillas* [*Chinchilla brevicaudata*], eagles, sheep, donkeys, cows, foxes, alpacas, llamas, skunks, *vizcachas* [*Lagidium peruanum*], pigs, guinea pigs. Thus there is also '*quiswar*' [*Buddleia longifolia*: used as fuel, its flowering is a biological indicator], *chilliwua* [*Festuca dolichophilla Presl.*], *kiñua* [*Polylepis incana HBK*], *jichu* [*Stipa ichu*]. You also find a whole variety of potatoes, maize, apples, broad beans, barley, pears, wheat, quince, a lot of prickly pears – white, purple and yellow; there is alfalfa for the little cattle too.

In my first engagement, my husband's parents gave him some *chacras* [plots of land located in the road to the community of Utalaque] in Collapunco; they said it was a place where sowing always gave good crops. But during the time we lived together, that is, five years more or less, things always went wrong for us, something bad always happened.

One year some worms appeared which rapidly destroyed the large beans; we could not contain the plague. Another year we sowed wheat; from its roots there came that black powder [*ustiago hordei.*], which pitilessly took the plants, from the roots to the ears. That disease rapidly walked from one plant to the next.

At another time the yellow powder appeared, *roya* [*puccinia pers.*] it is called by the technicians; it also completely wasted the little plants. We had a little money and with it my husband bought a remedy in Moquegua's agroveterinary shop. We spent the money in vain because it did not help a bit; in the end the *chacras* wasted.

In a '*patapata*' [terrace] we sowed barley, in another, oat, wheat, large beans, little potatoes, maize; every year we changed the crops, but, as I am telling you, disgrace was our companion. It even seemed that the cattle were enraged against us because they never passed by the neighbouring *chacras*. It was in ours that they walked and stepped with fury, they seemed to jump on the little potatoes, on the barleys or the large beans.

Their owners apologized to us, they would take care that their cattle did not trespass, they did not want to enter in litigation with us. However, their animals, with no prevention, without care, clumsily damaged the *chacras*.

In the depth of my heart I thought, why did we have so much misfortune? In the almost ten years that I lived with my uncle and aunt, I had never seen the *chacras* suffer so much. Our neighbours' *chacras* did not have such bad luck either. Could it be that it was because Francisco's parents gave them to us with such an ill will? They strongly opposed our living together ... So I thought in my heart.

On the other hand I suffered very much with that man; he was lazy, careless, irritable. Every time he went to the town, he drank, quarrelled with his friends, was thrown out from the shop. He would return home, with difficulty, and when he saw, it seemed that his eyeballs would come out; he would shout, kick whatever was in his way, threaten to hit me, throw the saucers, the jars. ... Sometimes he would hit me, kick me; he seemed to go out of his mind.

I did not know what to do, I would entreat him crying so that he would calm down, would offer him food, a little tea ... he would accept nothing. Some other times, when his rage was unbounded, I could not do anything else other than take my little boy in my arms and escape from the house; I would hide behind some prickly pear bushes or in the corner of a '*patapata*' where the grove was thicker. So there we would wait until dawn; my son cried, scared, and my grief was as deep as a bottomless pit of impure water.

During that period of my life it was as if I found myself in a dark, gloomy night. I felt lost, without finding a star that would help me emerge, without having the first clarity of the sun rays at dawn.

My neighbours had realized that we had a disgraceful life; they would look at me with pity and at Francisco with contempt. Even my relatives who lived nearby looked at our union with disapproval; they said that they reproached and scolded Francisco. They said nothing to me.

As we had gone to live together without the families' consent, we could not converse with them, I could not tell them of my sadness, I could complain to no one ...

When I met Francisco, I was 19, a sprightly young girl, I loved singing, I sang with my little siblings who are my aunt Eugenia's children.

I did the household chores singing. Singing I took care of the plants, of the little cattle; my word was singing. ... Now, after these years, when I go back to the time that I lived with Francisco, I realize that in that time I forgot singing.

My mouth, my heart closed, and, for my sorrows not to be heard, I learned to walk in silence. After years, when my son was born in my second engagement, a song again lives inside me.

I met Francisco in the city of Moquegua. By then, my uncle and aunt used to entrust to me the pieces of cheese which we made during the week to sell in the market or leave in our households.

When I was in the city of Moquegua, almost always I had lunch in the food stand of Mamita [Little mother] Estela. In the stand next to it, Francisco worked; he washed and passed the dishes to the customers and also cleaned the table, arranged the chairs.

Thus, little by little we got to talk. Since he was cheerful, playful, funny, he entertained me. When he finished his work, almost when the night fell, we sat to talk in the square. ... As I started to linger and to arrive late at the house of the uncle and aunt where I was staying, they realized that something was happening with me. They scolded me, became angry, said that they would talk with my parents; but I thought that it was empty threats. Thus almost a year passed; by then I already had relations with that young man.

His parents also live in one of the ravines of the Carumas valley; they were Aymara. One of his grandparents had been born in the community of Titilaca [near Acora by the Titicaca Lake], and the other in Pallalla [a community near Acora]; they say that it also belongs to the district of Acora in the province of Puno.

Another of his ancestors who first arrived in the valley of Carumas, was also from Laraqueri [a district in the province of Puno]. They were related with the Callas families.

Francisco is the fourth of the six children of the Quispe Mamani family; he is three years older than me. He studied up to the second year in secondary school; he then started working in different trades. Most of his time he had spent in Moquegua and Tacna, and visited his parents once a year in the time of carnival or in the patron saint's feast.

When my uncle and aunt found out that I was conversing with that young man, they worried a lot; they asked why I had not trusted them from the beginning, why I had not asked for consultation with the families. They advised me that I had to walk with care, straight ahead.

After some time, they said that this man was not suitable for me, that it was best to leave him, to forget all; that I was still too young to live with a man, that it still was not my time.

They were worried because in Carumas they were my parents. So it had been agreed when I came; one day they even said that it was best to return to my true parents' side. ... They talked with me in every possible way.

I did not understand what they were telling me, my ears were plugged, my heart too. I did not understand why my cousins had indeed had authorization; one was 14 and Elsa 17; she already had a child. In turn they did not want to support me; maybe it is because they are not my true parents, I used to think inside.

They did not know Francisco so how could they thus disapprove? How could they know that that young man was not suitable for me, that I could not have an understanding with him . ... So I rather began to feel enraged with my aunt and uncle, I did not want to listen to them; so little by little, I began to close my eyes, to plug my ears.

Now they did not entrust me with the cheese to go down to Moquegua; that made it worse for me, as if obstinacy became master of my heart. ... It was not like it used to be; without realizing I was changing, I was ill-tempered, I was indolent with my chores. ... I only thought of ways of meeting Francisco, and thus I only thought of going away.

One day, I bundled some things, the clothes I had bought for myself; I left what they had given me with such affection. ... Giving some excuse, I left the house very early in the morning.

I felt very cold the day I left, as if the icy wind of the early morning pierced my body, into my bones. ... While I walked, the wind turned around, jumped, danced, made the leaves in the trees move strongly; it made them whistle as if they were celebrating, raising dust.

That day it dawned late because it was cloudy, though it was not its time to be so.

When I arrived in Moquegua and lodged in my uncle and aunt's home, I lied to them, saying that I had permission to sell some clothes and also to buy something for the house. I think that my aunt and uncle believed me, because they received me gladly. ... I told them I would be gone soon.

After leaving my belongings, I went to the market looking for Francisco. Well, he was happy because we had not seen each other for more than two months. ... After three days he asked me to move to his room.

Thus, without ceremony, I took my things from my aunt and uncle's house with lies, taking leave from them and saying that I was returning to my community.

In the coming days, I did not leave the room so that they could not see me; I became bored. As I did not have anything else to do but cook, I had to go out to buy sugar, bread, onions, chilli for the meals.

Maybe on one of those days, my aunt may have seen me and followed me, because one day they knocked at the door. I went to answer and there they were, the two of them.

A row ensued; I had to allow them to enter into the room, so that the neighbours would not hear. You know that in those houses they want to know everything. They questioned me, scolded me, advised me.

At first, I did not reply; I was scared and frightened. Then, little by little I told them everything, but as I did not listen to their words, they also got angry. ... We will send a letter to your aunt Eugenia and your uncle Quintin, they said to me: how they will be suffering, you are ungrateful, they have raised you with such affection – with such words, they took leave.

On his side, his family, his uncles and aunts and his cousins, did not treat me well; they looked upon me as a bad person. One day his aunt insulted me in the street; all of them avoided my greetings.

Thus time passed by; I got pregnant. ... Shortly after, my uncle Quintin came; he demanded Francisco to arrange our lives. He treated me very curtly, returned my greeting, but did not want to converse with me.

So we left the city and went back to the countryside. His parents gave him land to sow in Collapunco. His parents showed their disapproval from the beginning. ... I did not know what to do. I tried with all my might to live far from his family; perhaps that was my mistake. I think that his parents would have helped me to nurture our union.

We began to live together in a house with a '*mediagua*' room [with one roof inclined to a side] and a very small kitchen by it, and with the things that I had in Moquegua and what my uncle had brought.

As time went by, his mood changed; he was no longer that cheerful, playful young man that I had met. ... He did not want to talk, much less to play. When he was drunk, he would say that his life had ended with me, that formerly he had enough money to give himself his whims, now all of it was spent in the household. He was unhappy with everything, everything bored him, anything would make him mad; he would curse, he began to work in the *chacras* with scorn.

One day I told him that it would be good to call one of his relatives, or perhaps some acquaintance who knew of an offering to the earth, since I did not know anyone in that place. 'Nonsense!' he said. 'Do you think that I am an ignorant man! ... I have spent so many years in the city, alone, and I have never done that nonsense. ... Besides, I do not even remember how my parents did it. ... Do not bother me!' Shouting in this way, he left the house.

When my first son was born, he gave him the name Henry. I did not like it, it sounded strange to my ears, but I accepted so that he would not get angry.

At that time I was happy, I thought that that child would sweeten our lives; that Francisco would change. ... But, fifteen days after the delivery, he came back drunk, he came in as if he were a madman, to insult me, shouting, trying to hit me. Thanks to the presence of my younger sister – Marta is her name and she is the daughter of my aunt Eugenia – he did not beat me. How mistaken I had been!

It became customary for him to come back drunk, my life was a suffering. The only thing I did was to use herbs to prevent me from having another child. The last thing he did, which when I recall – zass! – it makes the whole of my body shudder, it enters into me like cold. ... It was several months after when I got pregnant again. It was almost three months; he wanted to have a daughter and he asked me to get pregnant. Now, I also remember, that it was in this way that he had begged me to go to live with him. ... I had doubt in my heart, but in the end, I accepted; I believed that a daughter would make him change.

A short time after I told him that I carried a '*wawa*' in my womb, his temper turned worse; I did not know what I should do. ... The limit was when, one afternoon, as so many times, completely drunk, he would quarrel with someone whom I did not see and he started looking at me as if I were a stranger, an enemy. Even our son, who was playing peacefully, he began to annoy him, to shout at him, to insult him, trying to hit him. ... I came to his defence; then, like a madman, he came against me, gave me a punch in the face, he almost threw me to the floor. Drawing strength, I pulled my son by the hand and took him out from the kitchen; while leaving the house I held him in my arms, and I immediately started to run.

He was following us, throwing stones ... I think that out of fright, I could not even walk. ... As never before, I broke out shouting, calling our neighbours who lived nearby ... I must have been running, so scared that I did not realize that I was at the border of a terrace; a stone yielded and I fell with my son. I felt other stones falling with me, the only thing that I was able to do was to cover my son with my body. ... After that I remember nothing else.

I woke up in a neigbour's house, Susana Callacondo is her name; she was tending to me, she was curing my ankle which was out of joint, she rubbed me with hot alcohol and with a sharp pull, she put it in its place. For his part, her husband was preparing himself to make a plaster with black sugar cake [*chancaca*], '*Chirichiri*' [*grindelia boliviana*: used in osteo-articular injuries], '*acero*' [steel: a snake], alcohol, '*altamisa*' [*franseria artemis-ioides*], lime, '*coca acullita*' [chewed coca leaves for medicinal purposes]. This plaster is very good, and serves to heal bones which are out of joint or broken.

My tears fell like rain, I could not speak, the words did not come out of my mouth, I could not even tell them, thanks brethren! Because during the time we lived there, my husband did not want me to make friends with anyone, I seldom greeted them, sometimes hiding from my husband. On the other hand, he was jealous of the men and of the women. He said that we were ignorant people. As I did not stop crying, they gave me a cup of tea of valerian and chamomile. ... So little by little I calmed down. My son was also being taken care of, they had given him food and he was now playing with one of the younger children. When I saw him my heart calmed, I called him and he came running. ... He embraced me with much affection, he kissed me on the face, the head; ... I told him that I was allright. After looking at me for a while, he peacefully went back to play.

When I wanted to sit in the bed, I felt a sharp pain in the waist, as if it wanted to break in two. What a face I must have had, that sister Susana asked me what hurt me. I told her that I was pregnant, that I felt wet – blood it was, hot it came down! ... She also got frightened and went to look for her husband; the two talked and made an agreement to call on my aunt and uncle, who are like my parents.

I was ill for almost eight days, I lost the *wawa* [baby]; I felt very warm, feverish, my clothes were wet with sweat and they had to change me because I had very little strength left. ... They fed me, brought me tea for drinking, washed my clothes, combed my hair, washed me – they treated me as if I were their true family, 'How could it be otherwise?' they said. 'We all are a single family.'

My aunt and uncle also lodged in the same house, they also attended me with much affection; after some days, sister Susana told me that my aunt Eugenia had cried a lot in the courtyard when they told her what had happened.

During those days they did not tell me anything; no one mentioned Francisco, they did not ask where he was, what had happened with him, neither did I want to remember. However, I had a deep grief for the loss of my child, I felt weak; in falling, besides breaking my ankle, I had also injured my right side, which was very swollen where I had fallen on a large stone.

As the days went by, I began to heal; my uncle is knowledgeable in healing and he put plasters on me, gave me tea, rubbed me with herbs. Thus, little by little the swelling lowered, the green-purple which I had in some parts of my body began to disappear.

He called my '*animo*' [part of the vital force that comes out of the person and which produces a weakening, madness and even death]; that makes me always feel good, because inside I continued to be ill, I had much grief, I awoke crying of fright, I dreamed that I fell into a deep, dark gorge.

My aunt and uncle were worried, they felt a lot for me, they had talked with the neighbours. It is said that they called the *Varayoc* [traditional authority] of the sector and, through him, Francisco and his parents.

Three nights later, Francisco's parents, Francisco, the closest neighbours and the *Varayoc* came; the owner of the house received them, my aunt and uncle and sister Susana accompanied me in the room. They entered, greeted all one by one, and sat down. My uncle Quintin asked for permission to invite coca, to chew ['*chajchar*'] it, to achieve a good agreement; after a while the landlord asked for permission to bless [*ch'allar*] the house with liquor for the *Pachamama*, to ask her consent.

My uncle asked for permission and excused himself, then he spoke in the name of the family, in my name; he began to recount from the moment they brought me, when I came to live in these lands, the years I had lived nicely in my uncle's family. He recounted the way they had taught me to care for the cattle, the little *chacra*, the household, my siblings; he told them my way of being, that I sang all the time, that they laughed a lot because he said I answered singing.

After that he asked to be forgiven because without the consent of anyone, I had gone to live with Francisco. 'Surely we have not raised this daughter well, we have come even to the disgrace of losing a *wawa*,' he said. Then he asked the Callacondo family and the neighbours who were present, to recount how they saw our union, during those years.

Asking for permission, everyone spoke of us, they did not see well that we would have gone together without the consent of the families, the *Kollo-Achachilas* [mountain deities], the *Pachamama* and others. 'That is the reason everything has gone wrong for you two,' they said, 'why the *chacras* have suffered so much. For that reason there is damage in the animals.' 'The seeds weaken and have not taken strongly to the earth, for this reason the earth has taken her *wawa*,' someone else said.

Other voices added their views: Francisco is almost a stranger in our lands, he does not know how to nurture a *chacra*, does not know how to nurture a family, does not know how to live in the countryside. How come? His parents have neglected him, definitely abandoned him; he has grown in the city.

We have seen that they carry on a bad life; the husband is rude, he does not greet anyone, does not respect the families here, beats his wife senseless. Some of us are even distant blood-relatives and he has looked upon us with contempt.

The woman walks with the head bent down, she feels frightened, in her gaze you can see it, said an aunt. … She walks with no strength, without joy, as if the earth would have caught her. … How is that son of theirs going to grow, and if other children come, they will come only to suffer. That is not right!

Francisco's father also asked for permission and began to speak. He recounted how, being a child, Francisco was wilful, ill-tempered. He always tried to get his own way but he was also cheerful and playful; as he was growing it was difficult to raise him. 'My biggest mistake was to give him authorization to go to the city to work,' he said, 'before having learned his obligations with his relatives, with the community.'

He asked my aunt and uncle, me, his parents, the *Varayoc*, to be forgiven for the mistreatment that his son had given me, for the ways in which he had made me suffer; then looking at Francisco he said: 'Now it is your turn to speak, we want to hear you. You have made me endure shame, you have humiliated me with your behaviour, you need punishment.'

Francisco had a very frightened face, I had never seen him like this – he did not even dare to look at me. Asking for permission to speak, he knelt before all, it seemed a lie that he should be like this; he asked to be pardoned for his behaviour. 'I have not been a good son,' he said, 'neither a good husband, nor a good father. I have not known how to respect the relatives, I have made my family suffer shame, also my wife, my son. For this I beg your pardon.'

He also recounted which bad habits he had learned in the city; he admitted that the *trago* [alcoholic beverage] had increased the problems and disgraces that had befallen him. 'So I have to quit. So I promise you,' he said, 'that I am going to mend my ways.'

I was sitting on the bed feeling weak and trying to calm down, but I was overwhelmed by emotion; in spite of my efforts, tears welled up, all I had were tears. I could not say a word, as if speech had left me. All my bodies only remembered the suffering. All I did was weep. All were silent. Sister Susana handed me a jar with tea of valerian. I could not even drink, it seemed as if it did not enter in my throat. ... Gradually I began drinking, until I calmed down.

Making an effort I asked for permission and spoke, I apologized for not having received their word in its time; I apologized to the neighbours for not having behaved as my aunt and uncle had taught me. I had lived in Collapunco almost as a stranger, without knowing anyone, not paying attention to the families; I apologized because sometimes I hid myself to avoid greeting them. I told them that I behaved like that because I was afraid of my husband, so that he would not get angry.

Afterwards I also thanked them for their presence, for their concern; I thanked my sister Susana and her husband with all my heart, for the protection and care that I had received since the day I fell down. I will never forget their affection, their concern for my son and for me ... I also thanked them because they had given my little '*sullito wawa*' [foetus] to *Pachamama*; when as a consequence of the fall I aborted, they had buried it with my blood.

I apologized to my aunt and uncle for the suffering that I was causing them, I told them that it would not happen again because their words were good, sure, and I had not understood them.

Then I looked at Francisco, he seemed a stranger to me. ... How could I have lived so many years with him? In my inside, in my bodies, I asked myself this question.

I do not know where my strength came from after so many years silent, bent down, keeping all his scorn, when he said to me: 'Indian, shut up!', 'ignorant', 'silence!' ... 'What can you know!' Years I went through bearing his abuses – when he beat me up, when he threw me out of the house, when he threw the food at me, when with a kick he threw my little dog far away.

Looking at everyone I told them: I have been in error, I have made a mistake with the families, with my aunt and uncle, with the *'Ticsani qullu'* [mountain deity of the locality], with the *Pachamama*, with Saint Isidro the Farmer, I ask pardon to all, to all I ask protection. I do not want to live with this man any longer; please listen to me, do not forsake me.

The *Varayoc*, who listened to one and the other attentively, said: 'These are just a man and a woman who have strayed in crooked paths, they are not one for the other. A man with good heart would not make such great offences, he cannot and should not behave badly. That man here disrespects all of us who live here, even himself; because of him we could be punished.

'Pretty clearly *Pachamama* had become angry, his *chacras* have not flourished, his family has not flourished, even a child She has taken from them. Perhaps if they change they can improve. Let us see, sisters and brothers, let us reflect, *"chuyman arupa istasiñani"* [let us listen to the voice of the heart].' My uncle once again offered his coca leaves, 'We will ask the coca leaves,' he said. After a lapse of silence, again all spoke; they again asked me what I thought. Again I repeated to them that I wanted to return to my aunt and uncle's house, I asked them to give me shelter.

Francisco also begged for forgiveness and asked permission to go to the city to look for work; he said that after a time he would come back, to show how a man, a true son, must be, so that his parents would not be ashamed any longer. He said that he would stand by his son, and said of the plots of land that his parents had given him when he formed a family, half of them would be for his son. He said that if I wanted I could stay in Collapunco.

Almost at midnight agreement was reached; I would go live with my uncle and aunt for a time, half of the plots would be for raising the son whom I had had in that union. Every year I would sow and harvest, sharing half of the crop with the family of sister Susana; my uncle and aunt would also help me. The family of sister Susana would also take care of the house we were leaving, the little animals we would take to my uncle and aunt's house. That was the agreement, that is how it was left. Thereafter we all thanked and embraced each other, saying: 'Let it be well'.

Many years, many moons went by rapidly; my son grew, and it was quickly time for him to go to school. I lived near my uncle and aunt's house, there they helped me to raise my house and I began raising my family in Collapunco on the land of my uncle and aunt. Like that the cattle, the *chacras* and my son were raised – everything I nurtured with affection.

My uncle and aunt were always by me, we helped each other in everything; with more peace I became more of a woman every day. Suitors were not lacking, when I went to Huachunta to barter for leather or to bring alpaca wool, they proposed that I form a family, they offered for me to stay in the community. In Sotalajo, which is also close to Carumas, the same happened. At first when they said those words, I got angry; afterwards I did not pay attention, I did not listen.

Happy I walk in life, my son is my joy, the *chacras*, the little cow and the rest of the cattle filled my heart. ... Thus time went by.

One night in the house of my uncle Quintin, we were preparing the feast of the departed, we had to make bread, '*quispiño*' [a little piece of bread with quinua or *k'añiwa* flour], crackers; this year we would receive the departed well, as we had agreed. That afternoon when the sun was tired and wanted to go to sleep, visitors came. They were our relatives who came from Acora; they came with gifts, with bundles from my parents, my brothers, they came with fresh news from our relatives.

My uncle Sebastian has relatives in the community of Muilaque and came to help in the family of my uncle Quintin to change the straw roofs of a couple of rooms, before the beginning of the rains; there also arrived my cousin Mercedes, we call her Mechita out of affection.

Mechita is the daughter of one of my mother's brothers, she brought woven blankets, also '*llijllas*' [a quadrangular piece woven with bright coloured wools, also used to carry babies], she must be around 25 and was unmarried at that time.

After a good meal in the company of the visitors, we all began to prepare the food for the departed relatives; my uncle began to knead the flour to make bread – the 'bread *wawas*' which we call '*t'anta wawas*' [babies made of bread or cake flour]. Uncle Sebastian set himself to grind quinua to make '*quispiño*'; with my aunt and my cousin we prepared the dough for the crackers, and with the dough we made little doves, flowers, hearts, moons, suns, stars, little animals, little alpacas, little llamas and so on.

The day of the departed is a great celebration, it has to be done properly, it has to be especially prepared for the departed who have gone to another life, every year. We have many departed ones, a family it is, the grandfathers and grandmothers, the aunts and the uncles, the brothers, the sisters, who always accompany us, who protect us.

From Puno we brought all the food we prepared and the alcohol we offered to the departed relatives. You know that in the house, in the big room, a table is arranged, it is covered with a black cloth; on it are placed plates of fruit, crackers, '*quispiño*', bread, '*t'anta wawas*', roasted lamb, '*chuño p'uty*' [*chuño* steamed], boiled potatoes, '*habas p'uspu*' [fava beans boiled in their pods], sweets, *chancaca* [black sugar in pieces], cigarettes, maize *chicha* [slightly fermented beverage], quinua *chicha*, beer, coca cola, rum. ... Prettily it is decorated with flowers, with plates being placed in pairs.

The little Saints, Saint Father Isidro the Farmer, and Father Santiago [protector Saint, keeper of llamas, alpacas and vicuñas, also keeper of the storms with thunder and lightning] are also laid out; little candles are lit, and the best flowers, with the prettiest being placed on both sides. ... Raw food is also put out, so that the departed can take it with them and cook for themselves when they feel hungry.

So when all is ready, the departed come to serve themselves as they please; when they eat well, they are happy and accompany us with affection. The visitors also arrive: friends, uncles, aunts, *compadres*, *comadres* [godparents of one's children]; they come to greet our departed relatives, accompany us and offer prayers to the departed, speak to them so that they always protect us. The visitors are also invited to share food with the departed, and another part of the food they take with them in gratitude. ...

When we had discharged part of our obligations, that night we sat down to converse, to listen to the words they brought from our families.

Chewing the coca leaves, drinking a little rum, sitting in the kitchen while we readied ourselves for the meal, the words arrived; they told us that the rains were delayed, that the year would be good for grains, not so much for potatoes.

The cattle, the '*uywitas*' [little cattle] will suffer from drought, due to scarcity of pastures we said. ... So it always is, my aunt told us; every year they are different, the rain, the frosts, as we ourselves are – some are good, give us water, help us to have food, but they also get angry, curse, become capricious. For that reason sometimes they withdraw or come with violence and hit us – when we commit offences, when we do not respect the families.

So it was, recounted sister Mechita, last year in the month of December, in the days of Christmas, one night the '*Chijchi achachila*' came [*Chijchi* [hail]; *achachila* [grandfather], equivalent to the hail deity]. Furious, he went by the *chacras*, hitting hard the *chacras* of potatoes, of large beans, of quinua. He made his way from the top of the mountain, coming down to the *pampa* and in the lake he went in.

As if that were not enough, accompanied by thunderclaps, there came the lightning – very angry – looking for some family of '*j'aquis*' to punish them, making the sky rumble. The lightning bolts came out menacingly from between the clouds, with much violence, until it entered into a house by the right corner which faces to where the sun hides. Then it crossed the room, crawling on the floor; the right foot it grabbed, passing by the backbone through to the head, it reached and thus killed him.

That night it frightened all of us: the little cattle in the courtyard cried, the dogs did not stop howling. From afar it was heard how the *chacritas* suffered, all the *'j'aquinacas'* [*J'aqui* (person), *J'aquinaca* (persons)] – men, women, children. We came out to ask it to withdraw, to forgive us if we had trespassed. ... Afterwards, when the storm calmed down, whistles were heard, they were calling for a meeting; it still rained but we gathered all the same.

The lieutenant governor, together with the *'Waly chuymanj'aqinacampi'* [men with very good hearts, the ones who know, who are wise], their women were there; there were also some delegates, and the men of respect spoke. Afterwards we all came to an agreement.

One group, uncles, aunts, brothers and sisters, followed the path the *'Chijchi achachila'* had taken, to take stock of the damage done in the *chacras*, to the little cattle, to the house of some uncle.

Another group prepared itself to make a *'loj'taña'* [offering], with red-hot coals and incense; it is necessary to offer wine to *Pachamama*, to put oneself in the right relationship with her for her not to suffer, so that she does not get angry with the *'Chijchi achachila'*, so that his anger may pass, so that he does not return. To be forgiven one says to him:

> Saint Chijchi achachila
> if you were hungry and we have not heard you, forgive us,
> if someone has insulted you, we will find out.
> In your heart, let there be no anger,
> we ask you to excuse us, we ask
> that your anger do not come any longer,
> with a good heart return home and feed your grandchildren.

Other sisters and brothers went in aid of the family whose house the lightning hit. We have to look at the damage of the lightning, we have to look because they have fallen in disgrace.

Also another delegation of men and women had to find out why the *Chijchi achachila* had hit the *chacras* of the community so hard; for that, the people of greatest standing, with the authorization of the parents, had visited from house to house where young women lived, to find out who had aborted in the community.

As is known by all in the community, it is easy to take account of the *'tawacus'* [young women], of the women who are alone because the husbands are away on a trip, or of the young widows.

First those present were asked who had committed the trespass; as on other occasions, it was expected that the man and woman would admit their fault and feelingly ask for forgiveness. No one said anything, so they had to examine the breasts of the women, looking at their size; the colour of the nipples is a sign.

The *Chijchi achachila* comes like this when the life of a *wawa* that is germinating in the womb of a woman is taken away; when the young woman – hiding from her parents and from the families – enters into relations with a young man and when they have asked permission from no one. At other times, when a young woman deceives the husband of another woman; sometimes it is the opposite way round, when a married man woos a girl, thus in wrong ways they get together.

For that the *Chijchi achachila* brings the children who have not reached this life, from every town he gathers them. ... He takes out food from the *chacras*, for them to eat, for the children's parents did not give them time to eat in this life. They also had to take food for that '*machaj sullu wawa*' [new human foetus, new human being]. To take life when it is just germinating is a big mistake, a very great lack of respect to all: to the clouds, to the stars, to *Pachamama*, to the *Qullu achachilas*, to the river, to the springs, to the *j'aquis*, to the *chacras*, to the little Fathers, to the cattle – all are offended, disrespected.

It took almost two days to find the '*sullo j'aqui*' [human foetus]; none of the women had the signs, so it must be one of the absent ones, we all reflected.

We went on to the neighbouring communities – there also the *Chijchi achachila* had passed – and we asked for permission; and an agreement was reached between the authorities.

With their help we searched and in a '*musiña*' [a very small mud hut used by the *chacra* keepers in harvest time or when making *chuño*] we found a sister of our community; she looked sick. Through a brother we called her parents. ... She strongly denied it, she did not want to speak, she said that her throat ached. ... With heat from the cold she was [fever chills]; and she would not let herself be examined; however the '*chuyma j'aqui*' had seen in the coca leaves, so they insisted and began searching from *chacra* to *chacra*, from furrow to furrow, from shrub to shrub.

In the end, in the middle of some big potato shrubs, they found loose soil and there they dug. There it was, wrapped in some rags: the buried '*sullo j'aqui*'.

They picked it up with care, calling his '*ajayu*' [the most important vital force which is also possessed by the departed, it is related with the 'spiritual'], and we went back to the community; her parents also took the girl to the community with much shame. ... There all were waiting.

The father had to apologize to all. ... The girl also apologized for her error, for the damage that she had brought to all the families of the '*parcialidad*' [sector of the community].

The father made the commitment of passing the '*loj'taña*' to the Sacred Earth *Pachamama*, also gifting part of his produce to the most affected families who had suffered the blows of the *Chijchi achachila*.

On the other hand, the '*tawuacu*' gave the name of the young man with whom she had had relations. He was an agricultural technician of the local government; and he, after making the sister pregnant, like a dog with its tail between its legs, had fled.

A committee was formed and agreed to go to the town of Yunguyo to find him, to take to him responsibility for the harm caused in the community, in the *chacras*, and to the sister.

It was also decided to present a complaint to the police station; they asked for the arrest of this ill-hearted man, who had not learnt to respect his brothers and sisters.

This man had been born in the community of Challacollo, his parents made him study in Ilave through all of the secondary school and he ended up as technician in the José Antonio Encinas Technological Institute of Puno. The committee searched hard until they found him; they had found out everything about his life, his work, his parents, his families, his community – everything. They obliged him to present himself at the police station to admit his fault and promise to pay for the harm done. They told him if you do not comply, we will complain to your employer.

The man right away admitted his guilt; with his salary he took responsibility to buy seeds, to buy foodstuff for those who had less land and to whom the hail had dealt the strongest blows. ... Thus the matter was settled.

In the same way in the community, other people [men and women] found out why the lightning had entered the house of the Mamani family. Each and every one of those who live in the sector had gathered, called the relatives, prepared the wake. After the burial, with our family, we also went; there I heard the word of his closest relatives.

The man who had passed to the other life was a bad son, he was the only son of the '*K'ariri auqi*' [*k'ari* [tired]; *auqui* [old man]] Teodosio Mamani. This is a man who has walked a lot in life, distinguished by the families, strong for his age, he himself is still making his *chacras*, caring for his little cattle; they say he is reaching one hundred years, his wife had died ten years ago.

The man struck by lightning never remembered his father: he did not visit him, had not brought him food or clothes as a gift, did not keep him company; he did nothing – in sum, he had forgotten his father.

Many times we reminded him of his obligations, recounted one of his elder aunts. ... We gave him advice, spoke another of his elder relatives. ... We advised him to take care of and to nurse his father, another relative remembered. ... If it were not for the other families, how he would have suffered! Affection and company is what he most lacked, all said. ... We have to recognize the goodwill of aunt Martina Vilca who had given him one of her sons to accompany him, they said. Thus, without further ado, chastisement reached this son without heart: the lightning must have taken him because he has seen his father's grief, they agreed.

'Thus it always is,' said my aunt Eugenia, 'the old men, the old women we all have to nurture; one must not abandon them through no motivation because that also is our way in life. ... Clearly the lightning got angry, his heart must have had compassion, so punishment has overcome this ill-hearted man.' We passed all the time that our relatives were visiting very happily – we talked a lot, we laughed a lot, we stayed awake until late at night.

One day I accompanied my cousin Mechita to the town. Quickly the evening overtook us. 'We have to hurry up because very soon it will become dark and the night will reach us,' we said. ... As we were talking we arrived, just at nightfall. We wanted them not to notice, so we slowly approached the house; everyone was in the kitchen and from there the voices came.

No one noticed when we approached, all the elder people were gathered, but there was also another voice. I realized that it was Tata Mauricio Apaza's: he converses with the coca leaves, with the *Qullu achachilas*. ... That evening they were conversing about me, they were calling me.

I entered frightened. 'What is happening?' I asked. 'What did I do? Why are they mentioning me? ... Shut up, do not make a noise,' I told my cousin who was coming in a little behind me.

My uncle and aunt were consulting the coca leaves for me to form a couple. I got a little angry. 'Why do they have to mention me?' I said to myself. What do I want a husband for? Is it that I ask something for my son or for myself? All this I said in my insides. ... Then, taking strength, I called my cousin to accompany me and we entered. All my uncles and aunts received us with affection, invited us to sit down, and my aunt served us a hot cup of sage so that a cold would not take hold of us.

I thanked them and sat down to drink the tea; I did not say anything, I was mute, I just did not know what to say, my tongue was tied.

My uncle Quintin took the floor and began to speak; for a long time I had not heard him speak like that. As he was speaking my anger went away, as his words reached all my bodies, little by little, I calmed down.

'I would like you to listen, I want to speak with my heart,' he said. 'It is time that you have company, it is not good for a woman, it is not good for a man to live alone too long; you need a man who walks by your side, who walks with you together in life. You have to have support to raise your son, to nurture the *chacra*, to nurture the little cattle, the house. ... In life all goes in pairs, male and female, there is not one alone, you know well that in the plants it is like that: the rue there is male, and there is also female, the male sage has a female sage, it is the same with the small carnation [*clavelina*] male and female; much more with the animals and the '*j'aquis*'. It is just the same with the mountains, all have a partner, there are male *Qullus* and female *Qullus*; in the rivers, the lakes, the sea, are males and females; the '*warawara*' [star], the wind, the clouds also live like this. The departed also have to accompany each other in pairs, you know that when they are lonely in order for them not to suffer, a partner has to be found for them.

'For all to live well, together, "*loj'tañas*", "*sart'aña*" [a solemn and ritual visit effected with the purpose of commiting oneself to living as a couple] must be made, one has to do "*chinj'a*" [tie, when a couple is very closely united], one has to do for "*J'acasiñanacapataqi*" [so that one can live well, generate life].

'When it does not rain, when frost falls too much, it is a sign that something is happening, then consultations must be made, sometimes one has to help so that a "*tawacu*" lives together with a "*K'ollo achachila*", or also that one has to help to get together, to live together, to wed a young man with the "*mara*" [season, year], it all depends on what pair is sought whether male or female; in sum it always has to have its partner to walk in its company.

'You little Louise, you already have been living alone several years, we are very happy to share your life with us, but to go on like this is not good for all, there has to be someone to accompany you with affection, to nurture you and your son. Some man with a good heart must also be waiting that a good woman keep him company, nurture him, have children with her.'

Tata Mauricio also let his words be heard: 'To have company would be convenient for you. ... The coca leaves said that a partner younger than you is waiting. He is Quechua. The *Qullu achachilas*, our ancestors who have passed to another life, and *Pachamama* are also saying so. ... There is agreement among all, everything will go well for you in life if you listen to them. You are going to have other children, thus also you will see your *chacra* grow, your little cattle, the families. ... We must make an altar of sweet offerings for *Pachamama* so that she receives your son and you; finally you are going to live well.'

That's just the way it has been, everything they advised me that night has been accomplished; I will never forget it.

My second husband is named José Erquinigo Quispe, from Atuncolla. He was born in the community of San Martín Cueva; before coming to live in Carumas, he was also working in Tarata [Province of the department of Tacna]; there he learned Aymara, and he speaks Quechua, Aymara and Spanish very well.

He is ten years younger than I, but his mode of being is that of an older man, he is a *chuyma j'aqi* [a man with heart]; for that reason we get along well. Many women in Carumas live with younger men, it is just the same; no one cares whether the man or the woman is older or younger – the elders advise thus on their side.

When the '*sartawi*' took place, when he came to ask me to live together, an older relative accompanied him – an uncle who lives in Tarata where he has a bread oven. The evening of the visit to the house of my uncle and aunt he came in the company of his wife and the lieutenant governor of his annex [a territorial subdivision of a community].

His uncle is called Ancelmo Ccama Quisca and his wife is Carmen Cruz. They came accompanied with two donkeys fairly well loaded; they brought many presents, one carried big, delicious loaves of bread, and cakes of different shapes; the other donkey brought fruits: *camuesas* [sweet small apples, which are produced in the inter-Andean valleys], pears, grapes, bananas, watermelon, maize, figs. ... They arrived by the middle of the afternoon. We were also ready, we had put guinea pigs in the oven, potatoes, sweet potatoes, and had ready a '*p'atasqa*' [peeled barley] soup.

His relatives were respectful people. Before conversing they told us that they wanted to ask permission to *Pachamama*, to Aligrade, their protector '*Orku*' [mountain deity]; my uncle and aunt also quickly agreed. We called the *Ticsani Qullu achachila*, we raised red hot coals, we poured sweet wine on *Pachamama*. So his uncle and aunt conversed with mine and asked for their permission and consent for us to live as husband and wife.

We all conversed very nicely, we were happy, we laughed, we ate, we chewed the little coca leaves; we drank wine, *pisco* [alcoholic beverage made by distillation of grape must], and beer. ... When it was fairly late in the evening they accompanied José and me to the house where we were going to live, with *charango* [a small stringed musical instrument], singing and playing they accompanied us.

After ten years together we were married by civil law and by religious law, only a year ago. ... You should have seen the celebration we had! During those years we had made our friendships grow, the *chacra*, the little cattle, the house, the family; we already have five children; the eldest one is from my previous marriage. José loves him as his own kin; he is making him finish secondary school in Moquegua. Every month he visits him, invites him for a walk, to talk; they joke, they always get along well. For his part, my son is also a good person – he lets himself be loved. He calls José his father ... he has a lot of affection and respect for him.

We set the date of the marriage for August; it is the best month of the year – after that it's February. August is a good time to get together, to get married; don't you see, the earth receives us well, the *Pachamama* is hot. At that time the wind helps in grooming it, to prepare the next sowing, it is the beginning of the new year for the *chacra*.

That time is also a good one to raise a house, for that reason the knowledgeable people build their house in the month of August; it is always good to begin a new life, so that man and woman be born as one. As I say, August is the best time for raising the house; when it is born in this time it takes good care of all who live within the house; others also agree in roofing at this time.

In both cases, one prepares a feast, one must make '*Wilancha*' [a ritual for *Pachamama* and the *apus*, which is effected with the sacrifice of a llama or alpaca, on the occasion of building a house, sprinkling the blood on the walls] of a white alpaca or, as others prefer, a little black or brown alpaca. This is done according to custom – the little alpaca's blood nourishes the house, as it is a *wawa*. In its foundations an offering must also be placed, that is very important. ... Even the *mistis* [persons of non-peasant origin or who live in the cities] do this: all make *Wilancha*, with flowers they clothe it, with liquor they pour an offering.

We prepare with anticipation for the wedding to receive the relatives. Our acquaintances for their part also, when they found out, gave their approval ... and said that they would come with '*apj'ata*' [a present for festive occasions]. They also offered their help: 'Just tell me what we can do to help you.'

A week before, one by one our relatives started arriving; all brought something ... potatoes, maize, lard, *chuño, chalona* [dried meat], hens, eggs, guinea pigs, little pigs, and so on.

It seemed as if we were going to be *alferado* [a person charged with offering the necessaries of the feast in the central day]; we never felt so showered with gifts, the *apj'atas* came from the side of my uncle and aunt, from his relatives in Tarata, from my relatives in Chucuito.

The godparents arrived three days before the wedding to discharge their obligations. The older godmother and the godmother of the rings took charge of me, and the godfathers, of José.

The day following their arrival both godparents concerned themselves with the room where we would sleep on the night of the wedding; as when we joined together, the place had to be cleansed with the smoke of burning herbs that came from all places. On this occasion, it was not the relatives but godparents who performed the ceremony.

They brought different herbs from different places; they brought to-gether herbs from the *montaña* [jungle slopes] of Puno, from the shores of Lake Titicaca, from the *yungas* [tropical zone] of Bolivia, from the heights, from the coastal valleys and from the valley of Carumas.

Among them they agreed to gift the earth with a sweet *lojtaña* which they passed around at midnight of the second day before the marriage. From the preceding day a good meal is prepared for those who are present: my uncle and aunt, José's parents, the godparents, my sister and her husband, our children, my cousins and other relatives.

While we eat, each one tells about the preparations which are his or her responsibility, what is missing; the tasks for the following day are distributed – all have to respond, even the smallest children. It is said who is going to be in charge of the kitchen, of the guests, of the musicians, of serving the food.

At dusk my aunt and uncle's house was full, the neighbours were coming and going, the friends also; little by little the table setting was being completed, they brought plates, jars, pots, glasses, cutlery, firewood and so forth.

My husband and I looked at each other and laughed with happiness, our little children calmly played, the elder ones eagerly helped, my oldest son hurriedly came and went: carrying things, putting the house in order, helping prepare the *ramada* [a kind of arch built with eucalyptus branches or other trees, ornamented with flowers and/or textiles, to receive the newlyweds on their wedding day]. He looked at us happily from time to time. My heart was full of happiness; I felt like crying out of gratitude. ... What I had lived in other times seemed like a bad dream.

Also with anticipation the godparents saw the clothes we would wear the day of the celebration; my husband and I had two changes of clothes prepared for us. My godmothers brought three changes of clothes in all, nice clothes they were: skirts, hats, girdles – everything they brought to change clothes twice on the day of the wedding and for the rest of the days that the celebration would last.

At night I retired to the bedroom with my two godmothers, they had to accompany me that night, as the godfathers did with my husband. My children were in the care of my relatives.

The elder godmother took out her '*istalla*' [small woven bag made of coloured wool to keep coca leaves in] of coca leaves and offered some to each one of us; we chewed slowly, conversing about everything that had happened during the day. They were in charge of advising me, of listening to my questions, of telling me the good and the bad they had gone through. ... Chatting, we fell asleep.

It is very important to choose the godparents. They cannot be just anyone; they must be a well respected couple. Some are accustomed to naming as godparents those who are wealthy – the '*k'amiris*' [peasants who have the largest amount of land, animals, money]; some of these '*k'amiris*' are also good, respectable people; others are crooked. But it is always more important to find a couple with good feelings, who will support you in case of need.

Just before dawn we woke up. The godmothers first left the room, to receive the first signs of the day; they told me that everything was allright: that the morning star was exchanging greetings with the sun; the birds happily flew about singing; the smoke of the oven had a good colour and rose high, playing with the wind.

That day we all woke up early in the morning; some were preparing the food, others arranging the house, and the godparents taking responsibility for us. A task for the godparents is to prepare the waters for the bath; in readiness and with anticipation they boil water with rosemary, rue, broom, roses and small carnations. With these waters, the godmothers bathed me while the godfathers bathed my husband.

With those waters they made us bathe to clean us, to protect us, to attract happiness. ... They recounted that in their day those baths were taken when the couple were first getting together, and that in other places they are still doing so – but it is preferable that it also be done for the wedding, for the couple to flourish, the new family.

After the bath they dressed us, with smoked and cleansed clothes, and combed our hair. The hair must be very clean; it has to be washed with rosemary water and rinsed with the water of lily leaves. The grandmothers braided my hair with much care, they rubbed my cheeks with geranium flowers in order to give me more colour – my lips too; others say that they paint with *ayrampo*. They also dressed me very prettily.

During these days before the wedding the godparents accompany the couple constantly: they do not leave us alone at any time. They say that we are like *wawas* who are just being born, that we need their attentions, their protection, they even slept near our bedroom. They said that sometimes ill winds come or some bad intention can reach us; for that reason too they take care of us.

After having the morning meal the relatives took charge of completing all that was missing for the feast. All changed into their feast dresses, all of us gathered to go down to the road and board a truck that had been lent to us; thus we arrived at the town, which is not too far from the house.

In the town other families were expecting us; the musicians, our friends, all were in the square.

The priest was in the chapel and quickly he said mass; from time to time the musicians played, the children let off firecrackers. I just talked with Saint Isidro the Farmer, he is our patron saint, I asked him to accompany me to nurture my husband, my *chacras*, my children, my little cattle, the families.

I also thanked him because until now he always looked at us with approving eyes, with a good heart, he accompanied us – together with the *K'ollo Achachilas* and the *Pachamama* – to care for the house, the relatives. Before leaving the chapel, the godmothers left fruit and loaves of bread for the Saint, so that he could help himself and join the feast along with us.

The mass soon ended; with the band of musicians, the relatives and accompanying people we entered the mayor's house. There too we did not delay much.

In the square the musicians played loudly while they waited for us, and when we re-entered the square they threw shredded and coiled multi-coloured paper over us. Then the relatives said that all had to take a little walk around the square, dancing – so we did. As the truck was waiting for us to return, we all boarded to go to the house; some returned on foot, others returned on bicycles or motorcycles.

We went straight to the *ramada* which had been prepared with eucalyptus and *kantutas* [a native flower which flowers in the winter]; inside the *ramada* a table and some chairs were arranged, where the married couple sits with the parents; the godparents come and give us loaves of bread, fruit and beer; they clasp money inside our bosom and embrace us. ... They wish us well and then sit down by our side.

The rest of the relatives, neighbours, friends keep on coming and also give us their *cariño* [a gift of produce, beverages, utensils, animals], they embrace us tightly and for each the band of musicians play the '*diana*' [a melody offered in reciprocity for the gift received].

Afterwards the musicians played *casarasiri* [a musical piece played during weddings] and we danced. First I danced with my husband, the godparents, the parents; after that all those present joined in the dance and thus the celebration started.

They served *chicha*, beer, food for all; very happily all our relatives danced and sang with energy and joy.

When it is near dusk, the godparents accompany us to the room where we are to sleep; the relatives follow us and also the musicians but only the godparents enter the bedroom, the rest stay outside, playing loudly.

The godmothers help the bride to undress, they leave her with her undershirt; in the same way the godfathers leave the man with only his undershirt. After that they advise us to rest.

When they left and closed the door, the musicians of the band also left. Then the relatives, as usual, played *charango*, singing and dancing around the room where we were – very beautiful. ... It is always funny. They sang some songs for me, other songs for him – on one side the men sang, and on the other side, the women. When they believed that we had fallen asleep they left to continue dancing in the backyard.

Well, thus we feast. The celebration lasts three days; one day is the invitation of the husband's relatives, another day is the woman's family's invitation, and at the end we also give thanks.

When the families let themselves be loved, and care one for the other with affection and with calm, then we are never wanting; with full hands we are helped, all is just given.

CHAPTER 6

Education in the Modern West and in the Andean Culture

Grimaldo Rengifo Vasquez

Repeatedly we forget that the word 'education' is of recent coining. It was not known before the Reformation. The education of children is mentioned for the first time in a French document dated 1498.

In the English language the word education made its first appearance in 1530. In the lands of Spain, the use of the word and the idea of education was delayed for another century. In 1632, Lope de Vega continued referring to education as a novelty. Centres of apprenticeship existed before the term education entered into common usage. (Illich 1991: 20)

The concept of 'education' is new in the history of the West and it is found temporarily associated with the emergence of modernity in Europe. This is not to say, as Illich reminds us, that various ways of learning did not exist before the modern era. The question is in what moment education begins to become a substitute for nurturance.

Two elements associated with the theme of European modernity locate for us the points at which education appeared. These are: the separation of man from nature, that which Carlos Cullen (1977) calls the de-naturalization of man, and the de-sacralization of the world. Obviously, these elements are part of the processes of a slow, unequal maturation in the European cultural geography until, by the end of the bourgeois revolutions (1750–1850), they became dominant. With the de-naturalization of man, he thinks of himself as distinct and distant from nature and begins to call it an object. Freed also from divine tutelage, man replaces the sacral with explicable causes, determined through human reasoning about the way the world functions. Nature is no longer appreciated as a divine creation to be respected, but is instead an environment where human experience is realized. Curiously, one finds in the Judaeo-Christian myth of origin the idea that nature is there to be dominated by man.

However, to establish dominance over nature, a precise knowledge of her is necessary. Knowledge, too, is a concept that appears to have suffered transformations during the history of the modern West. As Pannikar tells us, referring to knowledge of the ancients:

Knowledge was understood as that ability of the human spirit through which man places himself in contact with reality through participation with it, and entered into communication through a spiritual renaissance ('con-naissance') [French for knowledge] by virtue of a natural communion with reality. (Pannikar 1992)

Peña Cabrera tells us that the intellectual of antiquity:

moves between things and not between objects. In knowing them, he assimilates them and becomes similar to them. In this sense, truth is how the thing really is. (Peña Cabrera 1984: 98)

To know presupposes a distancing between humans and nature, but this situation did not bring the ancients in the West to intervene, but instead to fuse, to assimilate themselves with nature.

Knowledge in the modern context, however, is different, because man no longer forms or feels part of nature; instead he sees himself as possessing her and his knowledge is instrumental: it is not knowledge for contemplation, but rather knowledge for the purpose of exploiting a nature that is supposedly there to be dominated. Francis Bacon (1561–1626) reminded us – besides telling us that knowledge is power – that in order to enter into the secrets of nature one has to liberate oneself from spontaneity, and possess a method that permits one to reach the truth while saving time and effort. This is the experimental method. On the other hand, Pannikar tells us that:

Modern man is afraid of chaos, he has a fear that reality is bad or is his enemy. He trusts only in his power, in his intelligence, only in what he can control. (Pannikar 1992: 20)

According to Peña Cabrera:

Knowledge is not only power, rather power requires knowledge to consolidate itself. (Peña Cabrera 1992)

The appearance and development of the concept of education in the modern West is not far removed from the avatars of knowledge, since modern Western education is found associated with possession and transmission of a knowledge that permits one to operate on nature in order to bring about its transformation. Abugattas tells us:

He who wants to know nature for this end is not a man of the Middle Ages, but instead [...] a being that has no precedents in the history of the West: this man is the individual. (Abugattas 1986)

The individual is a product of modernity. He emerges from the separation of man from nature and from the dissolution of the community, for he, as shown by Adorno and Horkheimer (1971: 55), is a solitary being – 'a being contrary to the natural being, a being who emancipates and distances himself from nature's simple relations'. This is the man who no longer trusts in ways of learning that are not systematic, and requires a method of learning about reality – a modality that from now on will be termed 'education'. To the extent to which the individual is equipped with information about the world and manages the stresses which allow its dissection, he is in a position not only to dominate nature, but better to compete with other individuals in this plan to conquer the world.

Thus, education will be the mode – invented and desired by modern humanity – to give to the individual the arguments and the most efficient manner to increase his domination over things. As Voltaire (1694–1778) euphorically said: 'language is embellished day by day; children are beginning to be educated rather than being nurtured' (Bemac 1956).

Later, education will be a matter of institutionalization; schools will become the exclusive channel of selection of people to attain the knowledge that will transform the world. In the case of the Andean people, it is a very different matter.

In the Andes it is common to hear the farmers who raise alpacas say: 'In the same way that we raise alpacas, they also raise us', or: 'just as we raise potatoes, the potatoes also raise us'. The quality of upbringing or nurturing is not an exclusive attribute of the human community, but also of nature and of all the communities that inhabit the world. This is so because the Andean human community has not disaffiliated itself from nature, but is a part of her.

If knowledge presupposes a relationship of distance between a subject and an object outside of oneself, it is not difficult to see that this method of locating oneself in relation to nature is not an attribute of the Andean human community. What is experienced between human communities, Andean deities and nature is a reciprocal dialogue – a relationship that does not presuppose distancing and the objectification of those who converse, but instead presupposes an attitude of affection and comprehension regarding the other's life. This dialogue does not lead to the knowledge of the other, but rather to mutual empathy, to a desire to attune oneself with the other's way of being, and together to generate and regenerate life. We are dealing with a dialogue that fecundates, engenders, and leads to wisdom. Wisdom for the Andean people is not associated with an accumulation of knowledge – to know a lot about many things – rather it is associated with the attribute of nurturing, where the sensitivity to know how to nurture is as important as knowing how to allow oneself to be nurtured. This reciprocal nurturing is what re-creates life in the Andean world, and not the power-giving knowledge that one can have about others. In this way of living the world, the appearance of education as a social justification for the conquest of nature could not have happened.

Wisdom in Andean life: nurturing and allowing oneself to be nurtured

In the Andean cosmovision, the world is perceived as a dwelling for a multiplicity of animated beings. The mountains, the waters of the rivers, the rains, the *huacas* or deities, the plants, the animals, the human community and the wind all have life. The Andean world is a world full of life where there is no room for the notion of something being inert or without life.

Beings communicate among themselves by means of their reciprocal dialogue. Since everything is alive, they all speak, they join in dialogue. For example, a Bolivian farmer says:

> We have great faith in what nature transmits to us. Those signs are not the result of man's science nor an invention of people of great experience. Rather it is the very voice of nature that announces to us the ways in which we should sow our crops. (Van den Berg, 1990: 38)

As well as being alive, the mountain is our grandfather; the Earth is our mother. The potatoes that are incorporated for the first time into the *chacra* are treated like daughters-in-law. In the Andean world, not only is everything alive and everything speaks, but everything has the attributes of a person and a relative. Don Jesus Urbano Rojas, an Ayacuchan artisan, says, 'I myself am the son of my parents, may they rest in peace, but I am also the son of *Pachamama*' (Urbano and Macera 1992: 164).

We are dealing with a world of equivalence, where all are relatives, all are important and necessary in the re-creation of life, and where no one feels self-sufficient. This incompleteness is what makes this reciprocal dialogue arise; the person who is self-sufficient does not dialogue or reciprocate. Completeness in the Andean world is achieved through the contribution of all to all. The *ayllu* is the microcosm where our lives fulfil the kinship relations of reciprocity, care and mutual nurturance.

This living world is, in its own way of being, dynamic – it is a continuous series of occurrences. What is, is important and not the fact; the fact congeals. To say that, for the Andean, the perception of the world is not 'photographic' but 'cinematographic' may be a useful way to explain it. Events and occurrences follow one another in a world that is perpetually giving of itself. It is not a matter of a given world – congealed and coagulated. What exists flows and is fluid because it is a living and life-giving world. It is a vigorous and bubbling well whose physiology moves to the rhythms of the cosmic diastoles and systoles.

In this way of living, each one is showing his or her way of being, each one is saying, is speaking. Each being expresses itself through 'signs' that are continually saying something about themselves and how their relations with others feel. The position and the luminosity of the stars, for example, 'tell' the farmer about aspects of the climate because the behaviour of the stars in that moment corresponds to a mode of dialogue with the other beings. Similarly the frequency, intensity and colour of the winds are 'telling' the farmer of the weather that is about to happen, because the wind presents a colour and odour that express the particular way it dialogues with other beings.

Nature 'speaks' to the farmer, just as the farmer 'speaks' to nature and to the *huacas* about diverse matters. There is no objectification here, no distancing from nature on the part of the human community; rather, it is 'a dance' where all are dancing fraternally to the sound of a natural music, in a cosmic dance in which we participate and to which we contribute. Here there are no individual musical scores, but a rhythmical communion. For example, the harmony that is expressed when a plant buds, or when the corn flowers, expresses the synchrony emerging from such a harmonious encounter between the beings that dance. It does not arise because of the repetition of a code learned beforehand. It is this harmony of circumstances, it is this *tinkuy*, which causes the sprouting of variability and diversity of forms of life, not the transformation of nature by the actions of man.

To make harmony germinate, one has to be attentive to the 'signs' of the other beings. These 'signs' (called *lomasas* by the Aymaras) are telling us about the behaviour of the other and allow us to achieve an empathy – a bond that unites, the encounter that causes germination – in so far as we know how or are open to dialogue with these signs, with the way of being of that person. The edifice of Andean wisdom builds itself in dialogue with a multiplicity of signs. All beings 'emit' signs but not all dialogue with the existing diversity. Abstraction consists precisely in removing the signs to keep only some of them which are considered important: this is the road taken by science. However, holism is different from abstraction; it is an attitude to life that does not remove what is complicated because it knows how to dialogue with everything.

In a ceremony for the *Ispallas* (deities of the first fruits) which takes place in February in the *altiplano* around Puno, the old potatoes ritually dialogue with the new (recently harvested) ones. They tell them: 'Just as we have nurtured these humans, you now also will have to do it.' In the Andean world nurturing is not only attributed to humans. Nature and all of its dwellers also have the attributes of cultivating, of nurturing. They nurture the mountains, the water, the trees and forests, the *quinua*, the llamas, the potatoes, the *huacas* or deities and the human community. It is a pan-nurturing world.

It is in the Andes, as among many primal cultures, that nature is everything; so reciprocal nurturing is achieved in a world of equivalent beings in which all forms of life, not solely the humans, share the dignity of being considered persons. No one is more or less than another. The *quinuas* are persons like the alpacas, the humans, and the *huacas*. Here we are not in a world of subject and object. The water and the stone are alive, and the interaction between the human community and hail, for example, is an interaction between persons. (The hail is named *compadre* – godfather – by the human community of Quispillaccta, Ayacucho.)

The human community has not distanced itself from nature, and works within it as one member among others. The *huacas* or deities, and the humans are part of nature. Since everything is nature, everything emanates from her; and everything is made clear and evident to us through emotions, and sensitivity, since 'the beyond', the supernatural, does not exist. The deity *Wiracocha*, considered by many scholars to be supernatural, is apprehended as a person present here; one is dealing with a real *huaca* with whom one dialogues (Valladolid 1992).

If a world, like the Andean one, is constituted of persons and not of subjects or objects, its members are not interested in 'knowing' the other, because they do not see the other as an object or a thing and also because they are not interested in acting upon or transforming the other. The focus is on attunement between beings – lovingly 'getting' the signs – for inasmuch as mutual conversation arises, nurturing flows. Dialogue here does not result in an action that falls on someone, but rather in reciprocal nurturing, that makes life flower and flow: it is personal, generating; it is seminal, it is a dialogue for life.

Dialogue in a feeling and living world is communication between sensibilities. One dialogues with the mouth, the hands, the sense of smell, vision, hearing, gestures, flowerings, the colours of the skin, the taste of the rain, the colour of the wind, etc. As everything is a person, everything speaks. The potatoes speak, the llamas, the human community, the mountains, the rain, the hail, the *huacas*. Language is not a verbal representation that congeals the person named; in a world that is alive, language also is alive. The one named is 'presentified'; it is not, as Westerners would say, a representation or a reflexive interpretation. The word pronounced causes the person to 'emerge', it is the very person that is made present by the pronounced word; we are dealing with a seminal word.

In regard to this, Castelnuovo and Creamer say:

> Rigorously, in order to speak of 'thought' there must exist a discrimination between the internal world and the external world, between the symbol and the symbolized. What is given in these type of personalities is a mode of thought, where there is no difference between the symbol and the symbolized. In such concrete 'thought', the word is not a symbol, it is the symbolized, in the same manner that the host is not the 'symbol' of Christ but is His body. For this reason, in these cultures, there are words that one cannot pronounce; to pronounce the name of the devil, for example, implies the presence of the devil.
> (1987: 31)

For the Andean, the *illa* of the llama is not a representation of the llama, but actually *is* the llama. The *illa* ritually accompanies the Andean as a stimulus for regeneration. It is not an object, a symbol or an amulet to bring luck to one's flocks by magic for those who possess it, rather it is a beloved llama delivered to the farmer by the *Apus* to be a 'guide' in raising his animals. Thus, it also makes no sense to speak of the symbol and the symbolized. The symbol is found at the centre of the construction of the subject in the modern West. Such a subject does not dialogue with reality directly, but with representations of the thing, whose meaning is arbitrary and imposed by the subject as a condition for controlling nature. For those who believe in a transcendent reality, the symbol permits them to continue affirming their beliefs, since they consider that the spiritual is an invisible reality that is made evident through the symbol. Because of this they consider rituals among primal peoples as a symbolic action opposed to real action in the world. It is different for the Andean people; as Frédérique Apffel-Marglin puts it (personal communication with Eduardo Grillo 1992):

> For those who live in harmony and dialogue with the world, this distinction between symbol and symbolized is noxious. The Goddess is not to be understood as symbol of the earth or of women. This way of understanding things leaves us in a dualism between the mind and reality, that is between nature and culture.
>
> The Goddess, by her existence, shows that women and the earth are one and the same [remarks made about Orissan farmers in India].

In the Andes, however, vision has an important role. On the obelisk Tello de Chavin, a monumental sculpture made four thousand years ago, everything sees. The *conches*, the plants, the sun, the Pleiades, the human community, the serpent – among other beings – are drawn with enormous eyes. This conception continues; in the Andean cosmovision, everything that exists shares the attribute of vision. The Andean priests of today, as always, appreciate life and health through the eyes and even can, during ceremonies, share such visions with those who participate in the ritual. Vision is an important attribute in dialogue. The eye permits us to 'see' the interior, anterior and posterior sides of life. This vision is also a 'generating' vision; it directs, makes us 'see', makes life that does not show itself to everyday vision 'appear' and 'germinate'.

A Cajamarquino artisan from the north of Peru, being asked for the model that gave form to his 'rock sculptures', said he did not have any, and commented that 'inside the rock was the form'. He 'saw' the form, so that the final artistic expression was the culmination of a mutual dialogue between the rock (that is alive) and the artisan. What is called craft is simply another way of nurturing, of making appear, of generating new forms of life.

In this vision, one does not see 'a separate reality', but instead the same life felt in an intense way, in all its plenitude and particularities. Hence, the *Ayahuasca* is not a drug that delivers a paradise to whoever takes it, rather it is a person who accompanies us in the ritual, because it knows how to 'see' and it 'makes us see'. We all see, but with distinct intensities. Whoever sees more does so because he or she has special attributes in order to see; also, those who have lived more see more. In this way, the elders can know how the weather will be tomorrow, or in the next season. An Andean priest can also tell us how life was yesterday.

The modalities of dialogue are multiple, and they do not take us towards action, but culminate in nurturing. We will briefly refer to two of them: the *chaco* and the *chacra*.

The *chaco* is a ritual way of nurturing nature. In it and in the preceding petitioning ceremony, the human community 'nurtures' nature. In the *chaco* members of the *sallqa* or of nature are gathered and bound, be they *vicuñas*, fish, foxes, partridges, forests, etc. The human community 'thins' or prunes what is strictly necessary. They take the old animals, others are sheared; they cut the branches that hinder the flowering of trees. In this way nature is 'pruned' to permit a regermination and invigoration, at the same time that the human community is nurtured and a beneficiary of the products of nature.

The *chacra* is another modality of reciprocal nurturing between nature, *huacas* and the human community. In the *chacra*, a portion of the soils that inhabit nature evolves into nurtured soils; part of the natural waters are re-created into water for irrigation; certain plants from the *sallqa* are nurtured and evolve into plants that are cultivated to increase their variability. The climate of the *chacra* evolves into a micro-climate; some animals evolve into breeds for stock. In this way part of the natural landscape is re-created into an agricultural and pastoral landscape. The *chacra* is, therefore, re-created nature since it is not nurtured to negate nature but to propitiate its dynamism and its diversity. In reciprocity, the potatoes, the *chacra*, nurture the human community.

The *chacra*, however, is not the only arena of agricultural life. The farmers say for example that the llama is *kayuni yapu* 'a chacra with feet'; there exists a '*chacra* of salt', '*chacra* of gold', '*chacra* of cattle', etc. In this way the '*chacra*' comes to be any arena where the human community, nature, and the *huacas* dialogue reciprocally in order to nurture life. In the Andean world, the *vicuñas* are considered nurturers of the *apus* (tutelary mountains). Similarly, in nature there exist 'goose *chacras* of the foxes'. The very *sallqa* is considered to be the '*chacra* of the *huacas*'. The human community itself is the *chacra* of the *apus*.

Guamán Poma de Ayala, a sixteenth-century Indian chronicler in the Colony, depicted Adam and Eve in a drawing with their *chaquitaclla* (Andean hoe) making a *chacra*. In spite of suffering evangelization, this Andean could not envisage members of the human community, even our 'first parents', not being *chacareros*. The *chacra* can be found at the very centre of preoccupation of the Andean human community. Therefore, in PRATEC, we say that the Andean culture is agrocentric.

If there is no knowledge, there is also no accumulated knowledge. Nurturing is a dialogue that re-creates itself, that appears in each circumstance. If there is one thing that characterizes Andean life, it is diversity. Usually this term is used to designate the phytogenetic variability of Andean nature. One also has to consider that this variability applies to the landscape, the *chacras*, the human communities, the deities and even the weather. There is not a day, or a moment in that day, when the weather is the same as that of the day before. Although there can be periods of humidity or drought, within these there exists a variability of circumstances. The accumulation of knowledge – in this context – can only contribute to its petrification.

To nurture in each circumstance, memory and recollection are useful, but they are only references for this act, since what is nurtured and what is made in this moment is an expression of the dialogue that is held at that moment by members of the human community, the deities and nature. It may be that there is agreement to make a canal or a terrace, but the way of making it would depend on the dialogue that is held with the coca, with the rock, with nature at each moment. One can know how to irrigate, but the way in which to do it at any particular moment depends on a combination of circumstances; it will not be a repetition of what has been done before, but will arise from an attunement with the circumstances of the moment. Here in the Andes we are not in the world of normalization, of industrial standardization or of a human wilfulness. Manuals for how to make things have only referential value in Andean villages.

The concept of the reproduction of knowledge is inappropriate here, because one activity is not the same as another. The concept of homogeneous zones of production does not fit here either, because the soils of one *chacra* are not the same as those of another – even when they are found at a similar altitude. That is why a peasant is not interested in teaching others how something is done. What he or she does is to *show* the way he or she does it. The one who dialogues and who sees the demonstration will not repeat it in his or her *chacra*, he or she will re-create it – that is, attune him- or herself to the particular circumstances of that specific *chacra*. That being so, the educational concepts of teaching – of apprenticeship – are worthless. These correspond to a normalized world, which is not comparable to the Andean one.

Experience does not lead the peasants to say 'this is how we do it', but it leads them to know how to dialogue better, to know how to nurture with more intensity, to be alert with respect to what the other says, to have an attitude of attunement with the others. Wisdom in the Andean world does not have to do with knowing *more*, but with knowing *how* to nurture and allow oneself to be nurtured.

Education in the modern West

Knowledge When Columbus returned after his 'discovery' of 'the New World', those who had supported him were as interested in the treasures that he brought back or saw, as in the way that he made the voyage, in his navigation papers and his knowledge of the seas. For them the gold was important, but it was also important to possess the knowledge that gave permanent access to these paths to riches and enjoyment.

Columbus's voyage also made possible the concretization of the idea and the method for its formation. Like many, he did not know the Indies. He had images, vague legends, representations of them, but neither he nor one of his patrons saw the Indies before he undertook the voyage. According to the Judaeo-Christian God, man is mind and matter and, additionally, is made in the likeness of his God; man can also conceptualize realities that, if they do not exist right now, can be created in the future.

The notions of the 'idea' (God) and of 'matter' (created world), like the notion of man in the likeness of God, are found in the Holy Scriptures. In them God said: 'Now we will make man. He will look like us and will have the power over the fish, the birds, the domestic and wild animals and over all the animals that crawl on the earth.' And so it was done. When God created man, he created him in his image:

> And God said, Let us make man in our image, after our likeness: and let them have dominion over the fish of the sea, and over the fowl of the air, and over the cattle, and over all the earth, and over every creeping thing that creepeth upon the earth.

> And God said, Behold, I have given you every herb bearing seed, which is upon the face of all the earth, and every tree, in which is the fruit of a tree yielding seed; to you it shall be for meat. (Gen. 1: 26–9)

There is no reason to believe Columbus was the exception and did not adhere to this mandate, which is so deeply entrenched in the mentality of modern Western man. It was not only the conquering/learning of a piece of foreign territory for the Iberian Christian Crown, but rather a dominance over the beings who live in this space that was sought. In time it was inevitable they would make this a place similar to what they knew – in other words, they would strive to negate what existed and struggle to transform it.

The example is interesting because it allows us to appreciate through just one illustration – five hundred years of European invasion – the overturning of the attitude of the European man with respect to nature and, at the same time, the changes to the concept of knowledge that had occurred. Knowledge was no longer the understanding of reality, as St Thomas had thought, nor was it the contemplation of reality, as was the way of the Greeks (St Thomas said that *intellectus* comes from *intuslegere*, to read within and discover the internal articulation of things, and in this way penetrate the works of God) (Peña Cabrera 1984: 99). Rather, one had to act upon the world to have knowledge of it, a knowledge which in turn could be used to act upon nature in order to transform it. From then on, it has been action on the world and not the contemplation of it that provokes knowledge.

When knowledge is a product of contemplation, nature conserves its dynamism, its equilibrium, since human intervention does not alter its cycles. This idea dominated Greek thought and it was still a predominant idea in the Middle Ages – certainly it was believed that one could access God through contemplation of his works. But when it is presumed that the world can be explained be secular phenomena alone, when God no longer mediates human explanations of the world, a process of meddling with nature is initiated that modifies its composition. This action requires the interrogation of nature in a planned way; this way is the experiment.

As Van Kessel affirms, this process will be made more violent in accordance with man's separation from divine tutelage. He tells us:

> With the secularization of Western culture, God disappeared from the horizon. Only Man remained, now an absolute and autonomous owner of the earth and its objects. Because he feels he is the owner, the relation of ownership has alienated him from his natural surroundings, in such a way that he conceives himself to be completely distinct from the world in which he lives, even transcendent and opposed to it. In addition to feeling that he is the owner, Western *Homo faber* conceives himself to be a creator, autonomous, and the author of all the miracles of modern technology. (Van Kessel 1991: 17)

These ideas, the voyages of Columbus and other events that occurred in central Europe (such as the discovery of the plough, which allowed the expansion of the agricultural frontier), were strengthened by the notion that nature was there to be exploited. Those who awaited treasures from the voyages of Columbus did not believe for a moment that what was brought back would not be a product of the efforts of their intrepid navigators – their daring had won the rights to it. It was clear that nature was there to be exploited, as, by extension, were all people who were not like them – in other words those who were not Christian: 'the infidels'. Moreover, the Crusades showed that they did not have to trust or keep trust with those who did not believe in the Bible. The forms of genocide that were carried out were no novelty to the Europeans of the time.

Knowledge does not have as its goal knowledge itself. If this were the case Columbus and those who promoted him would have been content with the contemplation and description of the New World that they had found; the then king and queen of Spain would have considered it sufficient confirmation of the adventure and as contribution to the knowledge of their time if some novel formula of the world that affirmed their religious faith and a worthy painting or poetry of the landscape and the towns from this part of the world were produced. But it did not happen that way. Instead of sending painters and poets to the New World, they chose to send soldiers – people with military experience interested in dominating the world.

As man distances himself from nature he affirms the notion of the individual, a being separate and opposed to nature. Knowledge will not be the result – as Pannikar affirms – of an empathy, an identification with nature, but rather the result of the captivity of nature's being through its objectification, his own distancing from himself. Therefore knowledge presupposes a fortuitous bridge between a cognisant subject and an object to be known, and knowledge becomes the administration of this obtained learning. The man who affirms knowledge considers himself to have triumphed over nature. Alternatively, to be without knowledge will be interpreted as ignorance and amount to an inferiority relative to nature.

As Abugattas points out:

> The individual assumes that nature dominates him, in accordance with his ignorance. The individual is liberated from nature if he is able to unravel its mysteries and can invert his relation to it, to fulfil the divine wish expressed in the Scriptures at the moment of creation; to know that man is the owner of all other creatures and should exert dominance over them. (1986: 100)

It is in this modern ideological context that education gradually appears as an invitation to the individual to fulfil his or her desire for dominance of the world.

But the actual dominance of all of nature and of the non-Western human community would have been inconceivable without science and technology. Science is not only the systematic knowledge of a method to gratify its creators: by definition it is practice, it must serve to transform the world; therefore, technology is not only the instrument but the realization of science.

With modern science this relation of the objectification of nature is deepened and so is the way of knowing. As Antonio Peña Cabrera tells us:

> The modern scientist, in contrast to the scholar in classical Greece, upon knowing something distances himself from it through the representation he has of it. Operation on the representation becomes the representation of the phenomenon of nature. In other words, the truth of a scientific theory does not proceed from mere observation, but rather from the mental construction from which one considers a phenomenon. The characteristic of modern man – Heidegger says – is not that he has an image of the world, but that he takes the

world as an image [...]. [Heidegger] adds further on that the process of modernity is the conquest of the world as an image [...]. What is it then, that Heidegger understands as 'image'? He himself says: it is the formation of the product represented. Finally then, the truth for modern man is what he makes it [...]. In this manner, to know nature is to question it so that it responds by means of the experiment. (Peña Cabrera 1986: 76)

The real work becomes a reference, the arena in which experiences take place, since what is of interest is the mental construction of an image of the world and the adjustment of the world to it. Here one does not dialogue with reality but with an image of the world, and what will be of interest for the future is Utopia – the edification of the non-existent paradises which can exist thanks to science and technology. The knowledge of reality through actions upon it will equal the capacity for knowledge of imaginary Utopias.

School The encyclopedists, amazed at the development of Western thought and at the rapid way in which machines transformed nature, considered that the road to progress was already laid out. What non-Western nations should do was avoid the tortuous road that they – the Westerners of the time – had had to travel to find truth. All that remained was to assimilate and reproduce what was already known. This could lead all of us to enjoy short-term happiness.

Institutionalization and not just an accumulation of knowledge was important. The school constituted the nucleus of the transmission of this world-transforming thought now located in the centre of the educational process. According to Ivan Illich (1992) the history of education is associated with an idea of the salvation of man which surfaced at the end of the sixteenth century.

> Man, much before the enlightenment, was redefined by his new pedagogical tutors as a being that, after being born to his mother, should be reborn with the intervention of an *alma mater*, a new 'saint' mother, the School. (Illich 1992: 6)

However, for the purposes of the encyclopedists, it required that knowledge be systematized (as outlined much earlier by Comenius 1592–1670, in his *Magna Didactica*) and the school spread worldwide. What began to happen later, in the second half of the nineteenth century, is that France designed and established an education system that goes from the school to the university – a system that spread all over the planet – at a time when the present division of the world into industrial countries that are producers of science and technology and non-industrialized countries was taking shape.

As Albert Merani teaches, referring to the French educative process that culminated with the reorganization of public instruction by Napoleon Bonaparte (1769–1821):

For the first time in history, education was organized as a unified totality, from primary school to the university, constituting a 'course' with distinct steps taken by the sons of the bourgeoisie who, beginning in the first grade would end by becoming one of society's 'professionals'. All of the steps were regulated with meticulous stipulations, and in this manner the didactic organism ended by becoming an efficient machinery capable of adequately preparing men for State positions, bureaucracies, the military and for science. In 1872, France applies the Law of Public Education, and from there, the example expands in all directions. The old nations of Europe to the very new ones of America adopt the system, and the right of everyone to know how to read and write, to receive freely the rudiments of a primary education, was sanctioned. (Merani 1969: 13)

As Illich says:

The new path of salvation became first a road for the privileged and later an inevitable super highway, carefully paved with good intentions ... Later, learning was seen as a result of the teaching of professional experts, parents or someone in between. In the nineteenth century, if a person knew something, but could not identify the agent of his knowledge, he was defined as 'autodidactic', he who teaches himself. (Illich 1992: 6)

While the industrialized countries consolidated their own positions of power and distributed the world's areas of influence among themselves, the educational systems that were implemented in the non-industrialized nations did not achieve the massiveness that is valued today. The world education enterprise was set up after the Second World War, when the areas of influence were defined, and after experts designed and launched on to the market the world development enterprise, as it was defined in the United States and announced by President Truman on a cold morning in January 1949.

The presupposition that runs through the corridors of the institutions of the world education enterprise is that of the intrinsic incompetence of the human being to learn by himself, and that of the world's only destiny; man is ignorant while he does not know the secrets of nature. Education, with science and technology, is to liberate man from the ties that hobble his rapid and efficacious knowledge of nature. On the other hand, if we want free men living in the one community destined for peace and development, the institutionalization and expansion of educational services should be an obligation for all.

For Illich:

'education as an institution' involves the supposition that each person is born as an individual in a contractual society that should be understood before it is lived in. According to this interpretation, no one becomes part of this type of society, except through a grace that is granted under the cloak of education. This education is something for which one should work. But this education is also something that cannot be obtained except through the mediation of an agency – the School – which for *homo educandus* is analagous to the Church for Christians. According to this 'reformed' vision of human nature, salvation continues to come through the book, although this book is no longer the Bible. The new book should be read in a new way, and this type of reading demands prolonged ceremonies that take place in classrooms. To put this new church into action, a new clergy of teachers came into existence who were supported by new necessities defined by the new vision of human nature. The brilliant power of the new clergy required justification. It was based on the dogma that proclaims literacy instruction as something necessary for salvation. ... In the course of the century, a new reason for obligatory and universal education was discovered; school was defined as something necessary for work. Democratic socialization, literate culture and the training of the work force became fused as a rationalization for existence that came from a transnational church. (Illich 1992: 7)

With school legitimized, institutions promoting and monitoring the new school order appeared (UNESCO, for example). The world was divided into educated countries and those in the process of being educated. Those not educated are those that ignore the secrets of science and technology, which are the weapons that permit development. If they desire development they should consume education. This undertaking achieves its first results when the system is installed everywhere, at the same time as the illusion of consumption attracts middle-class minds of the non-industrialized countries. In order for this illusion to be shared by everyone, the possession of the necessary capabilities that a good education can provide is required. When school becomes an anxious channel of mobility and a moulder of progress, victory is assured. For this purpose the quality and density of the information received for transforming the world is not important; power is established in so far as the notion of one world for all is massively consumed and diffused.

As we know, the division of the Western ideals is relatively democratic, but this does not happen with knowledge. With the development of large industry, it is the owners of capital – the largest imperialist companies, those that accumulate scientific and technical knowledge about production and the reproduction of machines – that dominate the world. In the words of Karl Marx:

The accumulation of knowledge, of ability and of all the general productive forces of the social brain, are absorbed by capital which opposes labour; these accumulations appear hereafter as a form of capital's property, or more precisely, of fixed capital. (Marx K. *Capital*, Part I, Chapter 13: 274, quoted in Vasconi 1976)

That which is produced in the countries that are centres of capital is reproduced in the relations between the industrialized and the non-industrialized countries. Non-industrialized countries are left with their humble task of reproducing in disadvantageous conditions a knowledge whose ideal has been internalized by the intellectual classes, whose capacities to generate their own concepts are submerged by their competition with scientific and technological knowledge created in the modern West. (A great achievement of world scholarship has been the creation of a universal middle class that makes an intellectual from Puno think in a manner similar to one from Brussels, with the difference that the one from Puno will always be a disciple of the one from Brussels but only with difficulty will he become a teacher.)

If education is the method invented to prepare the individual for systematic access to the secrets of nature, what is in crisis is not only the school – which long ago showed its irrelevance to the ideals that support its gestation and development – but also the very principles that are behind the concept of education. These are: the notion of the individual, that of subject and object, and of course the very theory of knowledge. Nature has shown disturbing reactions to this way of knowing, and in many cases it has been irreversibly altered and modified. The ecological damage caused to the atmosphere, the contamination of the oceans and rivers, the environmental pollution and so on are symptoms that show this way of learning is dangerous for the conservation of the biosphere because it leads to an intervention that alters and damages life-cycles. When they enter into conflict with life itself, not only are science and technology (along with their principles and realizations) called into question, but so are the very ideals of life established with the aid of development (employment, housing, social security, democracy, etc.) and, of course, the instrument that allowed the conquest of the world – education.

Here it is of little help to know that the crisis of the school is universal. It is certainly known that the industrialized countries receive twenty times more resources than non-industrialized countries. Even so, they are far from having resolved the problem: 42 per cent of the Spanish population never read, and 63 per cent did not buy books in 1990. Edith Cresson took a stance as chief of the French government, denouncing the 'educational archaisms of France'. The North American education system, for so long a model for others, is close to becoming a disaster area. The percentage of dropouts continues to grow along with illiteracy, which already includes – as a functional deficiency – more than half of the adult population of the US. The 140 million North Americans involved in the educational regime – as students, teachers or whatever else – question more and more what they are doing. The Japanese cannot claim victory either, although the demands of their educational system make them pay the price of the highest rate of child suicides in the world (Opciones No. 2, 1992).

Ivan Illich, the great critic of the school, is not left out of this debate; he tells us:

The societies which maintain in effect their commitment to obligatory and universal scholarship persist in a frustrating enterprise more and more insidious: the multiplication of dropouts and 'failed outs'. From the point of view that I have assumed, faith in scholarship can no longer be innocent. ... Throughout the world, three-quarters of the children that enter the first grade never arrive to the level that the law of their country defines as the obligatory minimum. (Illich 1992: 3)

In Peru, Raúl Gonzales Moreyra states the following in a document evaluating the educational situation:

School definitely produces a maladjusting impact of sociocultural origin on an enormous contingent of children. Thus Cardo's (1980) findings show the smallest number of students completing first grade to be found in the highlands and in the Amazonian lowlands. The corresponding failure is 45.4 per cent in the mountains and 49.9 per cent in the Amazonian region. On the coast only 25.4 per cent fail. That is to say, for almost half of the children from the mountains and Amazonian region that enter national schooling, the school is an agency of frustration and failure. The school, instead of offering itself as an agency to facilitate socialization, becomes in fact an obstacle. (Gonzales Moreyra 1989: 66)

On a worldwide level Illich affirms:

The poor majorities have understood more rapidly and with greater clarity than the governmental experts that the goals of development in health materials, education, sanitation, transport or housing have been stupidly defined and cannot become beneficial for the majority. ... The general director of the World Organization of Work declared that to believe in the possibility of sufficient employment in the future – in wealthy and poor countries – was no longer an excusable illusion, but rather obsessively objectionable fuel for false expectations. ... The typical teacher firmly believes that even cats educate their kittens and that the parents 'teach' their children to walk. ... Viewed from the outside, the school classifies people, intimidates them so that they accept bureaucratic judgement over their own abilities, prepares them for a world that no longer exists, trains their capacity to pretend. (Illich 1992: 7)

Therefore, the issue does not consist of merely searching for alternatives to school or decolonizing society in order to search for new pedagogical alternatives outside of school. Rather, the heart of the matter is for our people to abandon the modern Western cosmology, which has introduced into our nations an institutionality foreign to our way of being.

The school in the Andean world

School, as we know, began significantly to penetrate Andean communities after the Second World War. This is now the tortuous 'encounter' of knowledge to transform the world with child-rearing in order for the world to live. School knowledge is, in addition, the knowledge of the Western middle class from non-industrialized countries; it is the official knowledge of the State and institutions whose Western cultural contents are compulsively spread throughout native populations.

Andeans attend schools where they are inculcated with a knowledge through which to transform the world – a knowledge unfamiliar to them. The central ritual of school is the teaching of abstraction, analysis, generalization and experimentation – attributes of scientific thought. Abstraction, as we know, is not only to separate something mentally that in reality is united, it is a way of mentally tearing nature to pieces. This mode is contrary to Andean holism.

Shardakov explains this process taking place within the boundaries of the school very well. He tells us:

> The development of abstraction is manifest in students in the formation of the capacity to separate and isolate from objects and singular phenomena, features, links, and common and essential relations, and also to distinguish the features and accidental links of these objects and phenomena and disregard them. ... In the process of studying isolated objects or phenomena first they are separated and isolated, that is to say, their shared and essential properties and links are abstracted from those that are accidental; only later, through the synthesis and generalization of the first ones, is generalized and abstract knowledge in the form of concepts, laws, and rules obtained. (Shardakov 1968: 145–7)

This operation supposes a world capable of being disassembled, a machine-world made of essential and accessory parts. The experimental method, as we have known since Galileo's time, guarantees a coherent plan for the manipulation of nature which is, as Abugattas says, 'the manner invented or better still, generalized, by the moderns to dialogue with objects' (Abugattas 1986: 103).

This way of seeing life is different from the Andean cosmovision, which is of a living world where one is part of nature, with everyone being important in its re-creation.

A typical question is whether this knowledge penetrates or actually synchronizes with the Andean cosmovision. School, like the variety of so-called 'improved' potatoes, incorporates itself into the living world and expands the pantheon of nurtured beings. But since school, like the 'improved' potatoes, demands an artificialization and homogenization of the environment, its reproduction is limited by the high cost of maintenance that its presence signifies in a highly variable environment.

School as we know is 'monovarietal', it is the compulsory teaching of Western knowledge, and has as a goal something different from the nurturing of the Andean *chacra*. In the words of Toffler:

> Historically, the implicit function of compulsory schooling, was to habituate children to certain uses and customs necessary for the new economic organ-

ization of society that came about after the Industrial Revolution. School was the place to train and accustom them to complete schedules, to habituate them to repetitive tasks and to obey foreigners, characteristics with which the recently appeared factories were organized. (Toffler 1980: 59)

The Andean *chacra*, as we know, is not a factory. Just like what happened with the so-called 'Green Revolution' and the native potatoes, the school has not displaced the Andean way of living and seeing the world. The Andean way has incorporated the knowledge of reading and writing as another way of linking itself to the knowledge of the official modern culture, but has not used the knowledge to insert itself into that culture – that is, it has not become modern and rational – and has not been sucked into the Western aim to transform nature. School has always been of the State and not of the community, despite the participating and reforming intentions that exist in this direction. In contrast, the nurturing of the *chacras* has continued in the Andean manner and not as the school would like the agricultural life of the community to be.

In the Andean community, a person learns from nurturing, from what he or she has nurtured and not because 'they have told him so'. To nurture one must live the nurturing. This is not to say that we are speaking of a closed and autarchic people; the Andean way of being is that of dialogue with all cultures, and if that entails learning to read and write in a language foreign to one's own, that will be done. For a people who nurture, nothing is foreign – including school.

As with the Christian saints, Western knowledge has not been syncretized with the Andean. In its pantheon one finds the school along with cattle, barley, the plough, and the Virgin Mary and Christ. The saints have been incorporated as deities with whom *ayni* is performed, with whom one dialogues, but who are not worshipped (as was expected by the colonizing forces). Clearly, because of the compulsive way this 'incorporation' has been and continues to be carried out, some of these presences injure the landscape and the healthy nurturing of it.

These incorporations, despite the fact that many are erosive, have not replaced the Andean way of being, and those that remain are lived in an Andean way. Abstraction has not entered. Each llama and each *chacra* is not classified under a generic name, but rather continues to be called by name and treated like a member of the family. The Spanish language is known because Andeans are a people who have the capacity to speak many languages, but that has not prompted us to write a dictionary of our own language. There is also some knowledge of mathematical operations, but this also has not caused us to measure the world or to accept this view which Galileo held, that the book of nature is written in a mathematical language. The learning of history does not mean Andeans accept we are living in a world of linear and irreversible time any more than the celebration of Christian festivals has brought us to monotheism. There are many more examples of where the Andean way of being remains true to itself.

If the school's goal is to produce, through the application of formalism, human beings whose conduct can be predicted and controlled, the school is a failure in the Andes. The Andeans continue to be people whose conduct is flexible, complicated, subtle and unpredictable. Their activities derive from dialogue with nature and deities, and when working their *chacras* they attune themselves to the particular situation in which they live. The world continues to exist as a living totality and a re-creation in spite of school.

But it is clear that the colonizers do everything in their power to substitute the school for the Andean way. This compulsive, colonial, fundamentalist spirit is what damages, erodes and causes problems for the harmonious re-creation of life. But its victories, such as pesticides, have been passing; they have not achieved the death of nurturing. This is so much the case that in spite of the worldwide enterprise of development and education, the Andean world is one of the most diverse on the planet, nurturing a diversity of potatoes, *ocas*, *quinuas*, llamas, alpacas, *andenes*. And in the middle of the crisis of modernity and of the educational system, both locally and worldwide, the Andean people recover their spaces and empower themselves.

References

Abugattas, Juan. 1986; 'La naturaleza de la tecnologia' (The nature of technology). In Antonio Peña (ed.) *Filosofia de la Tecnica: Aspectos Problematicos de la Tecnologia en el Peru y el Mundo* (*Philosophy of Technology: Problematic aspects of technology in Peru and in the world*), Hozlo, Lima, Peru; Universidad Nacional de Ingenieria: 99–116.

Adorno T. and M. Horkheimer. 1971; *La Sociedad: Lecciones de Sociologia* (*Society: Lessons in Sociology*) Buenos Aires, Argentina; Proteo.

Bemac, Henri. 1956; *Dictionnaire des Synonymes*, Paris; Hachette.

Castelnuovo, A. and G. Creamer. 1987; *La desarticulacion del mundo andino: dos estudios sobre educacion y salud* (*The Disarticulation of the Andean World: Two Studies on Education and Health*), Quito, Ecuador.

Cullen, Carlos. 1977; 'Ser y Estar: Dos horizontes para definir la cultura' (Being and to be: two horizons to define culture), II Seminario Interdisciplinario del Stipendienwerk Latinamerika-Deutschland, Lima, Peru.

Gonzales Moreyra, Raúl. 1989; 'La educacion en el Peru: Estado de la cuestion' (Education in Peru: The state of the issue), Documento base, III Seminario sobre analisis y perspectivas de la educacion en el Peru. Pontificia Universidad Catolica. Facultad de Educacion. Consejo Nacional de Ciencia y Tecnologia. Lima, Peru.

Illich, Ivan. 1991; 'Alternativa a la desescolarizacion' (Alternative to deschooling).

In Illich, I. *La Guerra contra la Subsistencia: Antologia* (*The War Against Subsistence: An Anthology*) Bolivia; Ediciones Runa.

Illich, Ivan. 1992; 'La critica radical de la empresa escolar' (The radical critique of the schooling enterprise), *Opciones* 13, Suplemento catorcenal de El Nacional, Mexico, July.

Merani, Alberto. 1969; *Psicologia y Pedagogia: Las ideas pedagogicas de Henri Wallon*, S.A. Mexico; Grijalbo.

Opciones No. 2. 1992; *Suplemento Catorcenal de El Nacional*, Mexico.

Pannikar, Raimon. 1992; 'La recreacion del Nuevo Mundo: El fin de la era colonial' (The re-creation of the New World: the end of the colonial era), *Opciones* 20, suplemento catorcenal de El Nacional, Mexico, October.

Peña Cabrera, Antonio. 1984; 'Ciencia, tecnologia y sociedad en el mundo antiguo y medieval' (Science and technology in the ancient and medieval world) in *El factor ideologico en la ciencia y la tecnologia* (*The Ideological Factor in Science and Technology*), Asociacion Cultural Peruano Lima, Peru; Alemana.

Peña Cabrera, Antonio. 1986; 'Notas caracteristicas de la tecnologia occidental' (Characteristic aspects of western technology) in *Filosofia de la tecnica* (Philosophy of technology) Antonio Peña, ed. UNI, Peru.

Peña Cabrera, Antonio. 1992; 'La ciencia, la tecnica y la ecologia: Los limites de la racionalidad occidental' (Science, technology and ecology: the limits of western rationality), Summary. Intervencion en el curso de Formacion en Agricultura Campesina Andina, PRATEC, Universidad de Huamanga.

Shardakov M. N. 1968; *Desarrollo del pensamiento en el escolar* (*Development of Thinking in the Pupil*) Mexico; Gribaljo.

Toffler, Alvin. 1980; *La tercera Ola* (*The Third Wave*), New York; Morrow.

Urbano J, and P. Macera. 1992; *Santero y Caminante: Santoruraj-Nanpurej* (*Craftsman and Itinerant*), Lima, Peru; Apoyo.

Van Kessel, Juan. 1991; *Tecnologia Aymara: un enfoque cultural* (Aymara technology: A Cultural Perspective), Puno, Peru; CIDSA.

Valladolid, Julio, 1992; 'Estudios sobre agroastronomia andina' (Essays on Andean Agro-astronomy) Study Document No. 25, July, Lima, Peru; PRATEC.

Van den Berg, Hans. 1990; *La Tierra No Da Asi Nomas: Los ritos agricolas en la religion de los Aymaras-cristianos*. La Paz, Hisbol; UCD, ISET.

Vasconi, T. 1976; 'Contra la escuela' (*Against school*). In *Temas de educacion y politica* (*Themes on Education and Politics*) Lima, Peru; Tarea.

CHAPTER 7

Development or Decolonization in the Andes?

Eduardo Grillo Fernandez

We consider that the question 'Development or decolonization in the Andes?' is appropriate at this time because although it is clear to almost everyone that imperialism oppresses us and that we need to decolonize ourselves, nevertheless there is still a political consensus that development is the path that will lead us to liberation. This consensus does not realize that it is development itself which is an important instrument of imperialism to tie us even more firmly to the global market that it dominates. This is why in this work – that forms part of a series of reflections about Andean life carried out by PRATEC – we try to present the origins and reach of the concept of development. What has happened is that very deftly, imperialism has been able to legitimize the image of a Single World, whose paradigm is the form of life of the United States and where homogenous development is the norm; if somewhere development has not happened fully, then the view is that it is due to obstacles that have arisen – bottlenecks have occurred – which can always be resolved technologically. On this conceptual base, imperialism has constructed a global development enterprise which sells the promise of universal and uninterrupted progress. It is ready to give us its 'help' in the form of loans which increase the volume of our unpayable external debt. Nevertheless, after some fifty years of the functioning of the global development enterprise one notes that no one has achieved the hoped for benefits, apart from the West, which has made considerable financial gains.

Here in Peru and specifically in the department of Puno, Juan Bernardo Palao and Ignacio Garaycochea have coined the apt phrase 'archaeology of development' (Palao and Garaycochea 1989) to refer to the ruined vestiges of infrastructures for development scattered throughout the *altiplano*, whose antiquity is not greater than four or five decades. Because these are totally foreign to the requirements of the rural communities of the department of Puno, they have been left to deteriorate rapidly through the action of the weather, without being used at all, creating 'development garbage' which damages the landscape.

Faced with such irrefutable and consummate facts, we propose that the best way of achieving the betterment of the quality of life of the majority of our human inhabitants, of our nature and our *huacas* (deities), consists simply in having recourse to our own knowledge,[1] to our own capacities: to what we know and can do with certainty. It is time to reject the intromission of an exploitative imperialism and the desire for development that it has sold us. Only the culmination of the decolonization of the Andes will return us to ourselves, will return us to the sane and joyful life that we know how to live.

Imperialism and development

We will examine the intimate relationship between imperialism and development, reviewing in passing the concepts of Utopia, power, poverty, order and development.

Utopia The modern Western world, capitalist society, is the world of competition in which the human person is reduced to the individual – a product of the alienating disaggregation of the community – and delivered to its own fate without benefit of any shelter. The individual is the real support of a society that ignores him, that makes of him a disposable thing dependent on the hazards of supply and demand.

Work, which is the activator of society, is not for the individual a form of self-realization but rather a routine with no meaning or gratification. To this is due the profound anxiety that seizes people in the modern Western world, the profound anxiety of capitalist society. Due to this there is also a need to flee the present which manifests itself in the massive and sustained consumption of drugs which is endemic in North American and European societies.

But capitalist society also produces for itself its own legal drug: Utopia, that is the image of a world which does not yet exist but which can be constructed in the future. It too is a flight from the present. Utopia can only emerge as the expression of a profound discontent on the part of people with the world in which they live, as well as from the conviction that this world can indeed be modified so that it may be less cruel, less unbearable, less frustrating. Such a conviction, in its turn, has two prerequisites: its legality and its feasibility. The legality of the transformation of the world by man according to his desires is given by the Judaeo-Christian conception of the world. Its feasibility finds support in the doctrine of unlimited progress and in technology as the instruments of the dominion of nature by man. In the Judaeo-Christian conception, God created the world from nothing. In the first five days God created nature and on the sixth he created man. Finally on the seventh he rested and contemplated the perfection of his work. The creation of the world from nothingness is the greatest expression of power imaginable.

All-powerful God created the world through the divine Word, through the Logos. So then, in this conception, idea precedes matter. God is the Idea and the created world is matter. God said: 'let it be' and things happened. Matter in this context is nothing but the concretization of the Idea. But God made man 'in his image and semblance'. Therefore man also posseses the idea; he is a mixture of idea and matter. God is creator and all-powerful because He is Idea. That is why in the Judaeo-Christian conception, and only in it, man is also, to a certain extent, a creator.

In these conditions particular to Judaeo-Christianity, having been created 'in the image and semblance of God', man does not have to adjust (or fit) to the world – created by God – in which he is fated to live. Man is also a creator and, therefore, if the world becomes uncomfortable, not satisfactory – that is if his desires do not find full satisfaction in the world in which he lives – he can always create a different world. It is only a matter of modifying the world in order that it accommodates and satisfies his own desires. All this appears perfectly possible for the Judaeo-Christian and that is why his desires do not accept any kind of limits. Here one finds the roots of the unrestrained desires which characterize modern Western man.

Since in that world the first, decisive thing is the word – the idea – the manner to achieve the desired world consists primarily in ideating and verbalizing it, that is in formulating a Utopia. One has to create at the level of the idea a 'happy world' which does not exist here and now but which does not escape our capacity to create, to construct. In that way expectations take shape. Meanwhile, however, in the time that elapses between unrestrained desires and their satisfaction there appears in the modern Western world anxiety, anguish, unfulfilled desire, restlessness, nervous tension and frustration.

The search for happiness is an individual enterprise of each separated person in an atomized world only conceivable as the consequence of the unleashing of individual desires. The search for individual happiness is a movement that expresses the arrogance of the Judaeo-Christian 'creator man', who does not accept the world created out of nothing that his own God offers him.

The outburst of desires expresses itself, for example, in the fact that in 1980 one inhabitant of the US consumed on average as much energy as two Europeans, 55 Indians, 168 Tanzanians and 900 Nepalese (Strahm 1986: 14). Six per cent of the world's population lives in the United States yet the US consumes more than a quarter of the world's energy – 2.3 times more than all the developing countries put together (including the countries that produce petroleum oil) (ibid.: 15). Beaud, for example, tells us that the world consumption of energy, measured in millions of coal equivalent tons, has grown in the following way: in 1900 it was 1,000; in 1950 it went up to 3,000 and in 1986 it was 12,000 (Beaud 1988). But what is most tragic is that this individual with unrestrained desires that lead him to consume excessively − not only energy but whatever is within his reach − knows deep down that he does not get what he wants in that way: happiness, Utopia, are no longer made to a social scale but rather to an individual scale. He knows that he consumes palliatives and this exacerbates his frustration. And as for the doctrine of the unlimited progress of science and technology, Meadows et al. (1972) wrote the report which put an end to that illusion in their famous *Limits to Growth*.

The Austrian physicist Robert Jungk refers to the use of atomic energy as 'the new tyranny that threatens liberty, health and the survival of mankind' and he affirms the following:

> With the technical use of nuclear fission, a jump towards a totally new dimension of violence has taken place. At the beginning it was directed only towards military enemies. Today it threatens the very citizenship. This is because the 'atoms for peace' cannot be substantially differentiated from the 'atoms for war'. The expressed intention to use nuclear fission exclusively for constructive ends in no way alters the biocidal character of the new energy. The efforts to control these risks can only partially contain the dangers. Even their defenders find themselves obliged to admit that it will never be possible to eliminate them completely. The small (or large, it is a question of point of view) margin of uncertainty covers such a potential of disasters that it overshadows all the possible advantages.
>
> An atomic catastrophe produced by a technical malfunction, by human negligence or by a badly intentioned action would cause not only enormous immediate damage, but its effects would also be felt for decades, centuries, and according to the circumstances, even millennia. This mortgage on the future, this fear of the consequences of uncontrolled nuclear energy, will become the heaviest imaginable burden of humanity: whether it is a matter of persisting toxic wastes or of the spectre of a worry that it will never disappear.
>
> The supporters of the atomic industry are not unaware of these dark possibilities. They are certainly convinced of being able to protect themselves and their countrymen by introducing unprecedented security measures. If this protection were of a strictly technical nature it would be a matter for engineers to deal with and, given their exceptional costs, for economists as well. But this human discovery has even to be guarded, and in a manner stricter than any other, from humans themselves: from their errors, their weaknesses, their anger, their stratagems, their hunger for power, their hatred. And if one tried to make nuclear installations totally immune to all this, the unescapable consequence would be a life filled with prohibitions, controls and obligations which would find their justification in the magnitude of the dangers which at all costs had to be avoided. (Jungk 1979: 9–10)

So the path towards Utopia seems to have lost its way and does not lead to the desired happiness; rather, on the contrary, it may lead us to an all too real hell of violence and catastrophe.

Power We have already said in the previous part that the Judaeo-Christian God, in creating the world from nothingness, achieved the act of greatest power that it is possible to imagine. Power is thus the ability to achieve what one wants.

We have also said that by presenting man as being made in 'the image and semblance of God' Judaeo-Christianity gives him the possibility of transforming the world created by God and achieving Utopia. But it is clear that for such a possibility, which lives only in the idea, to embody itself in the world a series of preconditions are necessary – a series of very special prerequisites.

It was the bourgeois revolution and the Industrial Revolution during the eighteenth and nineteenth centuries which began to make the creation of Utopia a real possibility. During these times there began to be constructed the instruments needed to go from unrestrained desires to unrestrained actions which in increasing scale, from then until now, are being created for the effective achievement of a series of impressive goals. However, simultaneously, those 'achievements' have taken the planet earth to the edge of collapse. It is true that these revolutions were made in a context of secularization and desacralization of the world, but it is also true that they were inspired and took to the highest plane the ideas of both man's creative capacity and his capacity to achieve dominion over nature. These 'key ideas' of the bourgeois revolution and the Industrial Revolution are Judaeo-Christian ideas.

In his book on the bourgeois revolution Hobsbawm points out that there were three revolutionary waves between 1815 and 1848. The first one took place from 1820 to 1825. In Europe it was limited principally to the Mediterranean, with Spain, Naples and Greece as epicentres. But in 1822 the whole of South America was free; in 1821 Mexico achieved its independence and in 1822 Brazil separated from Portugal.

The second revolutionary wave occurred from 1829 to 1834 and affected the whole of Europe west of Russia and the North American continent. It marked the final defeat of aristocratic power by the bourgeoisie in western Europe. Nevertheless, in the United States (liberated from England by the treaty of Versailles in 1783), Jacksonian democracy went a step further: the defeat of the rich non-democratic oligarchs was brought about by unlimited democracy – by the votes of the colonizers, the small farmers and the city poor.

The third and greatest of the revolutionary waves was that of 1848. Almost simultaneously, revolution broke out and triumphed in France, almost all of Italy, the German states, and a great part of the Habsburg

Empire and Switzerland. 'The world revolution dreamt of by the rebels of this epoch had never been so near,' wrote Hobsbawm (1971).

The economic and social world of 1840, however, did not look very different from the one of 1788 except in England and a few other countries. The greatest part of the world's population remained peasants.

What happened to the land determined the life or death of the majority of human beings between the first bourgeois revolution in France in 1789 and the year 1848. The most catastrophic phenomenon of this period was the impact of both revolutions on the ownership, possession and cultivation of land. Neither the political nor the economic revolutions were able to undervalue land which was considered by the first school of economists – the physiocrats – as the sole source of wealth and whose revolutionary transformation was considered by all to be necessary, both as a condition and a consequence of the bourgeois society.

Hobsbawm points out that:

> Two major obstacles stood in the way of such an imposition, and both required a combination of political and economic action: precapitalist landlords and the traditional peasantry. On the other hand the task could be fulfilled in a variety of ways. The most radical were the British and the American, for both eliminated the peasantry and one the landed lords altogether. (Hobsbawm 1971)

Later the same author adds:

> The revolution in land tenure was the political aspect of the disruption of traditional agrarian society; its invasion by the new rural economy and the world market, its economic aspect. (ibid.)

The traditional opinion that has seen cotton production as the first step of the British Industrial Revolution is confirmed, as Hobsbawm demonstrates in *The Age of Revolution*. Between 1750 and 1769 the exportation of types of British cotton grew more than ten times. In commercial terms the Industrial Revolution can be considered as the triumph of the external market over the internal one: in 1814 England exported four yards of cloth for every three consumed internally; in 1850 the figure was thirteen yards for every eight.

The quantity of raw cotton imported by England rose from 11 million pounds in 1785 to 588 million pounds in 1850; the total production of cloth varies over this period from 40 to 2,225 million yards. The manufacture of cotton represented between 40 and 50 per cent of the value of all British exports between 1816 and 1848.

What is very important to note is that the rhythm of change diverged between the industrial zones in the period between 1789 and 1848. Of all the economic consequences between the two revolutions, the deepest and most long-lasting one was the division between 'advanced' and 'backward' countries, notes Hobsbawm. In 1848 it was clear which countries belonged to the first group: western Europe (minus the Iberian peninsula), Germany, northern Italy and some parts of central Europe, Scandinavia, the United States and perhaps the colonies established by English-speaking colonizers. It was equally clear that the rest of the world, except for a few small areas, under sporadic pressure from Western imports and exports or the pressure of gunboat diplomacy and Western military expeditions, remained backward or became economically dependent on the West. Until the Russians in the 1930s found ways to change things, the gulf between the 'backward' and the 'advanced' remained unmovable, unbreachable and ever-widening – a gulf between the minority and the majority of the inhabitants of the world. No other single fact would determine the history of the twentieth century more firmly than this one. Up to this point we have followed the arguments and assessments of Hobsbawm (1971).

Pearson has remarked with clarity on a fundamental characteristic of the 'advanced' countries:

> During the process of the 'decade of hunger' of 1840, through the economic depression, bad crops and true famine, until the 'year of the revolutions' 1848, the prophets of doom seemed convincing; what changed the darkness of those years into bonanza and popular optimism was, more than anything else, the access given to the European emigrants to the whole fertile temperate zone which remained to be conquered and inhabited. (Pearson 1970)

What happened then was that great numbers of Europeans left western Europe to occupy all the temperate lands that remained 'available', stripping the aboriginals – the original inhabitants of the lands – of their territories. This process took place over two centuries, from the middle of the eighteenth to the middle of the twentieth century. According to Kemmerer and Jones (1959) in the of 1870s and 1880s the Russian Ukraine, Argentina, Canada and Australia were already competing in the production of wheat and cattle with the United States. To this Pearson adds:

> One should mention one more consequence. The consequences of the afore-mentioned power takeover, that gave Atlantic peoples – less than 20 per cent of the population of the world – a power over the resources of our planet that they have been able to both maintain and increase, have not yet been exhausted. The years of occupation and the years of conquest, which they used to devise entirely original instruments of dominion and organization, gave them total freedom of action throughout the entire world: in 1945 they still ruled the greater part of the world and gathered in their territories 80 per cent of the resources, and they continue to enjoy the same participation in the profits of the whole world. In fact the disproportion continues to grow. (ibid.)

Proof of the efficacy of the instruments of dominion and organization that were managed by the imperialist countries against the others is provided by Brown (cited in Wortman 1976), who has established statistically: before 1940 the zones that are now called under-developed in Asia, Africa and Latin America exported wheat, rice, corn and other grains to the central countries of the capitalist system. But at the end of the Second World War, this trend began to be reversed and the less developed world thus lost its capacity to feed itself. Bairoch (1969) similarly notes: 'The Third World countries whose positive balance in the interchange of grains in the prewar period has gradually changed to a growing deficit, they import more and more wheat.' All this has not happened by chance.

What has happened is that with the end of the Second World War, the central capitalist countries decided to pursue a policy of food security which guaranteed them the production of necessary food within their own frontiers. In order to achieve this they gave high subsidies to the producers of food. Agricultural production is also dependent on the weather and in good years it is not possible to limit production to what is strictly necessary; rather a surplus is produced so as to cover any possible deficit in bad years. The surplus was stored and grew, year on year – becoming the so-called food mountains – requiring large expenditure for its preservation. It was then decided to give subsidies to farmers to abstain from producing grains and, at the same time, vast quantities of grains were destined for the intensive raising of animals for the production of meat. It was thus decided to put the surplus on the market, and they even gave some away in the form of 'food aid' to the countries of the Third World.

The 'food aid' expressed as a percentage of the total exports of food from the United States in the period 1955–59 was 39.2 per cent, in 1960–64 30.3 per cent, in 1965–69 22.4 per cent, in 1970–74 9.3 per cent, in 1975–79 5.4 per cent and in 1980 3.0 per cent (Santos 1983). One can see a strong movement from a politics of 'aid' to one of commerce.

The meaning of the commerce of export of food in the balance of payments of the United States in the years 1970, 1978 and 1980 is extremely interesting. The agricultural exports went from $7.0 billion in 1970 to $24.0 billion in 1978 and $41.0 billion in 1980. On the other hand, the commercial agricultural balance changed from $1.0 billion in 1970 to $14.0 billion in 1978 and $24.0 billion in 1980; in contrast, for those same years, the non-agricultural commercial balance was $1.0, $-48.0 and $-51.0 billion respectively (Lajo 1985). It is clear that the commerce of food has become big business for the United States; the affirmations of Brown and Bairoch, therefore, correspond to a phenomenon that is neither random nor spontaneous.

Large donations of food that continue for prolonged periods significantly weaken the agrarian capacity of the 'benefited' countries by competing with national production. Through this massive exportation of food imperialism is able to make the food demand of the big cities of the Third World independent of the agricultural and pastoral production of their own countries since their food provision depends on what is imported. First, food is donated in order progressively to deactivate the production of the countries of the Third World and then, when the process has reached a critical point, the commerce in grains transforms itself into big business for the exporter – the United States.

To have an idea of the agrarian policies in Peru consider that Billone, Carbonetto and Martinez (1982) – studying the evolution of the system of prices and the fluctuations of the transference of the potential excess in the productive processes in raw cotton, unhusked rice, sugar cane, hard yellow corn, coastal and highland potatoes in the period 1970 to 1980 – have found that those products with a total annual value of 19,511 million soles (Peruvian currency) on average, at constant prices of 1973, transferred only 1,300 soles (6.7 per cent) towards the workers' earning capacity (individual agriculturists, members of cooperatives and day labourers). In contrast 18,212 million soles (93.3 per cent) went to the related industries: 9,656 millions (49.5 per cent) to the providers of capital, 3,122 millions (16.0 per cent) to the providers of capital goods and 5,432 millions (27.8 per cent) to the industries of consumer goods. Such circumstances are strong disincentives for national agricultural activity.

Meanwhile the world crisis in production of 1973–74, due to the drastic reduction of stocks and the increase in the price both of grains and of transport from the exporting countries to the importing countries, made tragically evident the consequences of the 'food aid' policy of the rich countries. It was realized that the countries of the Third World had lost the capacity to feed themselves which they had retained until 1940 and that, simultaneously, hunger in a majority of the population had increased. With this, food became a key product in the global economy of the exporting countries, principally the United States. The world market in food was consolidated, with a few transnational enterprises achieving hegemony.

To highlight the violence that is brought about by loss of food self-sufficiency in our countries, it is sufficient to indicate that the Central Intelligence Agency (CIA) of the United States is well aware of its destabilizing effects. The CIA advised its government, in a famous document (Central Intelligence Agency 1974) to increase its influence in the Third World through the political manipulation of its food surplus.

Poverty The organization of society, as a function of the requirements of the development of capitalist production, reduces the human person to a state of desperate anxiety when he or she realizes that within the capitalist system he or she has become a thing – something impersonal, insignificant and disposable. As Marx states in *Das Capital*: 'The regime of capital presumes the divorce between workers and the ownership of the conditions of the realization of work.' The human person, being reduced to an individual member of society, has been despoiled to the point of remaining in the most denigrating vacuity, in the most frightful impotence, in the most miserable solitude. Philosophers as renowned as Heidegger and Sartre tell us about this.

The philosopher Karel Kosik in his book *Dialectics of the Concrete* (1976) makes the following reflection on this theme which is very relevant to modern Western man. For this reason it seems appropriate to quote extensively.

> The primordial and elemental mode to exist in the economy for man is preoccupation. It is not man who is preoccupied, rather it is preoccupation that has the man. Man is neither preoccupied or not preoccupied, rather preoccupation *is present* in both cases. Man can liberate himself from preoccupation but he cannot eliminate it. 'While he lives, man belongs to preoccupation' (Herder). What then is preoccupation? First of all it is not a psychological state or a negative state of mind which alternates with a positive one. Preoccupation is the subjective transposition of man's reality as an objective subject. Man is always situated by connections and relationships to existence itself, which is an activity, even though it can present itself under the guise of an absolute inertia and passivity. For the individual, to be preoccupied is to be entangled in the jungle of relationships which present themselves to him as a practical-utilitarian world. Therefore, objective relationships manifest themselves to the individual not in intuition but rather in 'praxis', as a world of work, of ends and means, of projects, of obstacles and successes. Preoccupation is just the activity of the isolated social individual. (Kosik 1976: 83)

> To be preoccupied is the phenomenological aspect of abstract work. Work is already so subdivided and depersonalized that in all its spheres – as much in the material as in the administrative and intellectual spheres – it appears as mere occupation or manipulation ... The substitution of 'work' for 'preoccupation' is not the reflection of a particular thought of a singular philosopher or of philosophy in general, rather it expresses in a certain manner the changes of the very objective reality. The shift from 'work' to 'be preoccupied' reflects in a mystified form the steadily deepening fetishization of human relationships in which the human world manifests itself in daily consciousness (fixed in philosophical ideology) as a world *already arranged*, of mechanisms, installations, relations and connections, in which the social movement of the individual develops as an entrepreneurial capacity, as occupation, as omnipresence, as connection – in a word, as a being preoccupied. The individual moves in *a system of installations and mechanisms* which he takes care of and is taken care of by, but having long since *lost* the awareness that this world is a human creation. His preoccupation or 'cure' fills the *whole* of life. Work has divided itself into thousands of independent operations and each operation has its own operator, its own executive organ, both in production as well as in the corresponding bureaucratic operations. The manipulator does not have in front of his eyes the whole product, but only a part of it, separated abstractedly from the whole, which does not permit a view of the product or work as a whole. The whole

manifests for the manipulator as something *already made* and its genesis only exists for him in the details, which by themselves are irrational.

To be preoccupied is the practice in its *alienated phenomenological* aspect which no longer alludes to the *genesis* of the human world (the world of men, of human culture and of the humanization of nature); rather it expresses the practice of daily operations in which man is implicated inside the system of *things already finished*, that is of arrangements and installations. In this system of arrangements man himself is the object of manipulation. The manipulative practice (work) converts men into manipulators and objects of manipulation.

To preoccupy oneself is manipulation (of things and of people) in which the operations repeat themselves daily, transforming themselves over long periods into habits which, therefore, are carried out mechanically. The reified character of practice expressed in the term to preoccupy oneself, signifies that the manipulation is not of the product being created but rather that man is absorbed by simply being occupied and he does not 'think' in the product. To be occupied is the practical behaviour of man in a world already made and given; it is management and manipulation of apparatuses in the world but it is not at all the *creation* of a human world. The fascinating success of philosophy which has given a description of the world of 'therapy' and of being preoccupied derives from the fact that this world constitutes the universal superficial plane of reality of the twentieth century. This world does not manifest itself to man as a reality *created by him* but rather as a world already made and impenetrable in whose bosom manipulation presents itself as engagement and activity. (ibid.: 85–6)

In preoccupation the individual always finds himself in the future and he uses the present as a means or instrument to realize his projects. Preoccupation as practical engagement on the part of the individual in a certain manner concedes a privilege to the future and makes of it the fundamental temporal dimension, in the light of which the present and the past are understood and *realized*. The individual valorizes the present and the past in terms of the practical projects in which he or she is involved, according to plans, hopes, fears, desires and ends. Inasmuch as preoccupation is an anticipation, it devalorizes the present and tends toward the future which *still* is not. The temporal dimension and the existence of man as existence in time reveal themselves in the preoccupation as a *fetishized* future and as temporality understood in a fetishized manner: the present is not, for preoccupation, the authenticity of existence – the '*being present*' – but rather an escape since preoccupation with respect to the present is found further ahead. In preoccupation the *authentic nature of human time* is not revealed. The future in itself is not the overcoming of romanticism and alienation. In certain aspects the future is, everything being said, an alienated flight from alienation, that is, an illusory overcoming of alienation. 'To live in the future' and to 'anticipate' is, in some sense, the negation of life: the individual as preoccupation does not live the present but instead he lives the future and, from the moment that he denies what exists and anticipates what does not exist, his life is reduced to zero, that is to inauthenticity. (ibid.: 90–1)

The preceding reference to the excellent work of Kosik presents to us the extraordinary anxiety of modern Western man, who perceives how his world has become a system of things already finished in which he is simply one more 'thing', finding himself snarled in the tangle of relationships which is the market. Work has become transformed into something so subdivided and depersonalized that it is only a matter of a mere occupation, of a simple manipulation in which man no longer has in front of him the whole product to whose construction he contributes but only a part of it which has been abstractedly separated from the whole. That is how the 'whole product' presents itself in front of the working man: as something which is strange and even hostile.

In Kosik's exposition we also see how modern Western man, carried away by his anxiety, tends to flee from the present to advance and live in the future – that is in what does not exist – thus reducing his life to inauthenticity.

Poverty is the exclusive consequence of the compulsive rationalization of society – masked with the postulated right of the individual to freedom – with the end of satisfying the requirements of the development of capitalist production: a development considered as an end in itself, as an inexorable end in terms of which man or life on earth become simple means.

In this respect Susan Hunt afffirms:

> Scarcity is the basic assumption of economics. ... The assumption of scarcity distinguishes Western civilization from any other known human condition. Desires have culturally established limits among all peoples except those belonging to economic societies. 'Economic' men and women are motivated by the assumption that material desires are naturally unlimited. Given that their desires have no limits, the means to satisfy them will always be scarce. Thus to conquer scarcity (or poverty) becomes the objective of human effort in economic societies – be they capitalist, socialist or communist. ... Each traditional culture is a well-defined aggregate of customs and beliefs that avoids the emergence of scarcity. (Hunt 1986)

It is therefore clear that scarcity and poverty belong uniquely to economic societies in which the material desires present themselves as unlimited, resulting in the fact that their satisfaction becomes scarce.

The North American economist J. K. Galbraith has written cogently about the reasoning behind poverty and its relativist nature:

> People see themselves beaten by poverty when their income, although adequate for survival, finds itself markedly below that of the community. Then they cannot have what the community considers the minimum necessary to have a life with dignity and they cannot therefore escape the judgement of the community about their marginalization. (Galbraith 1964)

From this definition derives the fact that everywhere – even in the wealthiest countries – there are poor people. On the other hand, this would seem to attempt to universalize a condition that, as we have seen, is valid exclusively in the economic or modern Western countries. The scarcities that one finds outside of modern Western countries do not derive from the unrestrained desires of the native population but rather have originated from the abusive exploitation of the imperialist countries that have depredated nature and the human community.

It is evident that the eagerness of economists to universalize and operationalize the definition of poverty, invoking the concept of basic needs to live in conditions of dignity, ends up being extraordinarily forced because such needs cannot be properly appreciated from outside – they vary from one culture to another and they do not obey any universal model. All this artifice of the economists to quantify poverty has as its only aim the effort to *conceal* the imperialist origin of the existing scarcities in the colonized countries. They try to make it appear as if poverty is an internal characteristic of our countries, while in reality it is a scarcity caused by imperialist exploitation and greed.

It seems to me that the following reflection of the poet and writer Roger Rumrrill is appropriate here:

> A cruel paradox of history: Spain five hundred years ago was the mouth that devoured the wealth of the plunder that was produced by the colonial system installed in the New World and that fed the European stomach: France, Holland, Belgium, England and the other countries of the prosperous communitarian Europe of the end of the twentieth century.
>
> Today on the eve of the celebration of the cisquentennial of the Discovery of America, Spain once more is the mouth through which enters to the European stomach the converted cocaine by an irony of the market in one of the most perverse products of the consumer society, but at the same time one of the most succulent businesses of the liberal societies of the West, comparable only to the arms trade.
>
> But the paradoxes or coincidences of history do not stop there; five hundred years ago two colonial powers of the time, Spain and Portugal, put down the bases of a system which on the one hand is one of the causes that explains the material and moral poverty of the ex-colonies and on the other hand is the origin of the prosperity and wealth of the ex-colonial powers.
>
> Five hundred years after the plunder continues and is even more depredating and brutal. Now, however, the plunderers need neither caravels nor harquebuses, helmets nor swords; instead they use sophisticated financial mechanisms and tidy transnational agents. This is so because the external debt, or the eternal debt in the case of the Third World, if it were converted into 'physical gold, the total value of the net convertible holdings that leave Latin America each year would be superior to all the gold and silver that Spain and Portugal extracted during three hundred years' as Fidel Castro reminded us at the summit in Guadalajara recently. (Rumrrill 1991)

Rumrrill's words highlight both the continuity and the increase of the imperialist plunder. Nevertheless, after what has been expressed, we do not agree to call 'material and moral poverty of the ex-colonies' a situation that has not arisen internally due to inflated desires but rather to the colonial plunder as he himself says.

With respect to the quantity of the Spanish plunder, the College of Economists of Peru has just demonstrated that Spain owes Peru $647,075 million (thirty-two times more than the external debt of Peru) considering only three facts: (a) the ransom of the Inca Atahualpa: $599,408 million; (b) the secret lowering of the Monetary Gift of the mintings effected in the House of Money in Lima during the time of Charles III: $38,569 million; and (c) the debt contracted by the Spanish Crown with the indigenous communities: $9,098 million (Roel and Pacheco 1991).

Order The established order has been imposed by the power holders and, therefore, it is entirely at the service of their interests. Nevertheless, in order to try and confuse us, it is postulated that order is in the service of universal interests. Established order is used to justify the violence that is exercised by power since it ordains the way to live according to the interests of power and then designates as violators and deservers of punishment those who do not fulfil a given imposed order and those who make evident their perverse nature.

Thus, then, the aggregate of principles, precepts and rules which officially regulate human relations in the countries of the modern West and that receive the name of 'Right' are nothing more than a compulsive arrangement in the service of power. The Declaration of the Rights of Man and Citizen of the French Revolution of 1789, the greatest achievement of political modernity, 'under the appearance of universality ... defines a situation that creates the best conditions for the bourgeoisie, but abandons without much support the vast popular majority', says Comblin (1989: 67–8), who later affirms that: 'The Revolution established a society where the poor had no place' (ibid.: 69).

In our Andean countries the 'right' has been copied from modern Western countries and has been made official without taking into account the characteristics of our own culture, with the sole aim of justifying the imperialist exercise of power against the great majority of our human populations, against our nature and against our Andean religiosity.

The same happens with the so-called universal order that emanates from economics and that has achieved hegemonic status with respect to the formulation and defence of decisions that vitally affect people. Economics postulates the absolute primacy of the global market in human relations. In this way imperialism is facilitated – an imperialism that exercises full hegemony in the global market and that administers the whole planet according to its whim, submitting the world to a single order imposed by it. Our economists and politicians insist on the necessity of our participation in the global market as exporters, to the extent that its motto is 'export or die'. With this they try to ignore a fact of transcendental importance: the imperialist countries, thanks to the exploitation that they have exercised throughout the whole world over many centuries, have developed a technology adequate to their interests and are every day more self-sufficient both in food and in raw materials — so much so that they almost no longer need our participation in the international market. In fact, in 1981 the total of world exports for all the industrialized countries (of the West and the East) was 71 per cent and for the 'developing' countries (including China and OPEC) it was 29 per cent. The exports from the industrialized countries to the 'developing' countries made up 19 per cent of the world total whereas the exports from 'developing' countries to the industrialized countries reached 21 per cent. The exports between industrialized countries reached 52 per cent of the total and between 'developing' countries 8 per cent (Strahm 1986: 134). Complementarily, Figure 7.1 shows the loss in importance in the world export market of the aggregate of 'developing' countries that do not export petroleum (oil) during the period from 1950 to 1985.

So, in which market are we going to increase our participation? A pathetic example is the network of electric interconnections that has begun to be constructed — a project that has been carried out by specialized transnational companies. We were not even successful in having copper included as a conductor, despite the fact that we are a copper producer; rather an imported synthetic material was used. The only part of this network which is of national production is the concrete bases of the high wire towers. This is what the logic of the market requires.

On the other hand, the external debt of our countries could be easily written off by the imperialist creditor countries. Proof of this, if proof were needed, is the enormous waste of resources witnessed during the Gulf War. Nevertheless, they continue to make us pay, cruelly hurting our people in order that we should recognize their power and authority and accept the imposition of their order. Both the requirement to pay the external debt and the blatant show of naked power that the Gulf War was, have as their sole aim the maintenance and reinforcement of a world order in the service of imperialism.

The official system of education is the fundamental instrument to inculcate in us a behaviour obedient to the order of imperialism, to the established order. They even prepare us so that we become its faithful servants and defenders. This is why the university-trained professionals, who are people who have spent fifteen to twenty years in the education system with the hope of finding a good position in the service of the established order, are the most efficient servants and defenders of the order imposed by imperialism and their attitude is almost anti the popular classes. Their merit is evaluated in terms of their loyalty to the established

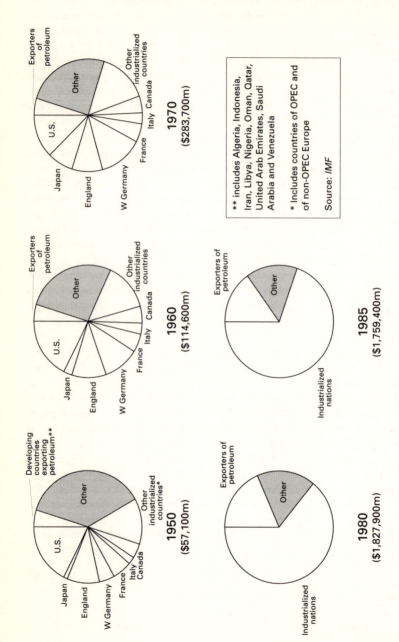

Figure 7.1 Global exports 1950—85 in percentages (annual exports in parentheses in US$m)

1950
($57,100m)

1960
($114,600m)

1970
($283,700m)

1980
($1,827,900m)

1985
($1,759,400m)

** includes Algeria, Indonesia, Iran, Libya, Nigeria, Oman, Qatar, United Arab Emirates, Saudi Arabia and Venezuela

* Includes countries of OPEC and of non-OPEC Europe

Source: *IMF*

order, which is considered to be unalterable. The education system teaches us what is put forward as the exemplary model of life, that is the one that corresponds to that of the middle classes of the imperialist countries. Thus it provides the normative status whose faithful accomplishment will make us 'succeed in life' – that is, reach the model of life postulated.

The intelligent Peruvian sociologist Raúl Gonzales Moreyra, in the First Encounter of Intellectuals and Academics over the National Project, expounded the following:

> I would say, and here I dare to make a very personal statement, that the underdeveloped countries are countries where very little in the future is predictable; the technology of futurology emerged in the developed countries where, unlike here, the normative structures that regulate the institutions, society and individuals, have a strong cohesion.
>
> We, the underdeveloped countries, are highly unpredictable because the normative institutional structures and the individual norms are fragmented and not highly organized. The regulation of conduct is due less to norms than to actual incentives – momentary, transitory and educational – which produce unstructured behaviour patterns in those countries that are largely characterized by chance.
>
> I would only give as an example that not one futurological institution was able to predict what was going to happen in Iran with the revolution or counter-revolution of Khomeini – whatever one wants to call it – a week before it happened and I think that there lies the heart of the relationship between person and society.
>
> The institutional norm only has meaning – whether it be a law or an administrative norm – if the subjects have internalized an aggregate of norms that regulate their interaction with the institutions and their interaction with themselves; and that is centrally an educative issue, in other words an issue of the educational content.
>
> It is the problem of the construction of persons that auto-regulate their exchange of values and auto-regulate their demands in function of their expectations and who do not reduce them but do not make them unrealistic either. It is fundamentally because this interchange of values, this individual development is articulated with a social development. This brings about a highly articulated social and individual development where randomness exists but is normalized and regulated by a basically normative system. (Gonzales 1986: 20–1)

This same educational psychologist goes on to say:

> Everything pushes us toward individual emigration which one sees in the brain drain, the flight of capital, etc., responses to situations concretely individualized which are those, in my area of interest, especially when it is a matter of the social project, that are related to the standardization of the personality. That is to say, we are all naturally reacting to stimuli: we value certain stimuli and come closer, and we negate others and move away.
>
> But in social life it is not a matter of living exclusively according to the randomness of the stimulated situation and its values, but rather to move on to

norms – that is to move on to the regulation of the situation of interchange of values. And this passage to norms implies the construction of a whole psychological structure which is the objective of a whole personal social education. (ibid.: 47)

Thus Gonzales Moreyra has brilliantly explained to us the rationale of education, that is the construction of a psychological structure that allows the subject to act according to the norms. But what happens in our countries is that the individual and the society, that is the protagonists of education, do not exist. Because of that our people display an unpredictable behaviour to those who observe them and who hold those assumptions. Here persons exist and *ayllus* (collectivities) exist. So it is not that here the institutional and individual norms are fragmented and poorly organized as Gonzales argues, but rather that this institutionality and individuality are foreign to us. Our organicity is different (Rengifo 1991). But obviously the task of education is universal: everywhere to form individuals and societies. Education tries to eliminate the cultural particularities of peoples.

The task of education is to make us functional to the order that suits imperialism. It is to normalize us and, thus, to make us predictable. But in our countries it is only the university-trained professionals who, after fifteen to twenty years of schooling, have been provided with a psychological structure that obliges them to proceed according to norms and to accept the assumption that all peoples, all over the world, are marching towards a unitary universal project hegemonized by the imperialist countries.

Development   After the end of the Second World War and the establishment of the new division of the world among the victorious military powers with respect to their zones of direct influence, the capitalist system and the socialist system were strategically configured and the 'Cold War' began between the two power blocs.

This gave rise to the classification of the capitalist countries into developed and under-developed, according to the size of the internal net product by inhabitant. This division, as we already know through the work of Hobsbawm (1971), is not new but was defined in its fundamental characteristics in 1848. But the difference during the postwar period became clear when the US led an attempt, with the aim of constructing a global development enterprise, to guarantee what some have called neocolonialism.

Friedrich Tenbruck, professor at the German University of Tubingen, in an excellent article (which we cite below at length) presents the corresponding process:

Until forty years ago there were no 'developing countries' and neither were there any 'underdeveloped' ones. These concepts first emerged then, tentatively, in the political language and the literature of the United States, but they were diffused by the international agencies (such as the International Bank for Reconstruction and Development, the United Nations, UNESCO) and by the corresponding disciplines which immediately appeared to give their services to the new practice.

The intention or at least the hope to better the destiny of the peoples on earth was, in any case, foreign neither to the Christian mission nor to colonialism. As a godfather to the United States's concept, twentieth-century evolutionism was also a major actor with its belief in the general problems of development, but it was a revolutionary step to declare development a global task and thus make it for some a regular obligation and for others a justified demand. Only after that was created the vision of One World, which since then has dominated over all the differences, in thought and in action.

The new message not only noted differences in development and development tasks but also converted rather homogeneous development in a normal and foreseeable case that had not yet happened – or rather had been obstructed – among given peoples. Thus countries that until now had been qualified as 'poor' or 'not developed' were transformed into 'underdeveloped' countries that had been left behind the expected development. It is only through and because of this [global development enterprise] that the expressions 'underdeveloped' and 'underdeveloped countries' were coined: terms that transformed the facts into an anomaly that had to be corrected rapidly, and thereby stigmatizing those affected. This issue was only later softened by the use of the idiomatic expression 'developing countries'. In spite of the fact that we make note of this, all the expressions have a value charge because they all arise from a uniform development of humanity as the valid and predictable norm.

From the idea of the global accord emerged the concept of developing countries, from the realization of the accord arose reality. The developing countries transformed themselves into reality to the extent that the overcoming of underdevelopment transformed itself into the truism of a normal permanent task. The majority of expressions that the reality of developing countries put in front of our eyes (such as aid to development, service toward development or ministry of economic cooperation) arose only with those institutions, activities and disciplines that were created in order to achieve the policy of development and that, at the same time, were arranged in order to fulfil the objective: a uniform and unitary development.

The 'developing countries' are the result of a politic that not only declared development to be uniform for all peoples as an objective worthy of effort or as a human precept, but also as a task that is capable of being achieved in the short term. Due to this it began with the optimistic conviction that the task could be realized rapidly and homogeneously as a technical issue, with no shortage of goodwill, specialized advice and a certain amount of investment. With the failure of this hope, the social scientists had to go to the field to study the previously ignored causes of 'underdevelopment' and the imperceptible premises of this appetizing development.

Pedagogy played a special role, with the recommendations of UNESCO introducing in schools at a global level an education in terms of a community of destiny, of peace and development in One World. Since then generations have grown up from childhood with this idea of a concrete global order, finding in it an ideal.

The Single World understands itself as a unified community of free peoples that feel themselves committed to a uniform and unitary development. ... At bottom, one finds a concept that simultaneously announced, diffused and imposed the Single World as the only possible order and, in any case, the only correct one. ...

The new idea of a correct order could only arise in a context of cultures which felt transported by universal messages directed toward the whole of humanity and, in that sense, felt themselves called by a worldwide mission. ...

Nowhere did this conception of the belief in progress emerge as strongly as in the United States, that had begun and uninterruptedly maintained its belief in progress and a missionizing consciousness. It was decisive that the United States believed that, in its own democracy, it possessed the universal recipe for progress. It understood its own history as the universal paradigm for a trust-worthy harmony between independence, democracy and progress and saw this paradigm in all the others. Even today – and this can be seen in foreign policy – all national liberation movements are seen as a spontaneous uprising of the people clamouring for a democracy on the American model, as if such as desire were chiselled in all human beings by nature, heart and understanding. ...

The programme found approbation in the developing countries without whose cooperation the whole project would have ended being simply a unilateral action of charity by the industrialized countries. Instead of coming from nations, this approbation came from small native groups which had either been educated on the European model or had, in one way or another, been in contact with European ideas. ... In the colonies there had emerged small élites based on education, from which later on would be recruited the élite leaders of the liberation movements and the future holders of power in the liberated zones. These achieved through their approbation the cultural understanding that allowed the realization of a politic of development. (Tenbruck 1989)

Tenbruck's article explains with great clarity the process of the construction of the world enterprise of development under the leadership of the United States. Imperialism has appropriated the suggestive word 'development' in order to dominate the enterprise of subjection that it has constructed in order to colonize us even more. The ideas of a Single World and of homogeneous, uniform and unitary development of humanity served as the basic pillars in this enterprise. At the beginning development appeared as a task achievable in the short term. Schools, as we have noted previously, took charge of inculcating children and the youth in the new ideas based on so-called universal messages directed at the whole of humanity. As one would expect, the actual way of life of the United States was proposed by the US as a universal Utopia. Complementarily one has to note that the acceptance of this project in the underdeveloped countries did not arise from the people as a whole but from those educated according to the Western model who took upon themselves its representation. In this way a unitary official scenario has been constructed for the legal realization of global development: some participate in order to fulfil a regular obligation in their quality of benefactors, others in order to present their demands justified in terms of being the benefited ones. Imperialism has imposed development as the only legitimate demand. There is no alternative road. In these conditions it even happens that any movement of national liberation is necessarily seen as developmentalist and is automatically legitimated when it is proclaimed as such. Whatever difficulties our peoples may experience are interpreted as symptoms of underdevelopment. So what needs to be done immediately, apparently, is to begin the task of development – and in order to do that one has to adjust to what has been established by the International Monetary Fund.

About this Paul Streeten writes:

> The most widely shared mentality in the years 1950 and 1960, codified by the report of the Pearson Commission about international development (submitted for the consideration of the World Bank in 1969), was dominated by Walt Whitman Rostow's doctrine of the stages of growth, according to which development is a linear course along which all countries travel.
>
> The linear point of view settled innumerable questions about the nature, causes and objectives of development. It tended to concentrate on restrictions or obstacles (especially the lack of capital), the elimination of which would liberate the 'natural' forces which were the impetus behind the continuous movement toward constantly rising incomes.
>
> Applied to the area of international relations this point of view called upon the rich countries to supply to the developing countries the 'missing components' and with those to help them to free up the log jams or remove obstacles. These missing components could be capital, foreign exchange, technology or administration. The doctrine offered a technique, foreign private exchange or investment. By breaking up the bottlenecks, the rich countries could contribute to development efforts several fold what it cost them and thereby accelerate the process of development in the less developed countries. (Streeten 1977)

As for the real function of the so-called 'development aid' in our countries, Ernest Feder describes his specific relation with the agro transnationals in the Third World:

> It is well known that a few firms commercialize the greater part of foods sold in the world. Some hundred corporations, each one with annual revenues in 1974 above one thousand million dollars, will now have a total volume of sales that can be conservatively estimated at some 300 thousand million dollars. These statistics show only the tip of the iceberg. I must once more insist that in order to appreciate the total power of agribusiness one cannot see it as if it was the sum of firms specializing in food. Rather it is a conglomerate formed by two gigantic groups of firms and organizations that operate in the whole world.
>
> A. The agribusiness transnational firms that produce or distribute (or both) agricultural food products or not; those that work in the production (or the

local assemblage) and the distribution of agricultural produce and those that act in the field of suppliers' services.

Nobody ever estimated the aggregate sales of products and services related with agriculture of all these firms, but the sum total must be truly fantastic, even taking into account that some of them can simultaneously carry out two or more of the activities mentioned.

B. Private or public organizations – national, bilateral or international – that directly or indirectly patronize or give financial and other types of support to overseas investments of the 'A' firms. Super private organizations are part of these for the planning of investment and the raising of funds; private banks; organizations for the bilateral and international financial and technical assistance and many other similar organisms.

The combined resources of these numerous organizations are also enormous. Their main function is to organize and improve the economic and institutional infrastructure and superstructure in the Third World in order to facilitate the old and new investments of the firms in group 'A'. Their resources are added to the weight that the firms that figure in 'A' can hurl upon the Third World. What few understand is that, most of the time, 'A' and 'B' work conspiratorially together so that the whole weight of monopolistic international capital that supports them is behind a counter-reform on a global scale. (Feder 1979)

This quotation from Feder makes clear that the so-called 'development aid', which takes place in the form of loans that enlarge our external debt, is in reality a contribution destined to facilitate the deployment of international monopolistic capital in our countries because it dedicates itself, for example, to providing an infrastructure that diminishes the costs of transnational operations.

Well now, as far as the issue of the Unites States's mode of life being the universal Utopia, the following reflection of Richard L. Clinton, professor of political science at the State University of Oregon, is apropos:

In admitting the ethnocentric concept of development we also leave out the growing evidence of social decomposition, the gradual deterioration of society in the advanced, industrial and very developed countries (like the United States). The continuous increase in crime, in mental illness, in alcoholism, in drug addiction, in divorce, in child abuse, in murder, rape and suicide, surely witnesses to something more than better information gathering and a more systematic management of data. As the historian Henry Lee Swint said several years ago, 'whatever is not riveted is getting looser'.

In reality many aspects of our culture that were riveted for many years are also getting looser: the youth in the ghetto terrorize the handicapped elderly and in general the children grow up without the structure of a global ethical conception of themselves and of the society in which they live.

We are constantly more aware of the waste and ecological destruction that our way of life implies, to the point that our scientific and technical methods indicate to us that many essential resources and the capacity of many ecosystems to withstand new aggressions are nearing their limits. Nevertheless we believe ourselves to be developed.

In pursuing development (defined as the increase of productivity and of per capita income) through industrialization and the creation of a consumer society, we have succeeded in generalizing our dependence on methods of production, modes of living, transport and even recreation that consume materials and energy in an intensive manner. In many parts of the world we have supported an agriculture based precariously on the availability of fossil fuels (for irrigation pumps, tractors, fertilizers made with natural gas, etc.). And, what is more important, we have contributed to the creation throughout the whole world of a 'growing expectation revolution'.

In one form or another our ideas about the 'developed' way of life have come to form the opinions and aspirations perhaps of the majority of the world's population. 'A chicken in every pot' is no longer an adequate electoral promise. In countries where many people are malnourished, an always growing proportion of those who vote or have political leverage want 'a car in every garage' when it is not, as the economist Nicholas Georgescu-Roegen said, 'a car for each two garages'.

In our delirium of technological innovations and of slavery to comfort and convenience, we have disseminated – as sorcerers' apprentices – a 'superculture of skyscrapers, airports, universities, films and rock and roll which sweeps the world as a great epidemic', to use the words of Kenneth Boulding. We have accepted in an uncritical way (and with us a good part of the rest of the world) this superculture as the central element of development. Notwithstanding, as many researchers and scientists begin to point out, we and a good part of the rest of the world are suffering from a tragic misapprehension.

We deceive ourselves at least in three ways:

• The majority of the world's population will never be able to attain what we call development. Simply put, the resources capable of sustaining a way of life that wastes so many raw materials and so much energy on such a large scale and for such a long time do not exist.

• Even if an inexpensive and practically unlimited source of energy were to be discovered – the eternal dream of the technological optimists – the disturbances occasioned by these ways of life, extended on such a vast scale, would alter in an important way the ecosystem of the planet. Even if no ecological disasters occurred, the heat that would be generated by such an expenditure of energy – both directly and through the accumulation of carbon dioxide in the atmosphere – would have perturbing effects on the climate of the planet and thus on agriculture.

• The human capacity to face and manage complex systems is simply not up to the tasks that are implied in the expansion and continued acceleration of the actual way of life. (Clinton 1978)

Clinton's argument, as laid out above, makes us see both the undesirability as well as the impracticability of generalizing to the whole of humanity the Unites States's way of life.

The Argentinian writer Ernesto Sabato adds his voice to the debate:

The Unites States, technologically the most developed country in the world, has only some 250 million of the 6,000 million human beings on the planet [4 per cent of humanity according to these figures]. And nevertheless they consume there 80 per cent of the drugs in the world. This is an a posteriori proof, as a philosopher would say, of what this paradise of technology is. (Sabato 1990)

But let us return to Tenbruck's article in order to appreciate the cultural imperialism contained in the concept of development:

Even when the great world politic has to renounce, as we hope, war, conquest and violence, only the form and means of confrontation would have changed through it, leaving aside neighbouring zones. Behind this domestication hides an intensification. Because while in the past only a few cultures clashed on their common geographical frontiers, modern development has put in contact all cultures among themselves through its universal presence and its interrelationship. The other hopeless face of this development is the confrontation of cultures, whose auto-affirmation is in question. And while we force a common and unitary development, it will acquire in greater measure the traits of a cultural struggle which finally will be more important for future history than the mere register of advances of development.

At the same time the bases of legitimacy and loyalty are substantially modified. The famous loss of sovereignty of nation states is only a part of this change. Before all powers were legitimated, in reality they had to attain recognition by world opinion. This is also valid for politics, for religion or other powers; this is also the case regarding the loyalties of the most diverse ruling élites, particularly (but not exclusively) in the developed countries. These have adopted science, education and training and their élites have in part adopted even the cultures and the languages of Europe. With the adoption of the industrial organization of existence, the relationship of the people with its own cultural history is put in question. In that sense the liberation of the colonized peoples has, with modernization, also increased their dependence on the developed countries in cultural terms. Their concern for their cultural identity is for them even more important than their development.

They observe that the United States and Russia are not only world powers who represent their own interests; they are at the same time the great centres of cultural prestige, through whom run cultural developments. Whether one likes it or not, it is the case, and has been for a long time, that the US and the USSR have fostered the (respectively) americanization or russification of their areas of influence – processes that, as is usual in history, are noticed only when they are finished. In this sense one must also note the gradual colonization of the old European cultures, whose spiritual independence has finally been homogenized. Just as in its time Latin was transformed into the lingua franca of the Roman Empire, English and Russian actually advance in their respective areas of influence toward the establishment of a lingua franca of the cultural intelligentsia – in part already well on the road toward the written language of science and advancing at the same time, through various lateral roads toward the consolidation of the vernacular language.

From all this emerge traces of a global cultural struggle whose end is still unknown. The confrontation of the cultural powers is part of the essence of development. (Tenbruck 1989)

The German politician Erhard Eppler is even more clear and direct about this when he says:

> For the majority of the countries of the Third World there are, at the beginning of the process that we call development, things happening that have nothing to do with a natural unfolding internally impulsed: the elimination of all the native structures, the destruction of social equilibrium. The most well-known example is that of the Inca Empire. There was there a balanced relation between man and the cultivated country, a well-organized community, with forms of social security. But the Empire did not develop and fell victim to the conquistadors. This may have been less spectacular in other places; it is possible that the organizational norms were more primitive in other places. But the introduction of the Europeans has always meant at the beginning the rupture of a development, the destruction of an equilibrium, the violent insertion in a world economic system and concretely, in general, the clearly defined role of providers of raw materials. (Eppler 1973: 9–10)

What is certain is that the construction of a Single World, of a homogeneous, uniform and connected development of humanity and of the way of life of the United States as universal paradigm that is promoted by the developmental movement has a clear homogenizing aim which intends to flatten all regional cultural manifestations. Nevertheless at the present time we are experiencing a situation of a clear resurgence of ethnic movements, whether they are in the former Soviet Union or in eastern and western Europe – contexts that until very recently were considered as definitely homogenized. Thus the relevance of ethnic cultures cannot be underestimated.

Paul Streeten reviews the efforts carried out by the World Bank to find concrete and operational paths of development:

> In 1954 Sir Arthur Lewis had predicted that subsistence agriculturists and landless labourers would shift from the rural areas to the modern urban industries that offered higher wages. This would increase inequality in the first stages of growth (as long as the rural inequalities were not considerably greater than the urban ones), but when all the rural poor had been absorbed in modern industry the golden age would begin and growth would be related to equity.
>
> The reaction to the growing dualism that had resulted from modern industrial growth was to return to the necessity of creating employment. Since 1969 the efforts of the missions of the International Labour Organization … have demonstrated that 'employment' and 'unemployment', as they are defined in the industrialized world, are not concepts that enlighten us for adopting in development a strategy that would reach the poor of the world. The experience of many countries demonstrated that 'unemployment' can coexist with a considerable scarcity of labour and with an under-utilization of capital. …
>
> The radical problem of poverty in the developing countries is not one of unemployment. It is the problem of working hard for long hours in non-remunerated and non-productive activities. This discovery has attracted attention

toward the informal sector in the cities. ... The problem was then defined as one of the 'working poor'. ...

With the concern for the 'working poor' attention was then transferred from dualism and employment to income distribution and equity. ... This concern emerged from two types of questions: (1) How can we make the small-scale informal sector more productive with an intensive use of labour? How can we eliminate discrimination against this sector and better its access to credit, information and markets? How does redistribution affect efficiency and growth? Does helping the 'working poor' mean sacrificing productivity or rather is helping small enterprises and small agricultural ventures an efficient way of stimulating growth?; and (2) How does economic growth affect the distribution of incomes?

It is an empirical question whether economic growth affects inequality and poverty and how both in their turn affect economic growth. The answers to these questions vary from one country to another and depend to a great extent on the initial distribution of goods, on the policies pursued by the govern-ment, on the available technologies, on the opportunities for external trade and on the growth rate of the population. Another empirical question is how the policies intended to reduce inequality and to satisfy basic needs affect individual liberties. ...

The actual insistence on the 'basic human needs' is a logical step on the road of development thought. The evolution from the concern for growth, employment and redistribution to basic needs indicates that our concepts have become less abstract, global, concrete and specific.

What is important in the focus on basic needs is that it permits us to reach in a shorter time an objective of higher priority over which there is broad consensus – and achieve that with fewer resources than would be required if we chose instead to increase only employment and incomes and waited to satisfy basic needs. (Streeten 1979)

Streeten clearly shows the operational difficulties of development which lead it to separate itself from its programmatic postulates. Already its first indicator, economic growth, is enormously reductive and was immediately criticized. Then they had recourse to employment – a concept that only makes sense in industrial societies where there are labour markets. In spite of this, growth and employment are indicators that are intended to include everything. But when one turns to basic needs one in fact accepts an activity that can only be marginal.

We have seen how development is something deliberately constructed by imperialism in order to channel in that direction, within a context managed and legitimized by itself, the demands of people in such a way that they end up being good business for itself. The postulates of a Single World and of a uniform and unitary development are, each day, increasingly false. In only one hundred and fifty years the world has been differentiated into two opposed conditions: imperialism and colonization. The growth of a few has been achieved at the expense of many others. It must be understood, therefore, that to adhere to development is to contribute to

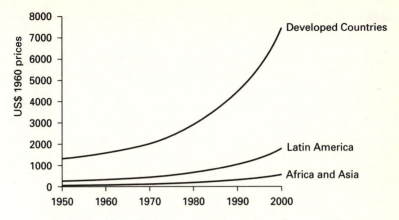

Figure 7.2 The widening gap: gross domestic product per capita

the legitimization of this imperialist enterprise and to betray the people. It does not matter if we call it eco-development, endogenous development, or some other term; what is at issue is to find anew the path that belongs to each people, what is at issue is to be ourselves once again, to reject imperialism and its colonizing instrument: development.

Figure 7.2 (which we owe to the British economist Barbara Ward 1971) shows us the growing gap to which the imperialist deceit called development has led us.

In order to appreciate how deeply the imperialist thesis of development has introjected itself as the only way in the thought of our intellectuals, let us consider what the Cuban leader and economist Carlos Rafael Rodriguez says:

> What Latin America asks for, what the underdeveloped countries clamour for, is not that the United States and other international economic centres such as the European Economic Community and Japan simply underwrite their economies as an act of international social generosity. That is not the issue. If we live in only one world, this single world must not be permanently subdivided among the haves and the have-nots. This opposition is not only morally unsustainable but practically dangerous. And above all irrational. Any economic calculations would show that if the underdeveloped world, with its 4 billion inhabitants, transforms itself into a developed world and the marginals of today become the consumers of tomorrow, the positive economic effects of such a change would not only benefit the South but would have repercussions of high returns in the North. Therefore we solicit not an act of charity but rather an action in which the intelligence of the leaders was used adequately. (Rodriguez 1989)

It is easy to perceive in the words of this old Cuban leader his endorsement of the thesis of a 'Single World' and his demand for development, presenting it as feasible and advantageous for all. Thus is evidenced his functionality to the interests of the imperialist enterprise of development.

On the other hand in the official Peru of today one does not see a frontal struggle against drug trafficking – a struggle that does not so much serve national interests as the interests of imperialism – but rather the handing over of our rain forest to transnational enterprises assuring them of high revenues and accepting their stipulations. On this matter, what Hernando De Soto in making an evaluation of his management as adviser to President Fujimori says, is enlightening: 'it has been possible to interest great multinational enterprises – which are the only ones capable of managing an alternative development and offering a market on a large scale – in this process' (De Soto 1992). The adviser continues: 'For them [the multinational enterprises] the primordial security upon which all the others can be constructed, [is] the willingness of substituting crops on the part of the agriculturists and the fact that the international community has stopped seeing them as criminals – converting them into valid and legal interlocutors, with identifiable properties and guarantees.' In this sense one has advanced, according to the adviser, in the 'Peruvian strategy of finding an alliance with the coca growers', as well as 'having gained the support of all the committees of producers of coca, on the basis of the com-mitment of introducing them into the market economy through the legal recognition of their properties as they have defined them, their democratic participation in the decisions that concern them, and the realization of structural reforms on the basis of agendas that they have made ... ' (ibid.). With such procedures it is said that the market economy becomes accessible to coca growers who, however, are already a part of it through their production and sale of coca leaves, which can be transformed into the basic paste for cocaine and later into cocaine. The change that is offered is that for the commercialization of their product, instead of dealing with drug traffickers, they deal with agents of transnationals. They will no longer grow coca, a species adapted over millennia to the region, whose cultivation dominates and whose leaves are relatively easy to commercialize; instead they will become subject to the strict norms of the cultivation of species imposed by the managers of commercializing transnationals in-terested only in 'the quality of exports', with the cultivators having to take all the risks of the substitution of the coca leaf. Hernando De Soto presents us thus with a good example of what development actually is: a good business, but only for the imperialists.

The Andean mode of being and decolonization

In the remainder of this chapter we strive to present characteristic features of Andean culture which make its decolonization both possible and desirable. Andean culture, as will be seen, is radically different from imperialist Western modern culture and, despite five hundred years of colonization, remains sufficiently vigorous to recover its autonomy.

Nurturance All who live in the Andean world are as we ourselves are; they are our friends. With them we keep company, with them we converse and reciprocate. We tell them what happens to us and they advise us. They also tell us of their own lives and trust us. We deal with each of them as a person and we converse with them face to face.

All that exists in the Andean world is alive. Not only man, animals and plants but rocks, rivers, the mountains and everything else. In the Andean world nothing is considered to be inert: everything is alive. Like ourselves, everyone and everything participates in the great celebration that is life: everyone eats, all sleep, all dance, all sing – everyone lives fully.

In the Andean world there are neither powerful nor self-sufficient beings; everyone needs everyone else to live. In the Andes the world does not exist as an integral whole different and distinct from its components; here there do not exist 'wholes' and 'parts' – these are only abstractions. In the Andean world there is symbiosis which is immediate to life – a symbiosis lived in the Andes in the form of mutual nurturance.

The *chacra* is a form of nurturance. In the Andean *chacra* not only plants and animals are nurtured; the soil, water and climate are not considered as given conditions but are also nurtured. Reciprocally, the *chacra* nurtures those who nurture it. We have here a nurturing culture in a living world. For that reason if anything is lacking it is nurtured. In Cajamarca, for instance, even today one can observe the peasants' manner of growing soils right from bedrock, a process that takes three to five years, using retaining terraces and special drainage channels that carry soil to the fields during the rainy season.

The Asociación Atusparia in Cajamarca has recorded the following testimony from Gregorio Castrejón Chilón, a peasant of the Plan Manzanas town in the district of Cajamarca:

> I have no inheritance yet, only small plots that I have bought. These plots were worthless and so their owners sold them. 'They are barren, they must be sold,' they said. The soil was in a pitiful condition; for that reason the owner was dissatisfied with his plot. ... I bought it like that, full of gravel [volcanic rock]; the soil was in a disgraceful state, very much neglected. I bought it in 1980 and I thought 'How could it be done better?' Soils do not recover just like that: it requires three to four years. I planted *aliso* [a native tree] sprouts at the edge of the plot the first years. Every single one dried but I planted again and today I have *alisos* that are five metres tall.
>
> Nowadays I plant maize with beans where before not even a shoot of grass would grow. Its former owner – the one who sold it to me - now wants to take it back. He has said to me: 'You have not given me enough money for it. I want it back' – as if he had toiled to make it as my plot now is.

Then don Goyo gives some details of the work that was done:

> Such was the *chacra* when I bought it in June 1980. It was a pitiful sight – no wonder the owner was unhappy. The same year, in November, I planted where a small patch of land remained. I planted oca, 3 *arrobas* with 15 bags of guano [manure]. I obtained 18 *arrobas* at harvest time. The following year I began to raise edges or lips so as to build terraces – the inclines from the top to the foot at the bottom – and started picking deep at the rock. As the edge raised, I traced others and that way, year after year, the lips were growing higher, making earth out of the gravel and improving the crops until now I have a good *chacra*. Thus, little by little, earth has been made and gathered in my plot. The edge or lip also helps when irrigating, directing the water to the borders so soil is not washed away. Taking care of it in this way my little *chacra* is now as you can see. (Castrejón 1989)

Gregorio Castrejón Chilón's excellent testimony relieves us of the need for further debate or explanation.

In a remarkable article, Sergio Cuzco, member of the Asociación Atusparia of Cajamarca states:

> It is frequent in Cajamarca to hear the peasants, the elder ones especially, refer to the plots of land as a personified being, which shows its own individuality through manifestations like the fact of needing 'affection', 'esteem', 'consideration', including having their own name like the other elements of the *chacra*. For that reason, commenting on the care and the arrangement of the fields, the peasants say that 'the *chacras* are also nurtured', thus placing the field on the same level of perception as the animals. (Cuzco 1990, 2: 213).

On the other hand, water is nurtured by making wells and filtering galleries as well as protecting the springs or *puquios*.

The nurturance of the microclimate in the *chacra* is done from the very moment of tilling the soil. Tilling assists the retention of rainwater or irrigation water since the tilled soil acts like a sponge, preventing rapid drainage and thus modifying the original microclimate. Microclimate in the *chacra* is also modified by building walls with stones or trees or mud, which protect it from wind and cold. In the same way, levelling the field, fertilizing with sufficient guano, and the association and rotation of cultivars all contribute to nurturing an appropiate microclimate in the *chacra*.

But there are other forms of nurturing the climate not only in the *chacra* itself but in the landscape where it lives. This refers, for instance, to the nurturance of irrigation and drainage. Irrigation permits water from the rivers to approach the *chacras* to converse and reciprocate, while drainage extracts from the *chacras* the excess water and restores it to the river. These works modify the conditions in its environment.

In the plains that surround Titicaca Lake there are around 80,000 hectares where there are remains of 'raised fields' or *Waru-Warus*. There, a special nurturing of the soil has been done, consisting of digging ditches where soil was extracted to raise the height of the strips of land between the ditches. This form of soil nurturing dates from around three thousand years ago (Denevan and Turner 1974) and was devised to improve drainage in case of floods resulting from a rise in the water level of the lake. In this way the effects of the climate in the zone are modified while simultaneously improving soil quality; the *chacras* are protected against frost, the plants' growth rate is improved and humidity is regulated.

Another very ancient configuration in the plains next to Titicaca Lake is known as *qocha*. These are depressions nurtured in the land as deep holes. Water rain is stored in the *qochas*, transforming them in ponds. The *qochas* are interconnected, linked by a network of canals. They can maintain water during rainless months, including the driest: September and October. It is also possible to decant water from one *qocha* to another. *Qochas* are used for agriculture and in the fallow period for shepherding. Likewise, they provide water for domestic consumption and for animals. This configuration covers an estimated surface area of approximately 528 square kilometres, located between the rivers Pucará and Azángaro (Flores Ochoa and Paz Flores 1983).

Perhaps the most beautiful form of nurturance of the Andean landscape is the so-called 'andenes' or terraces. Those which are located in the inter-Andean valleys with arid climate are supplied with irrigation facilities and their soil is levelled to prevent the surface drainage of water. Alternatively, terraces built in areas with abundant rainwater, be it in the northern Andes or on the eastern slopes, do not require irrigation water and their soils are sloped so that excess water is able to drain off.

Thus the nurturance of terraces modifies the form of the natural mountain slope as a series of ground strips whose slope corresponds to a good conversation with irrigation or with rain, where the soil is well conserved and the microclimate becomes warmer than before. The continuous slope of the mountain side due to the nurturing it receives, becomes a series of 'steps' and with it the surface exposed to the sun's rays grows remarkably and the microclimate becomes similar to that which occurs naturally only at lower altitudes. Thus, for instance, in the southern Andes, the terraces – by capturing more solar radiation and supplying irrigation water – make the cultivation of maize possible at altitudes at which it would be otherwise impossible (Isbell 1974, Earls 1976).

It is important to realize that the terraces, irrigated or rainfed, are not a localized phenomenon in the Andes but extend from east to west and north to south including the coastal area and the higher jungle. Luis Masson says that: 'It has been estimated that in Peru there are approximatively a million hectares of terraces in diverse conditions of conservation and use' (Masson 1986).

It must also be noted that the terraces are nurtured on the mountain slopes without the loss of the natural forms of these slopes; rather they adjust to them. It happens likewise with the beautiful Andean pedestrian roads (the so-called '*caminos de herradura*' or merchant roads) which have allowed the people of the Andes to communicate for millennia. This contrasts sharply with the awkward cuts made in the slope to build modern highways or irrigation canals without any respect for the landscape – and which often constitute serious erosion factors. In the first instance we have a case of a careful and loving nurturance; in the second the only concern is to achieve an alien purpose at minimum economic cost and dealing with nature as a hostile environment which has to be tamed.

Summarizing, the Andean world is a world of nurturance in which wisdom consists in knowing how to nurture and knowing how to let oneself be nurtured.

Equivalence Each one of the beings who inhabit this living Andean world is equivalent to every one else: that is, every one (be it man, tree, stone) is a person, complete and indispensable, with its own and inalienable way of being, with its definite personality, its own name, with its specific responsibility in the keeping of the harmony of the world. It is in such condition of equivalence that this living world relates with each one of the others.

In the Aymara region of Puno the *ispallas* are the deities (*huacas*) of the harvest. In the month of March, among many other rituals, there is one in the harvest of potatoes whose central event consists of ritually gathering in a shawl some old potatoes from the previous harvest (which are still kept in storage) with young potatoes newly harvested from the field. Culminating the ritual, through the Andean priest, the old potatoes say to the young ones: 'nurture these men as we ourselves have nurtured them'. Thus it is evidenced in the ritual that as humans nurture the potato in the *chacra* with dedication and love, the potato, in her turn, also nurtures humans as their food. This is why in the Andean world, wisdom – that is, the capacity to live – consists in knowing both how to nurture and how to let oneself be nurtured. In the *chacra*, humans nurture plants, animals, soil, water, climate and so on and they, for their part, nurture humans. This is the profound essence of the Andean equivalence: no one is self-sufficient; each one's life depends on every one else.

The living Andean world possesses a great diversity; it is a very heterogeneous world. From the biological point of view, the Andes possess the highest ecological diversity in the world, measured by the number of distinct ecosystems present on average by unit surface. In the same way, the Andean flora and fauna are the most diverse that can be found anywhere in the world. The number of different climates in the Andes is similarly great: from the cold of the perpetual snows to the heat of the deep inter-Andean ravines; from the coast and the higher jungle, from zones of very high rainfall as the high jungle and the northern sierra to zones of almost absolute dryness on the coast; from places with a relative humidity of almost 100 per cent in the central coast in winter and in some ravines in the Sierra in the western slope of the western Andean cordillera to other places, such as Ayacucho, where it is as low as 20 per cent. The Andean geology also presents an ample range of formations. In this Andean world, living and so diverse, a true equivalence of the heterogeneous takes place, because – I repeat – the life of each one depends on every one else.

In this world, as would be expected, for example each *chacra* is different from any other; each *chacra* possesses its own unique and incomparable personality. This is why if we find an Andean man in his *chacra* and ask him how potatoes are sown, he will answer, quite specifically: 'Here we sow it like this.' Certainly he will make it clear that he would sow differently in his other *chacras*. In each *chacra* potatoes are sown according to what is appropriate in the circumstances. For this reason in the Andes no one will ever say: 'potatoes are sown thus', willing to set rules for it. As each *chacra* is different, the conversation and reciprocity with each one of them is unique. This respect of each one for the others, and this understanding of the other as it is, is a sure basis for the equivalence of the heterogeneous. Here there is no aspiration whatsoever to normalize and to homogenize.

For a better appreciation of this equivalence of the heterogeneous let us give an example. The month of June is the coldest and driest in the Andes and for this reason life is at a minimum. The Sun, which is a major *huaca*, is very far from the Earth and, therefore, warms and illuminates it weakly. It is the time when the Sun shows its incompleteness and it is then that the human community, which has by then harvested its crops, makes ritual offerings to the Sun; it ritually offers *chicha*, the sacred beverage, to strengthen the Sun so that in December it shows itself in its full splendour and with its appearance, life as a whole overflows. Guamán Poma de Ayala (1980 [1613]) produced a drawing for the month of June in which he shows the human community represented by an authority who is offering *chicha* with the Sun and the constellation of the Pleiades as the winged messenger who gives the Sun its *chicha* vessel. It is thus evident that even the Sun, as a major *huaca*, is not self-sufficient but needs the support of the human community at a given moment in order to gather strength. Likewise, the month of July is also cold in the Andes and in this case, the respective drawing shows the fires with which the human community contributes to the warming of the Sun. All this takes place year after year, testifying that although the Sun nurtures us and is a source of life, it also needs us to nurture it. Similarly, during solar eclipses, we Andeans light our fires to contribute to the warming of the Sun 'who is dying', to help it to revive.

Another manifestation of equivalence in the Andean world is that we all have *chacras* and all herd a flock. As humans make a *chacra* combining the form of life of plants, animals, soils, water and climates which nature adopt with the *huacas'* assent, likewise the *huacas* have their *chacra* which is the nature's flora (or *sallqa*) and have their herds which are the human community and the *sallqa*'s fauna. In this context *chaco*, that is the sacred hunt and recollection which the human community undertakes in the *sallqa* (Rengifo 1990), is equivalent to the herding of llamas and alpacas in the prairies and wet plains.

Protection   In the Andean world there exists no loneliness. We are in a living world in which everything talks with us and everything sees us, which is shown, for instance, in the Tello Obelisk of the Chavin culture which dates from some four thousand years ago (De la Torre 1990, Valladolid 1991). The shepherd girl or boy, who have inspired poets who call themselves mestizo or creole to wax lyrical about the shepherds' loneliness, are in fact surrounded and accompanied by all those around them, the mountains, the lakes, the rivers, the stars, the plants and animals, who incessantly converse with them, tell them stories, sing to them, whistle with them and do *ayni* with them. The animals in their flock, the *Apus*, the pastures, the thickets, the trees, the rocks, the springs, the birds, the insects, are their friends and their relatives at the same time.

Ana De la Torre has written a beautiful book in which she shows the great familiarity of the children of the Kilish community in Cajamarca with nature, revealing their rich life experience and their exquisite sensitivity, which guarantees an extraordinary capacity for communication (De la Torre 1986).

Recently Grimaldo Rengifo has reached an understanding of the completeness of the *ayllu* and has perceived that, as has been said for a long time, it refers to a group of relatives. But it is now clear that the group of relatives does not restrict itself to the human lineage as has been asserted in the past, but applies to the entire kinship group, including each of the members of the local *Pacha* (microcosmos) (Rengifo 1991). The human family is not different from the large family, the *ayllu*, but is included in it. The *ayllu* then is the union of the human community, the community of the *sallqa* and the community of *huacas* who inhabit the local *Pacha*. The kinship unit thus constituted is very intimate and close. When we bring a 'seed' that has attracted our affection to a *chacra* from another ecological niche, and we offer it the best of our soils in the garden next to our house and we care for it with affection and dedication, she is already a member of our family: she is our daughter-in-law (*yoccha* in Aymara). Thus it is evidenced that the vegetal crops of our *chacra* are children of the human family that nurture them. Llamas and alpacas are also daughters in the family which herd them and care for them.

In Puno's Aymara peasant communities, when it is necessary to make a very solemn ritual to petition for rain, seawater foam is brought in special vessels as a central element of the required paraphernalia. After the long and strenuous trip to collect the foam, as a male element, it must then be wedded in ritual marriage with a virgin of the community without her being aware. In this way the seawater foam is taken into the community as a son-in-law and can now be used in the ritual.

In the same fashion, the mountain deities: *Apus, Mallcus, Achachilas* are the grandparents of the human community and of the community of the *sallqa*. Now, within the human community itself, all the generation of our parents are treated as mother, father, uncle or aunt. All members of the same generation are treated as brothers and sisters, and the members of the generation that follows are called son, daughter, nephew or niece.

The relationship can go on as long as it is wanted but it is clear that in the Andean world there is a strong kinship which unites each of the persons (humans, trees, stones) who are members of the local *Pacha*, and this kinship group is the *ayllu*. This is why a great longing for the *terruño* (homeland) exists in the Andes: no matter how long one has been absent from his or her homeland, one considers oneself in transit, a guest in foreign lands – one's *Apus*, the immediate references, continue to be those of one's *Pacha*, the place of our birth. Reciprocally, the *Apus* of our *Pacha* are always vigilant, caring for us and conversing with the *Apus* of the localities where we are being hosted, asking for our protection and for that of our descendants.

It is not that we are not welcome in other parts; on the contrary. In the Andes there exists a great fraternity and welcome for the foreigner, as long as one follows the rituals, and respects and reciprocates as is called for and does not attempt to impose anything. However, as in the Andes in general there is a great diversity, a great heterogeneity, no place is similar to our original *Pacha*: these are not my mountains, this is not my river, these are not my pastures, these are not my *chacras*, this is not my climate, these are not my songs, these are not my dances, this is not my food. Everything is there so that one does relate and reciprocate, and indeed, I relate and reciprocate. But it is not the same. It is not that one is unprotected or anything of the sort. It only happens that it is not the same. This could be seen, if one wishes, as a type of conceit: indeed, conceit is only possible in protection since without it there is nothing to do but to bear up and adapt. Here in the Andes it is not like that. We are always protected but our *Pacha* always calls for us because there we feel better than in any other place: our *ayllu* is there.

From the above it should be clear that in the Andean world, wherever we are, we are never alone because all that is around us is alive, friendly and converses with us, accompanying and helping us. However, not only what is immediately present accompanies us but also what is materially far away; the homeland also, in some way, lives in us. It is not then that we are homesick, it is not that we feel sorrow for being absent from our *ayllu*, because no matter how far we are from it, it always nestles in us. But the experience of the homeland is not full when one is far from it and that is why we are always coming back – in no way, however, do we live the absence. Absence is obliviousness and in the Andean culture it is not possible to forget the *pacha* of our *ayllu*: there is our family, there are our roots. It is true that we can face difficulties if we leave the homeland without the proper ritual to the *Apu* asking for permission to leave and asking at the same time for its protection while we are gone. But this can be arranged by making a '*mesa*' (ritual table) with a good Andean priest.

That the *ayllu* has a great capacity to recover its migrant members is shown in the following. It is known that in the Andes there have been three large drought and cold periods which seriously altered the landscape. The first took place four thousand years ago and was of undetermined duration; it corresponds to the Pan-Andean period called Chavin; the second took place between two thousand seven hundred and two thousand years ago and corresponds to the Pan-Andean period called Tiawanaku. The most recent one took place between the years 1160 and 1500 of our era and corresponds to the Pan-Andean period Tawantinsuyu or Inka (Absy 1980, Thompson et al. 1985, Grillo 1990, Rodriguez Suy Suy 1991). These drought/cold periods made the human population migrate from extensive areas which were left depopulated because the perpetual snows covered *chacras*, yards and pastures (Cardich 1975). These human migrations made possible Pan-Andean cultural epochs through the densification of the human populations in the middle and lower altitudes of the inter-Andean valleys as well as the coast and the higher jungle. However, at the end of each period of drought the snow line drew back to higher altitudes, leaving free the areas for cultivation and herding that had been covered. The members of the ethnic groups returned to their original region, to their *ayllu*, between places as far apart as Colombia and Bolivia. Of course the return migration, as in all the Andean living world, was not complete or exhaustive since some few groups stayed in lands along the way (for instance the Aymara group Tupe in the Cañete valley near and to the south of Lima) while other groups, not originally from the *ayllu*, joined the returning group (for example, the group of the Chimos on the borders of Titicaca lake). These great returns, after centuries of absence and several generations, show that the *ayllu* is not only the human group but it is indissoluble from its respective local *pacha* and from its *Apus*.

Harmony   Andean culture is impregnated by the feeling that the harmony of the living world, the harmony of the animal Andean world, is not given by itself but has to be nurtured continuously with the communal participation of every one of its members. In the Andean culture there is no place for discrimination. Every one of us (human, tree, stone) is an indispensable person for the attentive nurturance of harmony.

But in the Andean culture the nurturing of harmony is not the responsibility of a human community that arrogates to itself the universal representation to take decisions and implement them. Harmony in the Andes can only emerge from the communion of the human community with the community of the *sallqa* and with the community of *huacas*. And even then, it is not a matter of a decision taken by an assembly with opinions of the member communities. Harmony, in order to be constantly nurtured, must be revealed starting from the specific circumstance because it must not correspond to the will of the collectivity of the living world but to its physiology. The form of the harmony to be nurtured is not in the surface of the appearance but hidden inside the living world. It is as the sculptor in stone of Cajamarca said when someone asked him for the models that inspired his works: 'In the insides of the stone is the form' (Sánchez 1987).

To nurture harmony is to nurture the most favourable conditions for life and for regeneration which is the mode of being of life. Here, in the Andes, harmony does not serve the purpose of complying with the purpose of domination of one by the others.

As it is a matter of increasing life in a world of such diversity, it is not possible to find a unique form of harmony that applies to all the Andes or to large regions; each *ayllu* must nurture the specific form of harmony required for life there and, even then, this form of harmony is not always the same but varies with the circumstances. This requirement – to take the pulse of this living world which is the *ayllu* and to guide the nurturance of the suitable form of harmony – is a task of the whole natural collectivity: the human community, the community of the *sallqa* and the community of *huacas*. But at each moment, in every circumstance, there is a charismatic authority that facilitates life. It is clear that not all of us have the characteristics to assume charismatic authority; this role is taken on by people (humans, trees, stones) who obviously are those best able to orient themselves and others in the current circumstances, and they do not need to be candidates for the post or even formally elected. It is also clear that no one can be a charismatic authority for each of the very diverse activities of the Andean life in the *ayllu*. This guarantees that in each circumstance the most able will direct us and nobody will monopolize leadership; it will always be well distributed. We have already seen, for instance, that in the months of June and July leadership in the natural collectivity is in the charge of the human community which then makes offerings. But this is not so in other months, when the human community makes rituals to invoke the help of the other communities.

Although each *ayllu* is autonomous to nurture the form of harmony that is suited to it, there is nevertheless something that makes harmony among the *ayllus*. It is the common purpose of increasing life – that is, of improving nurturance, of improving the *chacras*, both the *chacras* of the *huacas* and those of the human community. Therefore, the nurturing of harmony in the Andes is agrocentric.

Now, the nurturance of harmony in the diverse Andean world can only be permanent if one knows how to converse and reciprocate with competence in extreme circumstances of drought and floods, cold and heat, so that life and regeneration continue whatever the circumstances. This stresses the importance and charismatic authority of the *Apus*, who have known the landscape of the *ayllu* since time immemorial and have witnessed extreme situations and the way life has recovered and continued. For this reason they can advise us from their great wealth of knowledge, if we know how to converse and reciprocate with them.

It is also appropriate to note that when a person of the human community requires to nurture a *chacra* he cannot proceed unilaterally by his or her own independent initiative, but must ask for permission of the assembly of the human community and for the assent of the community of *huacas* and of the *sallqa* too. To know the opinion of the latter two, a series of rituals must be undertaken in which their assent or lack of it is made clear. One only proceeds to nurture a *chacra* if one has the approval of all the groups. Therefore, in the Andes, the *chacras* are not only nurtured by the human community but are nurtured by *ayni* (work in reciprocity) among the human community, the community of the *sallqa* and the community of *huacas*.

Decolonization   Decolonization simply consists in the decision and corresponding action of recovering here in the Andes, fully and right now, the culture that is our own and which guarantees us healthy, creative, diligent and joyful life.

This implies the decision to break, once and for all, the colonial bonds – bonds which are often subtle and not clearly evident. We must, therefore, put an end to the difficulties which presently in the Andes injure the human community, the community of the *sallqa* and the community of *huacas*.

In this chapter we have tried to show that the path of the promised development is only a trap built by imperialism, with the complicity of a handful of native agents, to subject us to its interests.

However, the only option that our politicians, intellectuals and technicians have come to see is that of development – without realizing what that means. Therefore, their activity and purpose is only serving the maintenance of the colonial status of our country. This reality must not be hidden or disguised.

It so happens that in the political, intellectual and technical domains in the Andean countries, coinciding with the 'celebration' of the Fifth Centennial of the Spanish invasion, there is a strongly dominant trend which accepts colonialism as a given and irreversible fact; therefore, the only pragmatic thing to do is to try to accommodate oneself – setting up one's own firm, getting a job which pays good money, or taking advantage of one's university degree. Many have opted for university studies not out of a vocation – from a desire to know more and have a better critical awareness of their reality – but as a means of professionalization, as a means of maximizing their incomes. That is why they are not interested in getting to know our Andean world but instead attune themselves to the ideas that imperialism propagates. What they want is to sell their services to the highest bidder so that their individual life can be closer to their paradigm: the standard of living of the American middle class. So they are interested in knowing which branch of their profession is better paid in order to pursue the graduate courses which will improve their value in the labour market.

Those who devote themselves to research do not take up their own position but are attentive to scientific journals and to the latest technical advances in order to incorporate them in their work and thus obtain a better position in the market. They are also attentive to the fashions which predominate in the funding organizations for research and development to formulate 'saleable' projects.

In consequence, all the political programmes of the parties that function in Peru, formulated by university professionals, put their hopes in economic development, in the insertion of Peru into the international financial market and in our increasing participation in the world export market. But this is a well-laid trap of imperialism; we have nothing to gain and a lot to lose.

The Peruvian universities are not centres for reflection and critical study of the world and our country; they are not centres of original research. They are only places where what has been reflected upon or researched in the modern West is being repeated or quoted. They produce only professionals for the labour market, although it is increasingly difficult for them to find employment. So let us be clear then: one of the main obstacles to decolonization is our own politicians, intellectuals and technicians. But it is also true that a large number of them come from popular and peasant origins; they belong then to Andean culture and may come to assume a decolonizing stance, with discussion and clarification.

Let us now specify some characteristics of the decolonizing movement currently in place. We say that the decolonizing process is now happening because currently there is a great peasant effervescence which is expressed in very diverse forms, through which a remarkable process of peasantization and of communalization (official or not) is being affirmed in the countryside, with a sensible increment of the area put in cultivation in the 'jalca' and the 'puna' as well as in the higher jungle (including the cultivation of coca leaves). It can be said then, that in the middle of the prolonged crisis we are experiencing, the peasant is the one who shows himself most vital, creative and active. Even Andean migrants in the cities have re-created collective forms of life, which through redistribution of scarce resources, secure the survival of all its family members.

It is also pertinent to say that it is not a matter of creating one more political party because such formalism would become an obstacle to the displaying of the capacity of decentralized creativity that the decolonization tasks require. Neither is it a matter of employing violence to render inactive the apparatus of colonization. We consider that the appropriate thing to do is continually and repeatedly to affirm our Andean culture, rejecting the colonial structures, breaking away from the colonial structures, thus leaving them without function and rendering them obsolete. A clear example of this is the experience, at their truest moment, of the 'peasant *rondas*' of Cajamarca, which established peasant justice, leaving aside the official instances: police, lawyers and judges.

What has been said does not mean to postulate the perpetuation of the dualism of the foreign and the typical in the Andes, rather we consider that the most efficient and easiest way of eliminating the foreign is by disdain and disuse – that is, by breaking with the foreign and letting it expire by wasting away. The official in the Andes – that is, everything which is at the service of imperialist oppression – is just a scheme, a fiction, which when disdained disappears from the stage. At the same time, this is not to say that capital, today mainly embodied in the transnational firms, is a mere fiction. But we know that it is ever less enterprising and that it requires too many guarantees and incentives to invest in the Andes. Capital, on its own initiative, is going away. In these conditions we believe that violence, rather than liberating the people, on the contrary, justifies the presence and action of the police, the army, the magistrates and the rest of officialdom. For this reason violence gives sustenance to the oppressive system and thus legitimates it.

Now let us clarify what the decolonization task in the Andes is for us:

1. Above all, to decolonize is to affirm our Andean culture and to reject the imperialist pretention of homogenizing peoples, overwhelming one's own culture. Therefore, to decolonize is to break with the world development project, which imperialism has set up to affirm its power and dominance of the world market to homogenize and normalize, as it pleases, the behaviour of peoples, thus facilitating its dominating role. The International Monetary Fund, the World Bank, the Inter-American Development Bank, and the United Nations Organization are its instruments. For our country, the fact of participating in the world development project since its beginnings has only meant a holocaust to progress: the enormous external debt, the increasing misery of our people and the degradation of our nature – all of it for the exclusive military, political and economic benefit of imperialism. What

astounds us is the political consensus existing in our country about development as the only road to liberation, without realizing that development is in reality the imperialist instrument to subdue us.

2. To decolonize is to affirm the agrocentrism of our Andean culture. To nurture again the whole of the Andean territory: soils, waters, plants, animals and microclimates in the *chacra*. Only in this way will we be able to balance production and consumption in our country. Agrocentrism will help us recover our productive capacity to attain self-sufficiency in food. Then we will break our bonds with the world food market, attaining a fundamental autonomy: food autonomy. From the end of the Second World World War up to the present day the food dependence of our country has continuously grown. In addition, an aggravating factor has been that, with the growth of food imports, the hunger of our people has also grown, since our food production has increased at a lower rate than the population growth rate. As we have indicated (see section entitled 'Power' in the above text), the pressure of the world food market dominated by a handful of imperialist firms, as well as a 'national' agrarian policy subordinated to imperialism, have led us to the position of food dependence that we now endure. Food imperialism has been able, over the last fifty years, to break the link between food production and food consumption in almost all Third World countries, deactivating our productive capacity by establishing through 'food aid' that the people in our cities live not off what our own countryside produces but from imported food. However, without realizing the central importance of agriculture for the well-being of the Andean peoples, there is political consensus in the belief that agriculture must be subordinated to the macroeconomic policies of national development in order to provide cheap food to the cities competing in the market with food imports. Presently, from the political viewpoint, food self-sufficiency is not a priority in our country.

3. To decolonize is to reject the diagnosis, biased by adverse interests, which says that Peru is not an agrarian country. It so happens that simultaneously with the deactivation of our food production by the action of food imperialism, technocratic imperialism has evaluated our soils according to irrelevant criteria – supposedly universal – to try to 'demonstrate' that our soils are the worst in the world, and that therefore our increasing dependence on the world food market has no remedy. The land with agricultural potential in Peru, according to the National Office for the Evaluation of Natural Resources (ONERN) – the official body in charge of its measurement – is at best 5.9 per cent of our territory, whereas the world average is 25 per cent. But it is important that we indicate that this evaluation results from the simple application to our country of norms which emanate from the Department of Agriculture of the United States (Handbook No. 210) and

have been made official in Peru through a Decree (D.S. No. 0062–75/ AG, of 22 January 1975). As would be expected, what is evaluated with this method – restricting ourselves to the aspects it considers – is the magnitude of the lands which are suitable for the application of the technology offered in the market by the transnational firms (machinery, 'improved and certified' seeds, chemical fertilizers, chemical biocides, large irrigation schemes with dams, etc.) which will ensure sufficient profits to capital. It is thus an evaluation biased in the direction of the interests of transnational capital, although cloaked as an impartial and scientific application of physical, chemical and topographic protocols. It is a technique which evaluates the resources in function of the feasibility of profitable application of technology massively available in the market and controlled by transnational firms. It locates and measures the zones in which market technology is easily extended. Hence the interest of agrarian programmes in 'extension' and 'promotion'. From this perspective the wisdom of a people with a millenary culture is irrelevant. We reject this mode of action because Andean agriculture does not limit itself to considering the given conditions of the soil as a physico-chemical object but, in the wisdom of the Andean agrocentric culture, the soil is a living being, a person, susceptible of nurturance. However, it is also verified that in this case our politicians and technicians of all kinds have reached a consensus with respect to the need to support commercial agriculture to favour the development of capital in the countryside, while ignoring the virtues of Andean agriculture which does not require imported inputs to produce what we need and in sufficient quantities.

4. To decolonize is to recover the Andean *ayllu*, it is to recover our collective organic whole and our peasant mode of being. As has been indicated (see Rengifo, Chapter 3), the *ayllu* is a family unit which comprises not only the members of the human community which inhabit a locality but also the community of the *sallqa* and the community of *huacas* which reside there. Therefore, the *ayllu* is the kinship web which connects all members of the local *pacha* in a single family, in a single collectivity. The parental unit thus constituted is very intimate and close, to such an extent that when, in the long term, the human components of the *ayllu* have been forced to migrate due to extreme climatic conditions they have returned as soon as it has been possible, even after centuries and generations have passed between departure and return. However, with the European invasion and the colonization that began at the end of the fifteenth century, the *ayllu* has been strongly affected. The first to arrive in the Andes, even before the men themselves, were the pathogenic agents of diseases hitherto unknown in the Andes, which caused a demographic catastrophe in the human community and in the community of the *sallqa*. It has been estimated

that the human population in the Andes was reduced to one tenth of its original. The alpacas and llamas were also greatly affected by diseases and plagues like scabies; the fauna components of the *sallqa* were equally affected. The flora of the *sallqa* has also been affected by the pathogens brought by the invaders. To the action of the biological pathogens brought by the invaders have been added the actions of colonial rules that have worked against the Andean *ayllu*. Thus, the Viceroy of Toledo, to facilitate tax collection and the indoctrination of the human population, ordered the constitution of '*reducciones*' (reductions) or 'Indian commons', later called 'indigenous communities', through the concentration and resettling of a group of ancient *ayllus* in a given place. This was facilitated by the demographic collapse. Originally the Andean human population had a very dispersed mode of settlement, which allowed the dialogue with each of the diverse ecosystems of our *pacha* and reciprocated with each of the *Apus* that inhabited the particular place: in other words, the *ayllus* covered the whole Andean *pacha*. The '*reducciones*' meant the abandonment, on the part of the human community, of large areas of Andean territory in which intruders began to settle, forming *haciendas*, plantations, mining settlements and commercial centres. We consider that it is time to break with the human pilings called cities, which are the works of colonization. We consider that it is time to end the impositions of the world market and the market of our cities because both impoverish the Andean peasantry. We consider that it is time that the Andean human community renew the conversation and reciprocity with the whole of the *sallqa* and the *Apus*; it is time that the *ayllus* cover the whole Andean *pacha* again, thus recovering their fullness. It is now time again to nurture in the whole of the Andes' soils, waters, plants, animals and microclimates, that precious thing of ours – the *chacra*. We reject, therefore, the imperialist efforts to transform all the human inhabitants of the Andes into entrepreneurs – be they large, medium, small or micro – to link us to the world market: that impersonal and cruel environment in which we refuse to participate. The culture of the Andean living world is agrocentric. To be ourselves and live fully we have to 'make *chacra*'. To decolonize is to make Andean *chacra*, that is, to reduce the cultivation of rice, high-yield maize, asparagus and other crops imposed by the market and instead to promote what is ours: soft maize, beans, potato, sweet potato, *manioc, oca, olluco, mashua, maca, yacón, arracacha, tarhui* and many more. Let us nurture many fewer sheep and goats because they erode the soil and contribute to the degradation of pastures. We must nurture many fewer cattle because they now demand that 25 per cent of the area under irrigation of the Sierra be devoted to the cultivation of pastures to complement their food, while only 10 per cent is sown with potato. Each hectare cultivated under irrigation to feed cattle and to obtain meat and milk yields in nutrients only one tenth of what is obtained with any crop for direct human consumption. On the other hand llamas and alpacas are central figures of our culture and are very efficient in the conversion of Andean pastures into excellent meat and fibre; in addition the llama helps us in carrying the harvests of the *chacra* to the household storage areas as well as making long trips in which we reciprocate. We must then increase the nurturing of llamas and alpacas, and with it increase the well-being of the whole Andean collectivity, of which they are preferred daughters.

Let us next review some of the operative features of the path for decolonization.

- To show the radical difference between the Andean vision and the modern Western cosmology in order to highlight that 'to combine the best of the West with the best of the Andean culture' – with which some try to justify modernization, that instrument of colonization – is an eclectic and impossible stance.
- To show the radical difference between development and decolonization.
- To show that in the Andes both the improvement of the quality of life of the great majority of the human population and the improvement of nature's health are only possible within an endogenous process of vigorization and growth of Andean culture, which does not compromise with modernization and which points to decolonization.
- To show that, at a world level, Andean culture is one of the original cultures which is currently more 'complete', more 'entire', and that therefore its affirmation and flowering can be attained in a shorter time than any other.
- To show, in different places of the Andes, with concrete examples, the direct advantages that for the majority of the human population and for the landscape of the involved regions, are represented by the strengthening of the culture. This Andean process can offer useful experiences (neither models nor recipes) to other original cultures for their own decolonization work.
- To show that Andean culture is not an isolated instance in the world but that it can be said that it is one of the 'species' belonging to the 'genus' of the original ethnic cultures which everywhere struggle today to liberate themselves from colonialism in order 'to be themselves'. Let it be considered that the eclectic stance is not viable for the Andean culture and neither is it for similar ones.
- To show that modern Western culture is a special case, a particular reality: it is a unique experience which is reaching exhaustion having glimpsed already its 'limits to growth'.
- To show that the mode of being of the original cultures harmonizes

with the good health of the nature with which they are associated – that is, the re-establishment of original cultures implies the re-establishment of the health of the planet.

- To promote, on the basis of concrete experiences in the Andes, an inter-ethnic debate at world level on the issue of the affirmation of all cultures, to guarantee the harmony of each human community with its own religious experience and with the nature with which they are familiar.

- To show that the present resistance movements in the West are not alternative to the imperialist mainstream dominant there, but only variations not sufficiently differentiated. This is so because: first, they do not deepen the knowledge and the denunciation of the aggressive nature of imperialism and are content with the verification of the symptoms of environmental pollution; and secondly, they are not ready to sacrifice even a part of their excessive privileges to contribute to the fraternal harmony of the peoples of the world.

- To study the possibility of promoting new resistance movements in the West which could be an alternative to imperialism, to assist groups struggling for their decolonization – that is, for the affirmation of their own culture. It is considered that this process could find support in the increasing dissatisfaction of a considerable sector of the population of the West which no longer trusts in reason, is disenchanted with progress, and refuses to endure environmental pollution and rejects the nervous excitation produced by the increasing rhythm of technological change.

This is the extent of our enunciation of some of the operative features inherent to decolonization work. Finally, I would like to point out some of the progress made and make some remarks about it.

In 1992 (the time of writing of this chapter) PRATEC as a working group in the service of the affirmation of Andean culture had already completed five years in this task. It started in 1987 operating as the Project of Technologies of the NGO CEPIA and in 1988 it constituted itself as an independent NGO, the Andean Project of Peasant Technologies – PRATEC.

Considering the work we have achieved in these five years we see that our major contribution has been in building the bases which permit the cultural disalienation of Andean university graduates who, in a process of fifteen to twenty years of schooling, have been moulded into faithful servants of the interests of the imperialist colonizers and despisers of Andean culture. They are the politicians, the intellectuals, the scientists and the technicians who work in the Andes. They are the main obstacle to decolonization – to the affirmation of Andean culture – because their major ambition is to be recognized as members of the global middle class, with all the attendant trappings: cars, bank accounts, credit cards and career aspirations. To attain their goal, it is a prerequisite that they uphold the universality of the postulates of imperialism. With this dis-alienating purpose we have elaborated, from a fully Andean perspective, a discourse which shows both the perennial Andean culture and the modern Western culture that permits comparison on an equal footing.

The task has been particularly difficult in what pertains to the Andean culture because it does not express itself in an abstract and generic discourse but in the rich and incomparable singularity of life itself in which it is re-created, renewing itself continuously. Andean culture lives spontaneously and directly in daily life and reaches its highest intensity in the ritual celebrations that are always linked to the cycles of agricultural life. However, it is indispensable to make the discourse on Andean culture accessible in some measure to those who do not live in it as well as to devolve it to those who, having been born in it, have been separated from it by the school and the university.

Now to make a discourse on Andean culture runs the risk of reducing it, of systematizing it, which is not appropriate. In this way we could easily betray it. What is required then is highly committed, respectful and considerate work – that is, ritual work. In this sense, PRATEC has assumed the responsibility of making a holistic discourse on Andean culture in such a way that, starting from any issue – be it cosmovision, agriculture, water, soil, religiousness, art, education, etc. – we are always showing the living and indivisible world of Andean culture. This has been forged in a process of continuous learning in the living sources of the Andean world, without recourse to the chronicles of the first invaders or to the colonizer intellectuals of yesterday and today. We have thus achieved work, we say without false modesty, with no known precursors. What exists as available material on the Andean world are voluminous compilations of 'myths' and 'rites', as well as specific 'studies' whose authors strive to give account of the Andean in terms of modern Western science, which is incapable of comprehending it because science is at the service of the homo-genization of the world in order to finish with the cultural particularities of the peoples of the world.

So to elaborate a discourse on the modern West from an Andean position we have had to proceed radically. That is, we have searched both in the very bases of Judaeo-Christian religion, which gives it its ideological support, and in the concrete development process of capital, which is its material support. In this area we have had recourse to prestigious Western intellectuals who have made pointed critiques of their own world. In our writings we have made it clear that the behaviour of imperialism is inherent to its mode of being and not a 'deviation' from something that could have been better. Such a statement is one that many Western intellectuals and the Westernized from these latitudes are fond of making. Thus, in this sense, our discourse turns out to be original too.

From the comparison on an equal footing that our discourse allows, between perennial Andean culture and modern Western culture, we postulate that the affirmation of Andean culture in the Andes (and only in the Andes) is the best way to put an end, here in the Andes, to the damage done by colonization.

Our form of struggle for decolonization clearly differs from the one proposed by the 'indigenists' who demand only that the most basic services of Western civilization be extended to the indigenous peoples: schools, hospitals, water supply and sewage treatment. In this way they contribute in demanding what capitalist business knows best how to sell, while neglecting the millenary Andean process of transmission of wisdom and despising the capacity of Andean culture to secure good health for the population on its own terms. We also differ from political parties that operate in the Andes because all of them agree that only modernization and capital development in our countries can guarantee a solution to our difficulties. Finally, we differ from subversive armed groups because it is not a way of affirmation of the Andean but rather another way of imposing modernization in the Andes and a way of promoting the imperialist arms trade.

Some consider that our attitude is irreverent and that it does not do justice to the great advances of Western science and technology that day by day work marvels and, for that reason, merit universalization for the benefit of all peoples in the world. Those who make this assertion do not realize that these very advances which dazzle them have led the Earth to the brink of ecological collapse. They fail to see the fraud of globalization. Others consider that our attitude is romantic or a nostalgic desire to return to the past. Those who assert this do not realize that today in the Andes this culture is the most certain thing of all – because Andean culture is both the most widespread and the most vital. It has resisted and won in a five-hundred-year-long struggle.

In PRATEC we firmly believe that the flowering of each of the original cultures of the world, by the affirmation of themselves and not by denial of the foreign, would give back to humankind the joy of the sweet life, the enjoyment of the small but certain. (We cannot understand the fratricidal ethnic wars in eastern Europe.) With this the Earth which now agonizes, poisoned by the development of capitalist production, will also flower again.

Within this general conception, PRATEC does its own work in the Andes. Our work is not the wilful action of a vanguard but rather commits itself, jointly with other groups, in a respectful and careful manner, to the service not leadership of the Andean peasant process of decolonization. This process began the very moment that the invaders put their feet on our soil five hundred years ago and today is stronger than ever. This is our commitment; this is our reason for existing.

Note

1. Translator's note: the Spanish word used here in the original is *saber*, which is different from *conocimiento*. Unfortunately the English language does not have a similar differentiation. This is unfortunate since the members of PRATEC reject the term *conocimiento* to refer to their own knowledge and use the term *saber*. *Saber* is closer to 'know-how', whereas *conocimiento* refers to a more intellectual phenomenon. *Saber*, one could say, is an embodied form of knowing while *conocimiento* is a purely intellectual form of knowing.

References

Absy, María Lucía. 1980; 'Dados sobre as mudanças do clima e vegetaçao de Amazonía durante o Quaternario' (Data on the variations of climate and vegetation of Amazonía during the Quaternary period), *Acta Amazónica*, 10(4): 920–30.

Bairoch, Paul. 1969; 'Una revolución desconocida: la agrícola' (An unknown revolution: agriculture), *Ceres*, 7 (Enero, Febrero): 52–5.

Beaud, Michel. 1988; 'Intento de evaluación de los riesgos tecnológicos máximos' (An attempt to evaluate the maximum technological risks). In Grupe de Vézelay, *Jornadas de Vézelay sobre los riesgos tecnológicos máximos* (*Days at Vezelay on the Maximum Technological Risks*), Paris: 13–35.

Billone, Jorge, Carbonetto, Daniel and Martinez, Daniel. 1982 *Términos de intercambio ciudad–campo, 1970–1980: precios y excedente agrario* (*Exchange Terms City–Countryside, 1970–1980: Prices and Agricultural Surplus*), Centro de Estudios para el Desarrollo y la Participación (CEDEP).

Cardich, Augusto. 1975; 'Agricultores y pastores en Lauricocha y límites superiores del cultivo' (Agriculturalists and pastoralists in Lauricocha and the higher limits of cultivation), *Revista del Museo Nacional*, Vol. 41: 11–36.

Castréjon Chilón, Gregorio. 1989; 'Recuperando las *chacras*' (Recovering the *chacras*), *Tecnologías campesinas delos Andes*, 232, Plan Manzanas, Cajamarca.

Central Intelligence Agency. 1974; 'Potential implications of trends in world population', *Food Production and Climate*, OPR–401, Washington.

Clinton, Richard L. 1978; 'América Latina, la región que nunca se desarrollará', (Latin America, the region which will never develop), *Comercio Exterior*, 28 (7): 816–21.

Comblin, Joseph. 1989; 'Révolution Française, révolution bourgeoise'. In *Concilium* 221, Beaucherne, Paris.

Cuzco Lucano, Sergio. 1990; 'Los terrenos de las *chacras* se crían' (The soils of the *chacras* are nurtured). In PRATEC, PPEA-PNUMA (eds) *Sociedad y Naturaleza en los Andes*, Vol. 2. Lima: 213–20.

De La Torre, Ana. 1986; *Los Dos Lados del Mundo y del Tiempo* (The two sides of the world and of time) Lima; Centro de Investigacion, Educacion y Desarrollo.

De La Torre, Ana. 1990; 'Ideologia de la Naturaleza' (The ideology of Nature) in: *Sociedad y Naturaleza en los Andes* (Society and Nature in the Andes), Vol. 1, 78–92; Lima; PRATEC, PPEA-PNUMA.

Denevan, William M. and Turner, B. L. 1974; 'Forms, functions and associations of raised fields in the Old World Tropics', *Journal of Tropical Geography* 39: 24–33.

De Soto, Hernando. 1992; 'Texto de su renuncia a las funciones de Asesor y Representante Personal del Presidente Fujimori' (Text of his resignation to the post of advisor and personal representative of President Fujimori), 'Diario', *La República*, 29 enero: 8.

Earls, John. 1976; 'Evolución de la administración ecológica Inca' (Evolution of the Inca ecological administration), *Revista del Museo Nacional*, Vol. 42: 207–45.

Eppler, Erhard. 1973; *Hay poco tiempo para el Tercer Mundo* (*Not much time left for the Third World*), Madrid: Editorial Aguilar.

Feder, Ernest. 1979; 'El bloque de la contra-reforma' (The block of the counter-reformation), *Ceres*, 68: 20–4.

Flores Ochoa, Jorge and Paz Flores, Percy. 1983; 'El cultivo en qocha en la puna sur andina' (Cultivation in qochas in the South Andean puna). In Ana María Fries (ed.) *Evolución y Tecnología de la Agricultura Andina*. Proyecto Investigación de los Sistemas Agrícolas Andinos. Cuzco; IICA/CIID and Instituto Indigenista Inter-Americano.

Galbraith, John Kenneth. 1964; *Economic Development*. Cambridge, MA; Harvard University Press.

Gonzales Moreyra, Raúl. 1986; 'Intervenciones en el Primer Encuentro de Intelectuales y Academia sobre Proyecto Nacional' (First Encounter of Intellectuals and Academics on National Project). In Presidencia de la República, Instituto Nacional de Planificación (eds), *Proyecto Nacional.Primer Encuentro*. (Transcripción de la versión magnetofónica): 20–21 and 47.

Grillo Fernandez, Eduardo. 1990; 'Visión andina del paisaje' (Andean vision of the landscape). In PRATEC, PPEA-PNUMA (eds) *Sociedad y Naturaleza en los Andes*, Vol. 1: 133–67.

Guamán Poma de Ayala, Felipe. 1980 (1613); *Nueva Coronica i buen gobierno*. John Murra and Rolena Adorno (eds), México; Siglo Veintiuno.

Hobsbawm, Eric J. 1971; *Las Revoluciones Burguesas* (*The Age of Revolution*), Madrid; Ediciones Guadarrama.

Hunt, Susan. 1986; 'La invención de la escasez' (The invention of scarcity). 'Diario', *La República*, 5 de enero de1986. (Reproducido de Tecno-Política, México. Dic. 1985).

Isbell, William H. 1974; 'Ecología de la expansión de los quechua-hablantes' (Ecology of the expansion of the Quechua speaking peoples), *Revista del Museo Nacional*, Vol. 40: 139–55.

Jungk, Robert. 1979; *El Estado nuclear* (*The Nuclear State*). Editorial Crítica. Barcelona; Grupo Editorial Grijalbo.

Kemmerer, Donald L. and Jones, C. Clyde. 1959; *American Economic History*. McGraw-Hill Book Company, Inc.

Kosik, Karel. 1976; *Dialéctica de lo concreto* (*Dialectics of the Concrete*). México, D. F.; Editorial Grijalbo, S.A.

Lajo, Manuel. 1985; 'Revolución agroalimentaria: estrategia nacional y seguridad alimentaria' (Revolution in agriculture and food supply: national strategy and food security). In Edgardo Mercado Jarrín and Jorge Chávez Alvarez (eds), *Hacia un Proyecto Nacional*, Instituto Peruano de Estudios Geopolíticos y Estratégicos: 79–182.

Masson, Luis. 1986; 'Rehabilitación de andenes en la comunidad de San Pedro de Casta, Lima' (Rehabilitation of terraces in the community of San Pedro de

Casta, Lima). In *Andenes y camellones en el Perú Andino. Historia, Presente y Futuro*, Lima; Consejo Nacional de Ciencia y Tecnología: 207–16.

Meadows, Donella et al. 1972; *The Limits to Growth* (A Report for the Club of Rome's Project on the Predicament of Mankind), New York; Universe Books.

Palao B., Juan Bernardo and Garaycochea Z., Ignacio. 1989; 'Proyectos de desarrollo rural en Puno. Un avance descriptivo y apreciaciones 1950–1985' (Rural development projects in Puno: A descriptive preliminary report and appreciation 1950–1985). In Alberto Giesecke (ed.), *Burocracia, Democratización y Sociedad (Bureacracy, Democratization and Society)*, FOMCIENCIAS, CENTRO: 175–202.

Pearson, Lester. 1970; 'Pearson enjuicia el "Informe Pearson"' (Pearson judges the 'Pearson Report'), *Ceres*, 14, March–April: 20–5.

Rengifo Vasquez, Grimaldo. 1990; 'La *chacra* en la cultura andina' (The *chacra* in Andean culture). Documento de Estudio PRATEC.

Rengifo Vasquez, Grimaldo. 1991; 'Organicidad en la comunidad natural andina y organización social en occidente moderno' (The organic in the Andean natural community and social organization in the modern West). Documento de estudio. PRATEC.

Rodriguez, Carlos Rafael. 1989; 'Sobre la deuda externa' (On external debt), *Revista de la Casa de las Américas*, 175, July–Aug.: 126–32.

Rodriguez Suy Suy, Víctor Antonio. 1991; 'Visión endógena de la cultura andina' (Endogenous vision of Andean culture). In Greslou et al. (eds) *Cultura Andina Agrocéntrica*. Lima; PRATEC: 49–65.

Roel Pineda, Virgilio and Pacheco Linares, Félix. 1991; '500 años después ... ¡Que pague España!' (500 years later ... Make Spain pay!), *Domingo,* suplemento dominical del Diario, *La República*, 29 December: 26–30.

Rumrrill, Róger. 1991; 'Boca del narcotráfico Europeo' (Mouth of European traffic in narcotics), 'Diario', *La República*, 28 September: 18.

Sabato, Ernesto. 1990; 'Entrevista: Ernesto Sábato habla sobre la política y su literatura. Sobre antihéroes y túneles' (Interview: Ernesto Sabato speaks on politics and literature. On antiheroes and tunnels), *Perfiles*, suplemento del diario, *Página Libre*, 27 October: 8.

Sánchez Zevallos, Pablo. 1987; 'Intervención oral en la Reunión sobre la población de la sierra que AMIDEP organizó en Huaraz entre el 4 y el 8 de diciembre de 1987' (Oral intervention in the meeting on population of the sierra organized by AMIDEP 4–8 December 1987).

Santos, Eduardo A. 1983; 'El mercado mundial de cereales: Las opciones del Tercer Mundo' (The grain world market: The options of the Third World), *Comercio Exterior*, 33 (6): 551–5.

Strahm, Rudolf H. 1986; *Pourquoi sont-ils si pauvres? Faits et chiffres en 84 tableaux sur les mécanismes du développement. Nouvelle édition entièrement remaniée.* A la Baconnière/ La Déclaration de Berne, Switzerland.

Streeten, Paul. 1977; 'Cambios en la concepción del desarrollo' (Changes in the conception of development), *Finanzas y Desarrollo*, 14 (3): 14–16 and 40.

Streeten, Paul. 1979; 'Del crecimiento a las necesidades básicas' (From growth to basic needs). *Finanzas y Desarrollo*, 16 (3): 28–31.

Tenbruck, Friedrich. 1989; 'Sentido y límite de la política de desarrollo' (Trends and limits of the development policy), *Desarrollo y Cooperación*, 1: 24–6.

Thompson, Lonnie, et al. 1985; 'A 1500 year record of tropical precipitation in ice cores from the Quelcaya ice cap, Perú', *Science*, 299: 971–3.

Valladolid Rivera, Julio. 1991; 'Agroastronomía andina' (Andean agroastronomy). In Greslou et al., *Cultura Andina Agrocéntrica*, Lima; PRATEC: 171–207.

Ward, Barbara. 1971; *The Widening Gap*, Columbia University Press.

Wortman, Sterling. 1976; 'Alimentación y agricultura' (Food and agriculture), *Investigación y Ciencia*, 2, November: 6–17.

Index

New Paradigms in Development Studies:
Other Zed Titles

Zed has become a leading pioneer of a wide wariety of books critical of orthodox and largely economistic thinking in Development Studies from cultural, ethical, environmental, feminist and even more profound civilizational perspectives. Many of these books contain new approaches, often inspired by what is already happening among ordinary people at the grassroots of society. This new thinking has the potential to revolutionize development strategy and policy in ways that would really transform the lives of the poor and marginalized by respecting and building upon their worldviews, their culture and their material needs.

Frédérique Apffel-Marglin with PRATEC, *The Spirit of Regeneration: Andean culture confronting Western notions of development*

Cristovam Buarque, *The End of Economics? Ethics and the disorder of progress*

Raff Carmen, *Autonomous Development: An excursion into radical thinking and practice*

Arthur Lyon Dahl, *The Eco Principle: Ecology and economics in symbiosis*

Gustavo Esteva and Madhu Suri Prakash, *Hope at the Margins: Beyond human rights and development*

Denis Goulet, *Development Ethics: A guide to theory and practice*

Rajni Kothari, *Poverty: Human consciousness and the amnesia of development*

Serge Latouche, *In the Wake of the Affluent Society: An exploration of post-development*

Reinhard Loske, Wolfgang Sachs and Manfred Linz: *Industrial Societies and Sustainability: Proposal for managing the transition*

Manfred Max-Neef, *From the Outside Looking in: Experiences in 'barefoot economics'*

Manfred Max-Neef, *Human-Scale Development: Conception, application and further reflections*

Majid Rahnema and Victoria Bawtree (compilers), *The Post-Development Reader*

Carla Ravaioli, *Economists and the Environment*

Gilbert Rist, *The History of Development: From Western origins to global faith*

Wolfgang Sachs (ed.), *The Development Dictionary*

Thierry Verhelst, *No Life without Roots: Culture and development*